THE IRWIN
ASSET ALLOCATION SERIES
FOR INSTITUTIONAL
INVESTORS

HEDGE FUNDS

◆

INVESTMENT AND PORTFOLIO STRATEGIES FOR THE INSTITUTIONAL INVESTOR

◆

JESS LEDERMAN AND ROBERT A. KLEIN, EDITORS

McGraw-Hill, Inc.
New York • San Francisco • Washington, D.C.
Auckland • Bogotá • Caracas • Lisbon • London
Madrid • Mexico City • Milan • Montreal • New Delhi
San Juan • Singapore • Sydney • Tokyo • Toronto

ISBN 1-55738-861-X

Pinted in the United States of America

BS

4 5 6 7 8 9 0

PG

McGraw-Hill

*A Division of The **McGraw·Hill** Companies*

To John Cleveland
In appreciation of his support for the
Jackson Hole Community Housing Trust

Contents

Author Biographies

Ted Caldwell

Mr. Caldwell is president of Lookout Mountain Capital, Inc. (LMC), a registered investment advisor specializing in the evaluation, selection, and monitoring of hedge funds. LMC also publishes the *Lookout Mountain Hedge Fund Review* (see information at the back of this book), and advises several multi-manager hedge fund pools. Mr. Caldwell began assessing hedge funds in 1980, and investing in them as a private party in 1984. In 1990, he began gathering extensive data on hedge funds for the purposes of diversifying his personal investments, and in 1993 he established LMC.

Mr. Caldwell received his MBA from the University of Denver.

William J. Crerend

Mr. Crerend is chairman and founder of Evaluation Associates, one of the nation's oldest and largest investment consulting firms. Prior to forming EAI, he was vice president, Paine Webber, Jackson & Curtis' Investment Manager Evaluation Services. Mr. Crerend has served as corporate controller for the March of Dimes Foundation, and earlier worked for the Equitable Life Assurance Society.

Mr. Crerend received a B.S. in economics from Niagara University, as well as an honorary doctorate of commercial science.

Glen C. Dailey

Mr. Dailey is an executive vice president of Montgomery Prime Brokerage Services. Montgomery Securities is a San Francisco–based institutional trading, research, and investment banking firm focusing on U.S. growth stocks.

Previously, he was a managing director of Furman Selz Incorporated, responsible for the operations and systems groups of their prime brokerage division. Mr. Dailey, a frequent speaker at hedge fund seminars, began his career at A.G. Becker after attending Bernard Baruch College.

Michael E. Dunmire

Mr. Dunmire is president of Paradigm Partners, Inc. Previously, he served as vice president at the Frank Russell Company, where he was responsible for the research and evaluation of unconventional money managers for Russell Private Investment clients. He also has been partner and director of research at Cable, Howse & Ragen; manager of strategic planning at Seafirst Holding Company; director of investment research at Seattle First National Bank; and vice president and senior security analyst at Bankers Trust Company.

Mr. Dunmire, a chartered financial analyst, has a B.S. degree from the University of Pennsylvania and an MBA from Columbia University.

Martin J. Gross

Martin Gross monitors hedge funds and advises four funds of funds from Livingston, New Jersey. Since 1983, Mr. Gross has tracked and evaluated the performance of investment managers and has conducted other investment banking activities. A member of the New Jersey and New York Bars, Mr. Gross has practiced tax and corporate law in New York City, and worked in the corporate finance department of L.F. Rothschild, Unterberg, Towbin. He has written for *Barron's* and other hedge fund newsletters and often lectures at industry conferences.

Mr. Gross received his B.A. summa cum laude from Brandeis University, an M.A. from Brasenose College, Oxford University, a J.D. from the University of Chicago Law School, and an LL.M. from New York University Law School.

Bryan J. MacDonald

Mr. MacDonald is president and managing director of Investment Strategies International, Inc., and chairman of the board of directors of Investment Strategies International, Ltd. of Hamilton, Bermuda. His firm provides investment banking and advisory services to alternative investment managers interested in expanding their client base on a global basis. Previously, he was a senior vice president of Tremont Advisors, Inc., responsible for all product development and marketing for the firm. Mr. MacDonald has also held positions as vice president and group head of market and product development for Bankers Trust Company, as client service manager for Frank Russell Company, and as product manager for The Vanguard Group of Investment Companies.

Joseph G. Nicholas

Mr. Nicholas is the president of Hedge Fund Research, Inc., a research and consulting firm that tracks hedge funds and alternative investment strategies and provides consulting and advisory services on hedge funds to institutional and high-net-worth investors. He is also editor of the *Hedge Fund Research Journal* and president of Nicholas Financial, Inc. and Nicholas Securities, Inc., a registered broker-dealer. Previously, Mr. Nicholas was president and managing director of Hart-Bornhoft Group, a registered investment advisor. Earlier, Mr. Nicholas served as an attorney with the law firm of Fishman & Merrick, P.C., specializing in commodities and securities law, and held positions in finance and consulting.

Mr. Nicholas received a B.S. in finance from DePaul University and a J.D. from Northwestern University School of Law.

John P. Nicholas

Mr. Nicholas is vice president of Hedge Fund Research, Inc., a research and consulting firm that tracks hedge funds and alternative investment strategies and provides consulting and advisory services on hedge funds to institutional and high-net-worth investors, and is managing editor of the *Hedge Fund Research Journal*. He is also vice president of Nicholas Financial, Inc. Previously, Mr. Nicholas was an attorney in the corporate department of McDermott, Will & Emery, practicing securities, commodities, and corporate law. Earlier, he served as legislative assistant for foreign policy and defense to Senator Joseph R. Biden, Jr.

Mr. Nicholas graduated magna cum laude from Harvard University and received his J.D. from Northwestern University School of Law.

Lois Peltz

Ms. Peltz is the managing editor of *MAR/Hedge*, a 32-page monthly newsletter devoted to hedge funds as well as *MAR*, a 32-page monthly newsletter focusing on funds and trading advisors in the futures and currency arena. In addition, she supervises the two databases in these respective areas. Previously, Ms. Peltz was vice president and manager of marketing services/CTA selection at ML Futures Investment Partners Inc., where she was responsible for advisor analysis, alternative fund structures, the review of all current funds, and marketing support for futures funds.

Ms. Peltz graduated Phi Beta Kappa from Vassar College and holds an M.A. in international affairs from Columbia University and an MBA from New York University.

Joel Press

Mr. Press is a senior partner with Ernst & Young LLP, where he also leads the Private Investment Partnerships practice and is a member of the steering committee. Among his many activities, he provides broker-dealers and investment companies with audit, tax, systems, and business advisory services; advises clients on regulatory matters; has structured buyouts and compensation arrangements for investment advisors; and has designed new operations systems and established internal audit departments for broker-dealers. Mr. Press is co-author of *Security Markets Around the World*. He is a frequent lecturer on the securities industries, and conducts seminars on hedge funds. Previously, Mr. Press was head of the international financial services group at Spicer and Oppenheim.

Mr. Press received his B.A. from Long Island University.

M. Kelley Price

Mr. Price is a principal of Price Meadows Capital Management Inc., located in Bellevue, Washington, and general partner of several investment partnerships that utilize short selling as a core investment technique. His firm invests with 15 outside money managers, including four dedicated short sellers. In addition, Mr. Price is a general partner of eight single-manager funds and his firm provides back-office support and consulting services to several independent hedge funds.

Mr. Price is a graduate of Stanford University.

Paul N. Roth

Mr. Roth is a senior partner with Schulte Roth & Zabel. His areas of expertise include investment partnerships; investment advisers and broker-dealers; securities regulation, mergers, and acquisitions; financial transactions; and cross-border acquisitions into the United States. Mr. Roth is a member of both the American Bar Association and the New York State Bar Association, and was chairman of the committee on securities regulation of the Association of the Bar of the City of New York.

Mr. Roth graduated magna cum laude and Phi Beta Kappa from Harvard College, and received his J.D. from Harvard Law School.

Daniel S. Shapiro

Mr. Shapiro is a senior partner with Schulte Roth & Zabel. His areas of expertise include partnership and securities transactions tax matters and corporate and real estate tax issues. Mr. Shapiro is a member of the New York State Bar Association and the American Bar Association, and is active in numerous civic and philanthropic groups. He has also been a frequent speaker at seminars, and has had articles published in the *Journal of Taxation, Taxes,* the *New York Law Journal,* and *Tax Notes.*

Mr. Shapiro received his A.B. and J.D. degrees from Columbia University.

Mitchell A. Tanzman

Mr. Tanzman is a managing director of Oppenheimer & Co., Inc., the securities and investment firm. He is co-head of Oppenheimer's investment partnership and offshore fund business, which acts as investment adviser to a family of hedge funds offered to U.S. and international clients. These funds manage in excess of $800 million in assets in a number of different strategies, all on an incentive basis.

Mr. Tanzman received a J.D. from the University of Chicago Law School and a B.A. from Emory University.

David A. White

Mr. White is executive vice president with AIG International Asset Management Inc., responsible for marketing, product development, and investment analysis. Previously, Mr. White was treasurer and chief investment officer of The Rockefeller Foundation. Prior to that, he was staff vice president of capital management and trust investments at Unisys Corporation, where he implemented several investment firsts, including market neutral and currency as an asset class. He is a member of the Financial Executives Institute and a trustee of the Investment Fund for Foundations.

Mr. White received a B.A. in economics and mathematics and an MBA in finance and operations from the University of Michigan.

Preface

Over the past several years, hedge funds have attracted more controversy, excitement, and misunderstanding than any other sector of the capital markets. Politicians have accused some of the larger hedge funds of manipulating the world financial markets; the press has suggested that some hedge fund managers are wildly overpaid; and rumors of spectacular hedge fund gains and losses are the subject of Wall Street gossip.

Meanwhile, savvy investors have realized that superior hedge funds offer an outstanding tradeoff between risk and return — perhaps the best of any available asset class. But what are hedge funds? How do they operate? And how can institutional investors and wealthy individuals best incorporate them into their asset mix?

The answers are presented in this breakthrough book, the first ever compiled on hedge funds. It is the result of a year of effort by sixteen of the brightest and most successful experts on this dynamic industry. *Investing in Hedge Funds* covers every facet of the business and clears the clouds of mystery that have long surrounded a critical market sector.

Many thinks much be given to each of the contributing authors for the time and energy they took from their hectic schedules. We are also grateful to the superb staff at Irwin Professional Publishing, who made the timely publication of this important book possible.

Jess Lederman
Robert A. Klein

CHAPTER 1

Introduction: The Model for Superior Performance

Ted Caldwell, President
Lookout Mountain Capital, Inc.

Hedge Funds: Perception and Reality

How risky are hedge funds? Although broadly perceived by the investing public to be imprudent investments, in reality, most hedge funds are not. In order to gain useful insight into how many hedge funds provide superior returns with reasonable and controlled exposure to risk, let's begin with a better understanding of why they are *perceived* to be so risky.

Put an apple on a hedge fund manager's head and call it "the truth." Then step off fifty paces and hand a crossbow to a well-intentioned journalist with a steady hand and a mandate to "nail the truth!" As a courtesy, we will presume the hedge fund manager is blindfolded. If the journalist's best shot just barely misses, what happens? More often than not, the journalist's best shot ends up farther from the truth than the original fifty paces.

Over the past three decades, relatively few journalists have nailed the truth about hedge funds, while hundreds of misleading articles have been written by well-meaning journalists. The cumulative result is that "hedge fund managers—those flamboyant, dice-tossing speculators"[1] have an image problem.

There have been some glaring failures among hedge funds, and the media serves a useful purpose in disclosing as much as possible about them. But in general, the financial press grossly fails to convey how most hedge funds operate. Besides their focus on a small portion of hedge funds that are not typical of the industry, there are three primary reasons why the financial

---

[1] Riva Atlas and Dyan Machan, "George Soros, Meet A. W. Jones" *Forbes*, 17 January 1994, 42–44.

press so often misleads the public about the risk profiles of most hedge funds: A lack of good sources, an abundance of bad sources, and difficult risk management concepts. Let's consider each.

Sources of Information

Most hedge funds are private limited partnerships, prohibited from advertising. For legal and proprietary reasons, hedge fund managers have, traditionally, been very reluctant to disclose specifics about their operation, even to investors. They have rarely spoken with the press until recent years, and now, they seldom reveal much.

As a last resort, financial journalists came to rely (decades ago) on others in the financial services industry for information on hedge funds. They failed to recognize several major problems with this arrangement: To begin with, industry sources can only speculate what a hedge fund manager is actually doing, even when a source has direct information on some aspect of a fund's activities. Of greater concern, sources have sometimes been slighted in their efforts to provide services to a hedge fund manager, and quite frequently, the sources compete directly with hedge funds. Finally, many sources fail to grasp the risk management systems that hedge funds use.

In the mid 1970s, *Institutional Investor*[2] summed up the relationship between hedge funds and the rest of the securities industry like this: "Today, they [hedge funds] are still targets for an uncanny number of unsavory market rumors, the victims of smear campaigns accusing them of just about everything short of pilfering the napery from the New York Stock Exchange dining room. . . . hedge funds are so often branded as villains by other sectors of the investment community."

Seventeen years later, an excellent overview of the industry by *Business Week*[3] characterized the pattern more pointedly. "Bankers, security industry professionals, mutual fund managers—all are beating the drum. . . . It's no secret that Wall Street hates hedge funds." But why? "It's not just jealousy or scapegoating that makes the hedge funds anathema to the powers on Wall Street. Fear is another possibility—fear that the public may demand incentive-based compensation for their funds as well."

The concept of performance-based compensation may well be unsettling to an industry that charges according to the volume of transactions made or the total assets under management, regardless of whether the customer profits.

[2] John Thackray, "Whatever Happened to the Hedge Funds?" *Institutional Investor*, May 1977, 71–74.

[3] Gary Weiss and Joseph Weber, "Fall Guys?" *Business Week*, 25 April 1994, 116–120.

The investment services industry is highly competitive, and although most professionals exercise restraint in disparaging the competition, many have made hedge funds the accepted target. Over the past few decades, hedge fund rumor that is fed to reporters one day has become front page news the next! As a result, millions of readers have developed strong misconceptions about the risk profiles of most hedge funds.

There is a biting irony in the fact that rumor is often generated about hedge funds on Wall Street, because the operations that most closely resemble hedge funds are the proprietary trading desks of big banks and brokerage houses. One main difference is that most hedge funds take on less risk than many of Wall Street's proprietary desks.

Risk Management: Betting versus Gambling

The other reason why so many journalists have misled readers about the risks of hedge funds is that the concepts of risk management used by hedge funds can be difficult to understand. Many of the tools, and the lexicon applied to them, imply high risk to the average investor and to the journalists who write about their use.

Consider the word "bet," commonly used by hedge fund managers, but also by the entire investment community. Managers do not use the word "bet" to imply "gamble," but journalists often infer that is its meaning. Even though the inference of gambling is not correct, it is easily made when viewed in the context of tools like leverage, short selling, and financial derivatives. These are perceived by most investors as purely speculative tools, but many hedge funds successfully employ them to increase performance while actively managing risk.

Given some highly visible failures, it seems implausible, not just to journalists but to many good investors, that risk can be reasonably managed when using leverage, short sales, and financial derivatives. Yet it can! Let's approach some basic risk management concepts by personalizing them.

How much risk would you take with $1,000 of your hard-earned money, under the following coin-flipping scenarios?

1. Would you bet $1,000 on the flip of a coin?
2. Assume a win would pay you $1,200 against your loss of $1,000. Would you bet?
3. What if a win paid the same 1.2 to 1 ratio as in scenario #2, but you could bet in $10 increments and as many times as you wished? Would you bet, and if so, how often and how much?

4. What if you didn't have any cash to bet with, but you did have a bank CD you could borrow $1,000 against? Would you borrow against the CD to execute your bets from scenario #3?
5. Let's now assume the party you are betting against is a corporation with limited capital, making the same $10 bets and paying 1.2 to 1 to thousands of other people. You anticipate the company will go bankrupt long before you want to stop betting. Would you be willing to place an additional bet by selling short the shares of that corporation, in amounts equal to the winnings from your leveraged bets?

Scenario #1 is pure gambling, and if you answered yes, you are reckless with your money. Scenario #2 has an attractive payoff, but the downside risk is too great, at least for most people. Scenario #3 is appealing because your risk of loss on any single coin toss is acceptable, relative to your capital, and the odds heavily favor your making unlimited sums of money from a continuing series of coin tosses.

If you chose not to borrow against your CD nor to short the shares of the corporation under scenarios #4 and #5, you are not psychologically fit for investing in hedge funds. If you chose to bet under scenarios #4 and #5, congratulations; you are becoming an expert at utilizing leverage and short sales to increase performance, while prudently managing risk! Have you considered starting a hedge fund? (Affirmative answers to this question pose a problem that we will address later.)

Obviously, coin tosses that pay 1.2 to 1 do not entail any skills to come out a winner over time, so let's consider one more example.

When a "scratch" golfer makes a $2 bet on the flip of a coin, he is gambling. On the other hand, when he bets an eight handicapper "$2 Nassau, two down automatics, double the back and 18," he is *investing!* Never mind if you don't understand this bet. The point is, a scratch golfer fully understands the bet, and the odds are exceedingly high that he will collect a lot more than $2. Bets like this don't win many friends on the golf course (or on Wall Street).

Few financial journalists have taken the time to actually understand risk management as it is used by most hedge funds, relying instead on information fed to them by the competitors of hedge funds. Thus, most of their readers ("prudent men," many of whom acquired or held IBM at $170 in 1987) reject the suggestion that many hedge funds are very sound investments.

Given a better understanding why hedge funds are unduly perceived to be so risky, let's start over and develop a more legitimate awareness of hedge funds by reviewing their history and development.

A Brief History of Hedge Funds

In the beginning, a defining characteristic of hedge funds was that they hedged against the prospect of a declining market. Hedging through private agreements is as old as commerce, but most instruments for hedging in a securities portfolio are quite recent; so let's briefly review the evolution of tools for hedging securities.

Hedging is the utilization of a defensive strategy to mitigate or eliminate risk, and it usually entails giving something up. The creation of most tools for hedging in a securities portfolio came through the commodity markets. In turn, the catalyst throughout the development of commodities markets, going back to rice warehouse receipts in 17th-century Japan, has been the common desire for producers, processors and merchants to hedge against adverse price changes.

Over the past century, commodity exchanges in the United States have become highly developed to meet these needs. Producers of numerous farm, forest, oil, and mineral products sell futures contracts to hedge against price declines. While protecting themselves against future price declines, they forfeit the right to additional profits if prices rise. Likewise, users of these products often purchase futures contracts to hedge against future price increases, but they forfeit the benefits of future price declines.

Standardization of futures contracts on exchanges made them easily transferable, inviting speculators into the futures markets. Speculators provide two critical services. They willingly take on price risk that the hedgers don't want, and they provide tremendous liquidity, making the exchange markets more efficient.

During the 1970s, the exchanges began to develop a number of financial futures for hedging interest rate and currency risk. These developments were followed by futures and options on various equity indexes and options on hundreds of specific stocks. The number of financial instruments for hedging, or speculating, has grown exponentially since 1980.

In addition to standardized financial futures and options, traded on major exchanges, some banks and brokerage houses create a multitude of customized, off-exchange instruments. Some of these contracts are relatively simple and easily transferable; others are exceedingly complex and have very limited markets. Unfortunately, the "D" word (derivatives) is applied equally, if not reasonably, to the entire range of financial instruments, from the most liquid and stable futures and options traded on the exchanges, to the most illiquid and volatile "toxic waste" traded over-the-counter. In spite of the prevailing public perception, most derivatives render far more benefits than harm and they are here to stay.

Prior to the development of financial futures, options, and other derivatives over the past two decades, the only way to hedge against the market risk in an equity portfolio was to sell a basket of shares short. Information on the practice prior to the advent of hedge funds is sparse, but it was practiced by individuals, institutional investors, and securities brokers as early as the 1920s[4] and probably much earlier.

Alfred Winslow Jones[5]

In 1949, a scholar named Alfred Winslow Jones embarked on his fifth career, establishing what later became regarded as the first hedge fund. Take heart, baby-boomers; he was 48 years old!

Born in Melbourne, Australia, Jones came to the United States with his American family when he was four. After graduating from Harvard in 1923, he traveled the world as a purser on a steamer, and in the early 1930s he served as vice consul at the U.S. Embassy in Berlin (at the time Hitler came to power). During the Spanish Civil War, he reported on civilian relief for the Quakers. In 1941, Jones completed a doctorate in sociology at Columbia University, and his thesis, *Life, Liberty and Property*, became a standard sociology text.

During the forties, Jones became an associate editor of *Fortune*, then wrote for *Time* and other nonbusiness periodicals. The catalyst for becoming a practicing capitalist appears to have been the research Jones did for his article, *Fashions in Forecasting*, published by *Fortune*[6] in March of 1949. In preparing this piece, he became acquainted with some of the most highly regarded technicians, forecasters, and analysts on Wall Street. Several months before publication of his article, this amateur investor established his investment partnership.

Jones, who died in 1989, is remembered by those who knew him as a kind gentleman with a lifelong, active concern for unfortunate people. By today's standards, some of the social schemes he contemplated would be viewed as socialist; yet with a strange alchemy, Jones proved to be the quintessential capitalist, a man with remarkable entrepreneurial "compass."[7]

---

[4] J. Edward Meeket, M.A., *Short Selling*, Harper & Brothers Publishers, 1932.

[5] Information on A. W. Jones and his hedge fund was obtained through numerous personal interviews with individuals who worked for or with Mr. Jones, in addition to the cited literature.

[6] Alfred Winslow Jones, "Fashion in Forecasting," *Fortune*, March 1949, 88, 186.

[7] com•pass *n*.   1. the intrinsic quality that guides superior capitalists.   2. innate capitalistic genius. *Lookout Mountain Hedge Fund Review*, 1 September 1994, 1.

The Jones Hedge Fund Model

Relatively few people grasp the beauty and simplicity of Alfred Jones's original hedge fund model. He took two speculative tools, short sales and leverage, and merged them into a conservative investing system. His goal was to shift the burden of performance from market timing to stock picking, and he succeeded.

In 1950, short selling was customarily used for interim speculation in transitory opportunities. Leverage was customarily used for pursuing higher profits, subject to higher risk of capital loss. Jones's approach was unconventional. He viewed maintaining a basket of shorted stocks as a required asset allocation to hedge against a drop in the overall market. Given this method for controlling market risk, Jones became liberated to amplify stock picking skills with leverage!

Jones regularly calculated the exposure of his capital to market risk using the formula shown below. His method of quantifying market exposure is highly valued by traditional hedge fund managers for its intuitive relevance, yet it is largely ignored or misunderstood by academics and the financial media.

$$\text{Market exposure} = \frac{\left(\text{Long exposure} - \text{Short exposure}\right)}{\text{Capital}}$$

A typical asset allocation for Jones would look like this: Given $1,000 in capital, he would employ leverage to purchase shares valued at $1,100 and sell shares short valued at $400. His gross investment of $1,500 (150 percent of capital) would have a net market exposure of only $700 ($1,100–$400), making this portfolio "70 percent net long." Although Jones valued stock picking over market timing, he increased or decreased the net market exposure of his portfolio based on his estimation of the strength of the market. Since the market generally rose, Jones was generally "net long."

There are two primary sources of risk in an equity portfolio: stock selection and the market. Jones designed his system to maximize the former and minimize the latter. Of the $1,500 gross investment in the example above, $700 was unhedged and $800 ($400 long and $400 short) was "within the hedge." Investments within the hedge are comprised of equal value long and short selections, and are thus approximately "market neutral." The $700 unhedged portion was exposed to the risks from both stock picking and the market, but the $800 within the hedge was exposed principally to the risks from stock picking.

Like the risk, performance *within the hedge* depends on stock selection more than market direction. In a rising market, good long selections will rise more than the market and good short selections will rise less than the market, yielding a net profit within the hedge. Conversely, in a declining market, good long selections will fall less than the market and good short selections will fall more than the market, again yielding a net profit within the hedge.

As is usually the case, not all of the stock picks in our example are within the hedge. In a declining market, profits from within the hedge may mitigate, but not entirely offset losses from the 70 percent net long exposure outside the hedge. Even when profits within the hedge don't offset "naked" exposure, the portfolio is structured to decline less than the market.

In theory, Jones's hedge fund system would provide superior performance relative to well-managed, long-only portfolios. In practice, it did.

• • •

Jones set up his fund as a general partnership in January of 1949 and converted it to a limited partnership in 1952. In addition to hedging with short sales and the use of leverage, the third major characteristic of Jones's fund was its incentive fee structure. None of these three characteristics were original or unique when Jones established his fund, but the way in which he combined them was. He operated in relative secrecy for about seventeen years; but in time, his secret got out, and his system became the model for the hedge fund industry.

Jones initially considered using a "hurdle" based incentive fee, which rewards the general partner for performance in excess of an agreed upon benchmark, either fixed or variable (such as the Dow Jones Index). He settled on a straight incentive of 20 percent of *realized* profits. There was no asset-based fee, nor was there a "high watermark" provision requiring the general partner to make up losses prior to taking additional incentive fees. Expenses were paid 20 percent by the general partner and 80 percent by the limited partners, except that salaries were paid entirely by the general partner.

Significantly, Jones agreed to keep all of his investment capital in the fund. He clearly acknowledged that it was unreasonable for him to receive high incentive fees for risking his partners' capital, unless he took the same risks with his own. Since Jones was imminently aware of the premium his system placed on good stock selection, he became uncomfortable with its dependency on his individual stock-picking skills.

The compelling need for manager diversification moved Jones to convert his partnership into the first multimanager hedge fund in 1954, by bringing Dick Radcliffe in to run a portion of the portfolio. Over the years Jones had as many as eight independent portfolio managers at a time running money for the partnership. Many of these managers ran a model portfolio to demonstrate their stock-picking skills prior to being hired by Jones.

These portfolio managers were given tremendous autonomy, as long as they were not making duplicate or opposing investments. In essence, Jones had created a well-diversified fund of funds, at a time when there were no other hedge funds in existence. By 1984, there were some excellent hedge funds operating on Jones's principles, and at age 82, he amended his partnership agreement, formally becoming a fund of funds investing in a diversified selection of outside managers.

Jones never bid to create market neutrality by keeping all of his investments within the hedge. He did, however, seek to find a reliable measure for what he called "velocity," or the speed at which a stock's price would change in relation to changes in the market, as a stock-picking aid. Velocity was akin to beta, as we use it to quantify volatility. Jones and his portfolio managers toiled with the concept of velocity for decades, never finding a useful method for reliably predicting a stock's behavior.

Successful hedge funds afford an excellent environment for the incubation of new hedge fund managers, and Jones's partnership, as we might expect, produced the first fledglings. Carl Jones (no relation), who came in shortly after Dick Radcliffe, was the first of A. W. Jones's managers to set up his own hedge fund, City Associates, in 1964. Dick Radcliffe left a year later, teaming with Barton Biggs to establish Fairfield Partners.

Other incentive-based partnerships were set up in the mid 1950s, including Warren Buffett's Omaha-based Buffett Partners and Walter Schloss's WJS Partners, but their funds were styled with a long bias after Benjamin Graham's partnership. Under today's broadened definition, these funds would also be considered hedge funds, but regularly shorting shares to hedge market risk was not central to their investment strategies.

1966 to 1969: Proliferation

At the beginning of 1966, the hedge fund industry was still in its infancy with no more than a handful of Jones-style hedge funds in operation. A watershed event occurred that April with the publication of *The Jones Nobody Keeps Up With* in *Fortune*,[8] penned by Carol J. Loomis.

Mutual funds had become the darlings of the era, and like today, investors were spellbound by their performance rankings. Loomis' article shocked the investment community by describing something called a "hedge fund," run by an unknown (at least to the investment community) sociologist named Alfred Jones. It was handily outperforming the best mutual funds,

---

[8] Carol J. Loomis, "The Jones Nobody Keeps Up With," *Fortune*, April 1966, 237–247.

after deducting an inconceivable 20 percent incentive fee! Over the prior five years, the best mutual fund was the Fidelity Trend Fund; yet Jones bettered it by 44 percent, after all fees and expenses. Over 10 years, the best mutual fund was the Dreyfus Fund; yet Jones bettered it by 87 percent.

Needless to say, the Loomis article provided ample fantasy fodder for both investors and money managers. Investors estimated the impact of hedge fund investing on their portfolios and began inquiring how to find such an investment. Money managers estimated the impact of 20 percent incentive fees on their incomes and began setting up hedge funds.

But how do you run a hedge fund? Loomis covered that, too, providing a virtual blueprint of Jones's structure and operation. It's reasonable to presume photocopiers were working overtime on Wall Street and across the country, as the first great stampede into hedge funds got under way.

Although we don't know how many hedge funds were established in the three-year flurry following Loomis's article, estimates range from 140 to several hundred. Michael Steinhardt and George Soros were among those setting up funds at the time. The SEC found 215 investment partnerships in a survey for the year ending 1968 and concluded that 140 of these were hedge funds, with the majority formed that year.

This was the zenith of the "go-go years," and a bull market was raging. The broad equity markets, as reflected in the Value Line Composite Index, rose some 55 percent in 1967 and 1968. The legion of new hedge fund managers soon discovered that hedging a portfolio with short sales is time consuming, difficult, and costly, especially in a bull market. Jones observed that selling equities short is a strategy that simply does not suit the psychological makeup of most equity managers, in any market.

The intoxicating combination of incentive fees and leverage in a bull market seduced most of the new hedge fund managers into using high margin with only token hedging, if any at all. These unhedged managers were, as we say, "swimming naked."

1969–1974: Contraction

A favorite axiom of hedge fund managers who continuously allocate the substantial effort and expense required for prudent hedging in a leveraged portfolio, even in bull markets, is this: "You don't know who's swimming naked until the tide goes out."

In the final few days of 1968, the tide started out. Between then and the end of 1974, there were two powerful undertows in the equities markets, separated by a period of relative tranquillity. Although the second of these (1973–74) is more renowned, the first (1969–70) was more damaging to the young hedge fund industry, because most of the new managers were swimming naked. For the 28 largest hedge funds in the SEC survey at year end 1968, assets under management declined 70 percent (from losses and withdrawals) by year end 1970, and five of them were shut down. Smaller funds fared worse.

From 1969 through 1974, the broad market, measured by the Value Line Composite Index, declined more than 70 percent. Blue chip stocks, measured by the S&P 500 with dividends reinvested, fell only 5 percent over the 1969–70 downdraft; yet the broad market declined some 43 percent. The following two years were the eye of the storm, when the blue chips rose some 36 percent, and the broad market rose about 10 percent. The second downdraft, 1973–74, took the blue chips down about 37 percent, and the broad market fell a devastating 57 percent.

From the spring of 1966 through the end of 1974, the hedge fund industry had ballooned and burst, but a number of well-managed funds survived and quietly carried on. Among the managers who endured were Alfred Jones, George Soros and Michael Steinhardt.

The lesson of these broad market undertows has been lost on many hedge fund managers swimming naked in the 1990s.

The New Modalities

The financial press has influenced the creation of hedge funds since the mid 1960s. Indeed, the correlation between revealing articles on hedge funds and the creation of new funds was dramatic in 1966–68. Although the relationship may not have continued as one of cause and effect, there have certainly been strong parallels ever since.

In the decade following the 1974 market bottom, hedge funds returned to operating in relative obscurity, as they had prior to April of 1966. The investment community largely forgot about them. During this period, comparatively few hedge funds were established, but among them was one of the best.

In May of 1986, an imposing face on the cover of *Institutional Investor*[9] compelled readers to explore *The red-hot world of Julian Robertson*. This cover story, by Julie Rohrer, was prominent among several articles that reintroduced investors to the astonishing potential of hedge funds. Rohrer reported that Robertson's Tiger Fund had been compounding at 43 percent during its first six years, net of expenses and incentive fees. Performance prior to deducting expenses and incentive fees had been about 50 percent per year. This compared to 18.7 percent for the S&P 500 during the same period.

[9] Julie Rohrer, "The Red-Hot World of Julian Robertson," *Institutional Investor*, May 1986, 86–92.

Importantly, the article established that Robertson was an investor, not a trader, and that he always hedged his portfolio with short sales. This was textbook Alfred Jones investing, not high-stakes gambling. Rohrer's piece also shed light on how, in 1985, Robertson began adopting newly developed financial instruments to prudently and profitably improve on Jones's original model (although she never mentioned Jones). Robertson called these instruments, not available to Jones in his prime, "the new modalities."

Robertson had made his first significant "global macro play" in early 1985, anticipating the dollar would decline against Swiss francs, deutsche marks, sterling, and the yen. His Tiger Fund, and offshore sister fund Jaguar, spent some $7 million on foreign currency call options, limiting downside risk to less than 2 percent of capital. Over several months, profits from the bet exceeded several hundred percent of the capital risked.

Citing this example, Rohrer demonstrated how a good manager, operating from a base of well-hedged equities, developed strong convictions from the best available information, and, calculating risk, acted affirmatively on those convictions to generate exceptional profits. In essence, she showed a new generation of professionals on Wall Street the difference between a well-run hedge fund and traditional equity management. Many of her readers proved to be latent hedge fund managers who set up their own funds in the following years.

In the mid 1980s, Julian Robertson used the phrase "new modalities" to describe innovations in financial futures and options; but looking back from the mid 1990s, the phrase is equally if not more useful in describing the diversified evolution of hedge fund styles. Hundreds of hedge funds with specialized investing systems, bearing no resemblance to Jones's equity hedging, have been established since 1980.

The menu of incentive-based managers now includes: A variety of sector equity funds, dedicated short funds, convertible and merger arbitrage funds, technical trading funds, distressed securities funds, global macro funds, developed market funds, emerging market funds, a variety of market neutral funds, fixed-income and synthetic debt funds, derivatives funds, and more. In addition, there are funds of funds which, like Alfred Jones back in the 1950s, seek to diversify risk among different managers.

Many of these new funds actively control risk by hedging via one or more methods, but many do not. Most use leverage, but relatively few leverage beyond two times capital. A small minority uses enormous leverage, yet many use little or no leverage at all. A large number of these funds have exceptionally talented managers, but many do not.

Somewhat confusingly, all of these newer funds are now considered "hedge funds." The single unifying element between Alfred Jones and many of these new funds is that all have justified incentive-based fees with the promise of superior performance. Many deliver, but many do not!

Considerable caution must be used when reviewing performance statistics for the hedge fund industry and its various segments. Even the best statistics are skewed by asset weighting (or a lack thereof), voluntary selection, and a strong survivor bias. It's highly unlikely that hedge fund performance statistics accurately reflect the true, weighted-average return to investors for any segment of the industry.

Nonetheless, for decades the hedge fund platform has attracted much of the best investment talent available, along with numerous "wanna-bes." Hedge funds have repeatedly produced a disproportionately large share of the remarkable returns at the extreme right of the performance bell curve. In all probability, they will continue to do so.

Finding Superior Performance

Commingling assets with better hedge fund managers has provided immense gratification for many investors over the years. Which managers, in retrospect, will have provided comparable gratification to investors a decade from now? This is a challenging question.

The science of investing ponders the past, while the art of investing focuses on the future. Finding good hedge funds requires a reasonable mix of both, and we should focus our attention to the areas that will help the most. In the long run, the three key variables for hedge fund performance are motivation, opportunity, and compass. All three can and should be evaluated for any prospective hedge fund investment.

Motivation

The motivational dynamics of Alfred Jones's original hedge fund model run straight to the core of capitalistic instinct in managers and investors. The critical motives for a manager are high incentives for superior performance, coupled with significant, personal risk of loss. Hedge fund investors should seek to maintain both of these motives in their selections.

Early in the history of the industry, new managers began to alter Jones's formula. Many funds that were set up after 1966, adopted a 1 percent asset-based fee, in addition to the incentive fee. Most of these attached a "high watermark" requirement in exchange for the inclusion of an asset fee, but many did not.

The original justification for augmenting incentive fees with an asset fee was the presumption of a correlation between size and performance. One does exist. Smaller managers can provide superior performance, because the most profitable inefficiencies in the market are relatively small. But smaller managers, lacking efficiencies of scale, have relatively high overhead. As such, the asset fee was justified to help defray the expenses of small funds.

Hedge fund investors accepted this rationale, and the prevailing fee structure for the hedge fund industry became 1 percent of assets plus 20 percent of profits, subject to a high watermark. Although this is the "standard fee" in the industry today, others exist. These range from George Soros' Quantum Fund, with a 1 percent asset fee plus a 15 percent incentive fee, to some newer funds with 2 percent asset fees and 25–30 percent incentives.

Some long-term hedge fund investors argue that there was implied in the standard fee, and sometimes clearly articulated by hedge fund managers, a commitment to remain small. Jones's motivational dynamics work exceedingly well for most smaller funds, even under the modified standard fee structure, but not so well for larger funds. A range of structural modifications could bring good motivational dynamics back into play for even the largest funds, but consideration of these modifications goes beyond the scope of this introduction.

The fact that "standard hedge fund fees" entitle managers to "mutual fund fees" in a bad year, but mutual fund fees plus 20 percent of profits in mediocre and good years, has not been lost on hordes of new entrants to the industry. To the degree that investors permit, a migration toward "entitled" hedge fund fees will continue, without a corresponding migration toward superior performance.

There is distinct irony in the evolution of motivational dynamics for hedge funds, particularly as assets under management grow. Alfred Jones, who advocated entitlements for the poor, designed his fund with purely capitalistic incentives. Today, we acknowledge that entitlements can actually harm the poor; yet increasingly, we accept entitlement fee structures for hedge funds.

The original and continuing justification for incentive fees in hedge funds is the inherent promise of superior performance—not average performance, not absolute performance, but superior performance. Prudence dictates that investors fundamentally grasp Jones's motivational dynamics and seek to replicate them in the hedge funds they choose.

Opportunity

Superior performance can only be achieved when sufficient opportunity exists. This may be self-evident, but the shifting tides of opportunity often are not.

Although a gross oversimplification, comparing the level of opportunity for different hedge fund managers (or management styles) to the level of water in reservoirs is useful for visualizing the impact of opportunity on hedge fund performance. Mobility for a boat varies substantially as the water level in the reservoir rises and falls. At very low water levels, a boat may become stranded. In addition, mobility may become restricted due to the overcrowding of boats in the same reservoir. At times it becomes more sensible to tow a boat to a fuller or less crowded reservoir.

What happens if a boat grows into a ship? Ships are more suited for the high seas and can enter relatively few reservoirs. If a ship does enter a reservoir, it is restricted to only the deepest channels, while small boats move freely about it. A drop in the reservoir's water level can be disastrous for a ship.

Opportunity is influenced by internal and external factors. External variables are often somewhat quantifiable for a given style of management. For instance, distressed security managers are directly impacted by the number and size of bankruptcies and debt restructurings. Risk arbitrage managers are impacted by the level of merger activity. Emerging market managers are impacted by the aggregate flow of capital into and out of developing economies. Almost all styles are impacted by increased competition.

The most obvious internal variable influencing opportunity is size of assets under management. As hedge funds grow, they may be forced out of investment styles that were central to performance in earlier years. A number of hedge fund styles are affected by growth in this manner, but some are not. If the performance for a given style drops as assets under management grow, the fund is restricted by "capacity limits."

Unfortunately, capacity limits are not often distinct. They vary not only with size, but with size relative to external opportunity. Consider two hedge funds with the same investment style and equal management, one at (or near) its capacity limits but the other well within its capacity limits. Both will likely prosper when opportunity abounds, but in a "dry period" the fund operating well within its limits will likely perform much better. (The qualification for equal management in this example is important, because many small funds appear to operate well within capacity limits; due to limited management resources, they may be operating beyond their capacity limits.)

Relative opportunity for different hedge funds can be evaluated on a continuing basis. Some multimanager investors and fund of funds managers adjust asset allocations according to the perceived levels of opportunity for different manager styles; others simply make equal allocations to different style managers for diversification.

Compass

The English language lacks a term that singularly characterizes innate capitalistic genius. We use the word "compass" here, as a noun, to embody the intrinsic qualities that guide superior capitalists.[10] This concept takes us back to our coin-flipping scenarios, and the problem posed by an affirmative answer to the question (page 4) of whether you have considered setting up a hedge fund.

Flipping a coin requires minimal dexterity and no talent. On the other hand, Jones's traditional model for hedging and using leverage in an equity portfolio is exceedingly difficult to successfully execute, for managers lacking compass! The same applies for most other styles of hedge funds.

More than anything else, compass equips an individual with an eminent estimation for both opportunity and risk. It embodies an aggregation of qualities, most of which are probably acquired during an individual's formative years. Unlike investment technique, compass is neither taught nor learned at even the finest universities. An individual with compass can easily obtain the tools for hedging, but an individual with the tools for hedging cannot easily obtain compass.

So how can you discern if a manager has compass? The determination is most reliably made through direct observation. Historical performance records are poor indicators of a manager's compass, unless studied in the context of the specific strategies that produced the record. Indeed, impressive performance records from highly concentrated, unhedged management styles can attract unsophisticated investors by masking enormous unmanaged risk to capital.

It takes a great deal of effort to differentiate whether high performance comes from high-stakes gambling, or from competent risk management by an individual with true compass. It's effort well spent.

Of the three key variables for hedge fund performance, compass is the most critical for superior performance. As such, it's appropriate that we conclude with the views of Alfred Jones for good hedge fund management, revealed in *The Money Managers*[11]:

> *A money manager, Jones says, must have "an interesting set of abilities." He needs vitality, aggressiveness and good judgment, of course. But beyond that, Jones stresses the fact that he must have two sets of balances. One is "a balance between boldness and caution." The other is a blend of "gullibility and skepticism." This, Jones explains, is because "a money manager doesn't dream up ideas. He gathers ideas from other*

---

[10] **com•pass** *n.* 1. the intrinsic quality that guides superior capitalists. 2. innate capitalistic genius. *Lookout Mountain Hedge Fund Review,* 1 September 1994, 1.

[11] G. Kaplan and C. Welles, *The Money Managers,* Institutional Investors Systems, Inc., 1969, 118.

sources. I've seen both extremes and the ultra-gullible is the worst because he can be led up the garden path. But being too skeptical is not very good either."

Successful money managers must also be tuned into the latest fads. "He must know what is coming into vogue, into fashion," Jones says, "because that is what he wants to have [before everyone else]."

An investor who adroitly evaluates hedge funds in the context of motivation, opportunity, and compass will find funds that deliver superior long-term performance! Then, upon making a reasonable allocation of capital, he or she becomes a more "prudent man."

PART I

Hedge Funds in the Investment Portfolio

CHAPTER 2

Institutional Investment in Hedge Funds

William J. Crerend, Chairman
Evaluation Associates Capital Markets, Inc.

Institutional investors have yet to fully embrace the opportunities that exist in investing in hedge funds. Whether it be confusion over the proper classification of hedge funds within the asset allocation policy, concerns over liquidity, disclosure of information, high fees, UBTI or other commonly voiced apprehensions, there are clearly barriers to entry that have kept hedge funds from being flooded with sizable, institutional assets.

It is our contention that pressures on performance over the next decade from investments in traditional asset categories, which in the prior decade offered returns well in excess of their historical averages, and an improved understanding and less skeptical attitude toward hedge fund investing, will provide the catalyst for institutions to gravitate toward investing in hedge funds and other inefficient, nontraditional asset categories.

This chapter will provide some perspective on institutional investing and describe briefly why we believe hedge funds will eventually have a role in the management of institutional assets.

Evolution of Institutional Investing

To understand the relationship of hedge funds to the institutional fund sponsor universe it is necessary to first go back about 40 years to the beginning of the private pension system in the United States, and to that of its close relative, the world of endowment funds.

In the 1950s, equity investment in these funds was small. Fixed income was deemed the only thing really safe and suitable for trust funds and fiduciary assets. A few things happened to change the attitude toward equity.

The S&P 500 returned 19 percent on an annually compounded basis for the 1950–59 period. Yes, the 1950s even outperformed the 1980s! Second, final pay benefit formulae were introduced to U.S. pension funds. These replaced career average plans, and, in so doing, effectively transferred the ultimate adequacy of pension benefits from the employee to predominantly the employer. Accordingly, the employer became instantly sensitized to the fact that higher investment returns meant lower costs and, equally as important, that benefits, driven by inflation, would be higher than before. Equity became important to institutional portfolio management and the banks offered to manage them in a prudent manner. This was tough competition for the insurance companies that had previously dominated the pension investment business, but saw only the risk, rather than the opportunity in equity investment. Additionally, by today's standards, inflation was not a problem over the period either. Average annual inflation for the 1950–59 period was 2 percent and throughout 1960–69, 2.5 percent. As such, with 8 percent average annual compound returns for equity through 1960–69, it was a fine period for real returns. Actually, for the 20-year period ending in 1969, real returns for equity averaged 11 percent per year. Who could resist that appeal?

By the mid to late 1960s, brokers and mutual fund-related investment management entities began to compete with the banks for this new equity business. Indeed, some good people left these organizations to start their own firms, many surviving today as sizable investment management entities.

Pension funds made the transition from banks to these new organizations with ease. This loss of business was hardly felt by banks, however, as the growth in institutional assets was sufficient to grow their businesses, even in the face of these successful new competitors. In addition, their market share remained quite hefty because many institutional dollars remained under bank management, mostly because equity investment was still relatively new to clients and potentially a volatile asset class. This was brought home by the disorientation of 1969 (S&P 500, down 8 percent) concurrent with an upward movement in interest rates (Salomon High Grade Long Term Corporate Bond Index, down 8 percent), the latter triggering the beginnings of what we now call "active bond management." Then 1971–72 produced the famous "nifty fifty" markets followed by big down legs during 1973–74. At best, sponsors learned that equity as an asset class could be volatile.

Also, we should not forget ERISA in September 1974, released almost at the exact hour of the end of the worst downturn in U.S. equity markets since the Great Depression. It was an attack on corporate responsibility for the funding adequacy and risk management of U.S. pension funds, and through its re-definition of the "prudent man," essentially beatified registered investment advisors and re-beatified banks and insurance companies. Language of the act was very scary. Its principles crept over to non-ERISA-covered employee benefit and endowment funds as well. The message— fund sponsor fiduciaries, who benefited little or nil from serving in that capacity, were crazy to do much of anything other than "U.S. stocks and bonds." Surely real estate, venture, and international were to creep in as asset classes but would never dislodge domestic equities and fixed-income investments.

The 1980s were a wonderful return to good times with the stock and bond markets up 18 percent and 13 percent respectively. This reinforced institutional focus on traditional equity investing. That same buoyant period also caused a catch-up need to go global. The Europe, Australia, and Far East (EAFE) index of Morgan Stanley Capital International was up 22 percent for that same decade. While EAFE (and now emerging markets as well) carries currency risk, it is not dominant in the possible total return available from the asset class and, most important, it is essentially the same process used in equity investment in the United States: buy good companies at a reasonable price. Nothing fancy, just more of the same in foreign lands.

Striving for Investment Returns

It is important to remember that pension and endowment funds are not in the performance business as such. Put simply, foundations and endowments on average seek to achieve sufficient returns necessary to satisfy their required levels of disbursement: 5–6 percent annually, plus inflation. Roughly, that nominal target would be 10 percent, the average return for U.S. equity over the last 65 years. Pension funds get a little more complicated but with a similar nominal target. Since neither pension nor endowment funds pay taxes, a 10 percent nominal return over long periods of time, assuming 3–4 percent inflation, would be fine. The fact that the normal return approximates that of the U.S. equity market over long periods of time and is the largest of the asset classes in institutional funds is no accident. Equally as important is that a 50/50 stock-bond asset mix would have achieved that target as well over most periods in the last 10 years.

While the glorious investment environment over the last decade enabled most institutional funds to achieve or exceed target return objectives, the road to comparable bottom line results for taxable entities, by contrast, was a bit more challenging. We believe the predominance of taxable entities in hedge funds is no accident, in the positive sense. The imperative of performance is clear: Individuals need to pay taxes as well as deal with inflation, and a simple illustration brings that point home:

Pre-tax investment performance	20%	15%	10%	5%
Tax assumption: 40%	(8%)	(6%)	(4%)	(2%)
Inflation assumption: 4%	(4%)	(4%)	(4%)	(4%)
Net after tax & inflation:	**8%**	**5%**	**2%**	**–1%**

In general, an individual, particularly one living off the returns of invested assets, needs to seek 15 percent or more potential rates of return. Anything lower begins to marginally compete with, or underperform the after-tax return on municipal bonds. Accordingly, from a historic basis, traditional long U.S. equity returns (10+ percent) for taxable entities makes sense only in specialized circumstances such as capital gains qualifying investment results in low tax rate states, preferreds for corporations, finding exceptional investment managers, or periods of exceptionally high returns in the U.S. equity markets. Such exceptional returns have been the case for rolling five-year periods since the early 1980s. That, plus exceptionally low short-term interest rates have caused substantial investment in managed traditional equity by both taxable and tax-exempt investors. The question is: Will the returns and related investment continue? From a historic perspective, it seems unlikely. It seems that while the historic average annual returns of 10+ percent from equity are still reasonable to expect, we have been earning well above that for some time. Consequently, it may be fair to expect that we are going to earn below that for a while. We are not certain when, but we think it is coming.

If we are right, it portends a change in institutional perspective. Not only do bonds offer little more than prudent ballast to institutional portfolios, hardly offering real returns over the long term, but now equity itself is to be challenged. If 10 percent is the nominal target, where might it be had? And can it be had in sufficient size so as to "replace equity"? The answer is no, and, as such, we may well be entering a period of strain on investment returns for institutional funds. If so, in our opinion, institutions will begin sampling and reaching for returns outside of their normal spectrum, and that is happening already. There is bottom fishing in U.S. real estate; emerging markets equity is beginning as an asset class; EAFE country equity investment, now at about 5 percent, will rise over decades to perhaps 20 percent of total portfolios; private equity investment in emerging markets is in an embryonic stage, and we are finally seeing the early signs of institutional investment in hedge funds and other nontraditional strategies, broadly defined.

Why Invest in Hedge Funds?

If our thesis is correct that we may be entering a period in which returns from traditional asset classes revert to or below their historic averages, then what characteristics do hedge funds possess that may appeal to an institutional investor striving to attain a defined investment return during perhaps a less buoyant investment climate? Broadly defined, hedge funds are private partnerships wherein the manager/general partner has a significant personal stake in the fund and is free to operate in a variety of markets and to utilize investments and strategies with variable long/short exposures and degrees of leverage. It is the hedge fund manager's opportunistic approach, flexibility, responsiveness, and orientation toward producing absolute returns from which his or her compensation is typically derived, which is part of the appeal of investing in these vehicles.

The investment strategies employed by hedge fund managers are quite diverse. We generally define the categories of hedge fund managers as:

- *Market neutral*—balanced long/short positions
- *Opportunistic*—variable exposures to markets, investments and strategies
- *Futures/currencies*—forwards, futures, physicals, securities, and options
- *Event-driven*—deal arbitrage and bankruptcies

As shown in Figure 2-1 (which represents the range of returns by category—high to low—and the quartile distribution of those returns), the median manager return for each of the hedge fund categories (as displayed by the bold horizontal line within each bar) has exceeded the S&P 500 and the average (long only) traditional equity manager over the last five years ending 6/30/94. In fact, the median opportunistic hedge fund manager, for example, has nearly doubled the return of the S&P 500 over this period (16.8% vs. 8.5%). Furthermore, as displayed in Figure 2-2, the returns for the strategies are attractive on a risk-adjusted basis. Finally, by blending hedge funds with traditional asset classes (e.g., S&P 500), portfolio diversification is generally enhanced. Figure 2-3 illustrates how incremental allocations of the four categories of hedge funds to an all S&P 500 Index portfolio improves diversification.

Therefore, with a possible strain on investment returns on the horizon, we believe that the flexible and opportunistic investment style of hedge fund managers provides for greater investment return opportunities versus traditional asset classes over the next decade.

Gravitation into Hedge Funds

Certainly foundation and endowment funds have been more visible in hedge fund investing than pension funds, but they have not been many in number. In the years ahead they should maintain their lead, at least for awhile, because their need is more immediate. Foundations and endowments need to disburse 5–6 percent per year, and inflation, while currently low, will not

FIGURE 2-1.   Performance Comparison—Hedge Funds
Five Years ending June 30, 1994

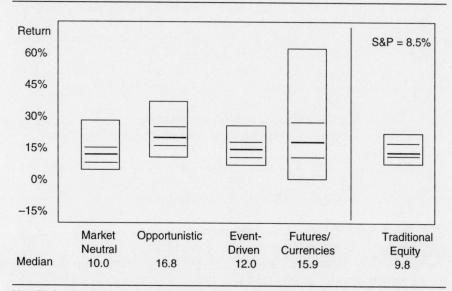

Median	Market Neutral	Opportunistic	Event-Driven	Futures/ Currencies	Traditional Equity
	10.0	16.8	12.0	15.9	9.8

Note: Hedge Fund categories reflect EAI manager universes, net of fees from 6/30/89–6/30/94.

FIGURE 2-2.   Risk/Return Comparison—Hedge Fund Manager Categories

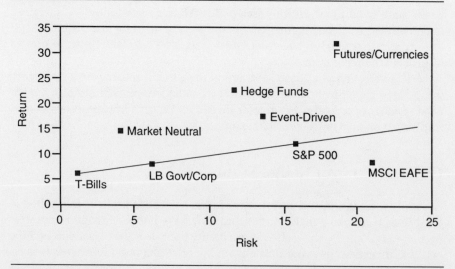

Note: Hedge Fund categories represent EAI manager universes, net of fees from 1987–1994:2Q.

FIGURE 2-3.   Diversification Enhancement
Incremental Allocations of Hedge Funds

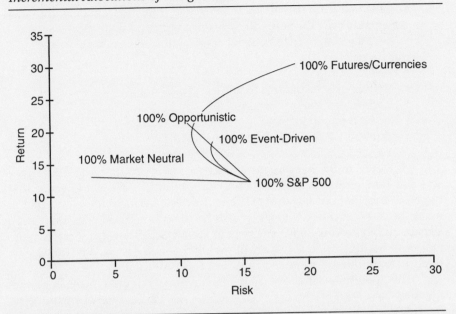

Note: Hedge Fund categories reflect EAI manager universes, net of fees from 1988–1994:2Q.

abate materially. Any shortfall from 10% ± will be painful if it is sustained over a few years, and investment goals will be more stringently targeted.

Pension funds, on the other hand, have time to react. Asset valuations are generally averaged over years so residual cost calculations, which are partially derived from these averages, will take some time to surface. However, the sheer size of pension funds makes them a force in any transition no matter how slowly they might be moving.

Conclusion

Ultimately, the $5 trillion that is our estimate of pension, foundation, and endowment assets will orient a small portion of those assets to hedge funds. When they do, some predictable things will happen, including:

- Some hedge funds will become very large (some would argue this is already happening).

- Since bottom-up (micro) management cannot absorb big assets, top-down (macro) will become dominant.
- Some hedge funds will fail to make that transition competently; arguably only the best will have the adaptive skill to do it.
- Returns relative to traditional assets will suffer unless leverage is increased.
- Fees will drop.
- Portfolio disclosure will increase.
- Practitioners will proliferate.
- Regulation will increase.
- Ultimately the area will be institutionalized.

However, in the interim, the challenge and opportunity for fund sponsors and hedge fund practitioners will be substantial. We would argue that the best, and first in, will do well. It is a decision best made with FIFO in mind, because after some years, it will be time to rephase back into traditional equity markets and management for attractive returns. Our guess is that most institutions will not adapt rapidly enough and, as a result, will be inadvertently pursuing either a LIFO or LILO philosophy.

The attainment of above 10 percent average annual returns is getting tougher than anytime in the last 10–15 years. The nature of institutional investing is not to be opportunistic on a cyclical but rather secular basis. We believe what is coming will require more of an opportunistic approach.

CHAPTER 3

Investing in Hedge Funds: Investment Policy Implications

David A. White, Executive Vice President
AIG International Capital Management Inc.

A primary message of this chapter is that the percentage of assets to be allocated to hedge funds should not be determined or influenced by Markowitz mean-variance optimization techniques. Skill-based strategies (a less loaded, more general terminology than the overused, narrower phrase hedge funds) offer several interesting attributes for asset allocation practitioners:

- Low correlation with traditional asset classes.
- High expected risk-adjusted returns.
- A source of return not explained by the Capital Asset Pricing Model.

Mean-variance optimization models love these attributes. Usually, the assumptions for skill-based strategies need to be tightly constrained, because the optimization models allocate very large proportions to these strategies. Normally, fiduciary committees find the unconstrained output unacceptable. As a result, the mean-variance theoretical allocations leave us without an acceptable mathematical answer to the question of how much to allocate to these strategies. After discussing why mean-variance analysis is not appropriate for the allocation issue, the chapter concludes by discussing the practical issues that plan sponsors should consider in reaching conclusions on how much to invest in hedge funds.

The Opportunity

There are three sources of returns which the hedge fund manager is positioned to exploit particularly well. In comparison to traditional managers, the hedge fund manager should be able to provide higher alphas, since relative outperformance against a benchmark is not the primary objective.

First, the hedge fund manager minimizes "dead weight." Dead weight in a portfolio results from securities owned into which the manager has no insight. For example, in a long equity account, the manager may maintain a market weighting in oil stocks in order to control tracking error within an acceptable range, even when the manager has no insight into the energy sector. The proportion of the portfolio which is held to control residual volatility (volatility relative to the benchmark) is the proportion that will not add value. In a hedge fund, in general, only positions about which the manager has conviction will be held. Portfolio risk and residual volatility are controlled with swaps or options, which require less capital than holding dead-weight securities. Consequently, a higher proportion of the skill-sector manager's capital is invested in securities about which the manager has convictions.

Second, because skill-sector managers can utilize leverage, often very high leverage, small inefficiencies can produce good returns when leveraged. For example, if 28-year Treasuries are trading five basis points cheap to 30-year Treasuries, a strategy of buying the 28s and selling short the 30s will produce very good risk-adjusted returns if leveraged 30 or 40 to one. But a strategy of purchasing the 28-year Treasuries in an unleveraged account is not very attractive.

Third, hedge fund managers are constantly scouring new or alternative markets for attractive investments, without the limitations often found in guidelines or policies established by pension or endowment fiduciaries. The probability that high risk-adjusted returns will be realized is increased, because skill centered managers are opportunistic and move into inefficient markets earlier than traditional managers. An example of a market with few participants and large inefficiencies was emerging markets debt and Brady bonds in 1993, and defaulted real estate mortgages in 1994. The absence of purchasers provided very good returns for the pioneers in these markets. This lack of inhibition, so common among hedge fund managers, generally leads them into the most attractive markets ahead of the typical institutional investor.

These three elements taken together—minimized dead weight, leverage, and opportunistic attitude—form a logical, strong case that the skill-based manager should produce higher alphas than traditional managers. These strategies often will be highly volatile, but there is increased probability of success from sources (i.e., skill) not explained by traditional finance theory. Since the strategies do not depend on a particular economic environment, expectations are that returns will not be correlated with traditional capital market sector (equity, fixed income, etc.) returns.

Other Attributes

Hedge fund managers' returns are dependent on skill. In the case of directional traders (the so-called macro hedge funds), returns are also a function of skill, since exposure to capital market sectors is adjusted frequently. The Capital Asset Pricing Model (CAP-M) holds that returns are compensation for bearing undiversifiable systematic risk. Further, adherents of the efficient market theory hold that active managers cannot add value.

Skill-sector managers, therefore, operate in defiance of some long-established "truths" of finance. Returns are dependent on skill and are not a function of bearing capital market risk. Measured in beta or duration, the exposures of skill managed accounts are close to zero. The Rockefeller Foundation regularly monitors betas in its hedge fund portfolio and the highest positive beta is found in the risk arbitrage accounts, where it is approximately .40. In most skill-based strategies, capital market exposures are hedged to remove unwanted market risk and difficult to forecast market action. In long/short equal amounts of equity—a strategy popularized in 1991 by institutional investors such as the Unisys pension plan, the Weyerhaeuser pension plan and The Rockefeller Foundation—beta is explicitly maintained at zero to produce returns from stock selection skill only, independent of the equity market. Early expectations for this strategy were that the "quant" managers who first researched and implemented it had found a method to mint 15 percent T-bills. Within the strategy's first two years, these hopes were dashed as it proved impossible to create 15 percent T-bills.

Long-term track records for the skill-based strategies are short. The explosive growth of hedge funds did not begin until the late 1980s and though accurate databases for this period are now becoming available, good quality data before 1987 is virtually nonexistent. The proliferation of approaches and increasing specialization did not begin until recently. A good source of accurate data for people interested in following the performance of the alternative assets segment of the investment industry is the quarterly article in *Barron's* written by E. Lee Hennessee of the E. Lee Hennessee Group. Objective and free from headline bias (which results from the press's tendency to report on managers whose results are at the extremes), her group's data is available to the general interest reader inexpensively for the price of a weekly publication.

Terms and Structure

The standard terms of hedge funds usually favor the manager. Institutional investors who are accustomed to a separate account structure will not find the norms in the hedge fund industry familiar. Investors should not be surprised by the stiff terms usually demanded by the manager.

Investments are generally made in partnerships (LP) or limited liability companies (LLC). These structures are often explained by 100-page disclosure documents which warn the investor that the strategy is subject to high risks, that everything could be lost, and that, most likely, the strategy is not suitable for anyone. It states that portfolio listings are never available, that the manager is only liable for fraud and the grossest acts of negligence, that there are many sources of unresolved conflicts of interest, and that the investor can get his or her money back only infrequently (annually with advance notice is common). In effect, full control is given to the manager, and the investor's rights are tightly constrained.

The message of this section for asset owners is to begin behaving like owners and to negotiate every term as if this were a separate account. To achieve favorable terms, it will often be necessary to establish separate accounts, but pressure can be brought to bear on the managers by investing only in deals with the best terms when the structure is an LP or LLC. To limit conflicts of interest, it is important to demand that all fees be included in partnership income and that involvement by the manager in other businesses be limited. Investors should seek to minimize the "lock up" period to one quarter or less, perhaps by agreeing to pay redemption fees for unscheduled withdrawals. Require errors and omissions insurance at least at the 10 percent of assets level. Since some hedge fund strategies may be limited in terms of how much capital can be profitably deployed, place limits on assets under management. This encourages the manager to stay within the original strategy and not seek ideas with higher liquidity. In this case, high fees work to the investor's advantage, as participation in the strategy is rationed by price.

Fee structures in skill managers are of the incentive variety. Apart from the level of fees, it is important to understand the fee structure and how it motivates the manager. An incentive structure without limits might encourage the manager to take risks well beyond what the investor would like. A high fee structure that starts at the first dollar of income does not motivate the manager to take any risks, particularly when there is a long lockup. Thus, in evaluating proposals, one should favor strategies that pay the incentive only after a hurdle rate of return is achieved and place an upper bound on the amount payable to the manager under the incentive formula. Finally, management fees should be sufficient to pay the manager a fair wage, but should not be high enough to make the manager wealthy. Some investors are beginning to demand that the management fee be subtracted from the incentive fee to communicate this point more effectively.

A term found in the majority of hedge fund fee structures is the "high water" mark provision. Under this provision, the manager cannot collect an incentive fee if cumulative returns are below the basis or hurdle above which the incentive fee is calculated. For example, in year one, given success, the manager will be paid a high incentive fee. In subsequent years, given failure in year two, the manager will not be paid a fee until success moves the asset balance above the cumulative benchmark. Even worse, the possibility exists that the manager could "owe" the investors a rebate of year one fees, because of negative cumulative performance. Experience with this formula suggests that it may not be as good a deal for investors as originally perceived. If a fund underperforms, the manager is motivated to quit and move to a new fund that is not below high water. Indeed, some of the personnel turnover at hedge funds in 1994 is attributed to this cause. A preferable structure, perhaps, would to make incentive payments only on a multi-year basis to smooth out the manager's income. Alternatively, consideration might be given to trading away the high water provision altogether in favor of a lower percentage incentive.

Examples of Skill-Based Investing

It is difficult to define with precision what a hedge fund or skill-sector manager is. Many definitions exist and a particularly popular, but unenlightening one, defines it as anything with a 2 percent flat management fee and a 25 percent incentive fee on the first dollar of profit. Indeed, the fee schedule charged by all of Rockefeller's hedge fund managers is of this form. But the problem with this definition is that it fails to describe the investment activity undertaken by the skill fund manager. Perhaps it is best to explain the concept by examples:

- Managed futures
- Currency as an asset class
- Convertible bond arbitrage
- Short selling
- Long/short common stock
- Capital structure arbitrage
- Risk arbitrage
- Leveraged mortgage derivative arbitrage
- Yield curve arbitrage
- Proprietary trading
- Volatility trading
- Traditional concentrated growth and value equity

The inclusion of managed futures at the top of this list is intentional to make a point. It means that returns from managed futures investing is the result of skill and that managed futures is not an asset class. Consequently, the claim that managed futures is a separate asset class that deserves an allocation based on mean-variance analysis is to be rejected. Managed futures managers argue vigorously that economic risk premiums are created because the primary users are hedging price risks, and through the mechanism of the futures market, transferring the hedging insurance premium to the futures buyer. While interesting in theory, it is difficult, if not impossible, to disentangle any systematic return "premium" from analysis of managed futures long-term time series data in the time-tested risk-premium framework originally set forth in 1982 by Ibbotson and Sinquefield for stocks, bonds, and bills.[1] Nonetheless, even if it is not an asset class, managed futures trading is a potentially high-alpha strategy and deserves to be included in any diversified skill-sector portfolio.

The strategies listed above do not have systematic duration or beta to produce returns. In leveraged mortgage arbitrage, for example, the manager may hold a long portfolio of mortgage-backed securities derivatives with duration of 50 to 60 years. To reduce the overall portfolio's downside duration to zero, the manager sells short an appropriate number of T-bond futures, hedges with put options to eliminate downside risk, or sells short other rich mortgage products. Because the portfolio has no duration, the returns arise from the manager's skill at selecting positions and managing the hedge.

The high return nature of these strategies is best illustrated by the returns of the nation's most successful securities firms such as Goldman, Sachs and Salomon Brothers. Both derive a high proportion of profits from highly leveraged proprietary trading activities. These firms are, perhaps, better examples of successful hedge funds than the specialized strategies listed above. Because of Federal Reserve Regulation T, which limits margin lending to customers using common stock as collateral, regulated broker-dealers are able to lever up much more than their customers and earn higher profits from such basic activities as futures arbitrage, convertible arbitrage, and statistical long/short trading. Institutional investors should consider lobbying to reverse this provision which reduces capital committed to certain equity strategies and gives the broker-dealer community a significant advantage.

Hedge funds can take many forms. But the source of return is not from the CAP-M theorized risk premium for bearing undiversifiable risk; it is from skill. Leaving aside the theoretical question of whether or not these returns should exist, E. Lee Hennessee Group's database for the seven-year

---

[1] Roger G. Ibbotson and Rex A. Sinquefield, *Stocks, Bonds, Bills, and Inflation: The Past and the Future*, Institute of Chartered Financial Analysis, 1982.

period ending December 31, 1993, showed that its hedge fund universe produced returns approximately 40 percent above the S&P 500 with dividends reinvested. At the end of 1993, the Hennessee Group's universe contained over 400 funds, up from 100 in 1987.

Many managers and consultants have shown that the addition of hedge funds to a diversified institutional investment program over the past seven years would have materially improved risk-adjusted results. Mean-variance optimizations with 5–20 percent exposure to hedge funds make the case that a substantial allocation to hedge funds would have dramatically improved overall performance. When plotted on the traditional linear capital market line showing T-bills (cash), the Salomon Broad Investment Grade Index (bonds), and the S&P 500 (stocks), hedge funds plot north (higher) of equities in the return dimension and to the west (lower) in the risk dimension.

Investment Policy Implications

Given the existence of high-quality data on skill-sector managers, can plan sponsors begin using historic hedge fund results with the same confidence that they use historic returns for stocks, bonds, and cash to establish asset allocation policy?

Two considerations suggest caution when using actual hedge fund data to form expectations. First, there is an interesting theoretical issue raised by the different sources of returns for hedge funds and asset classes. Second, there are several practical issues regarding hedge fund data, and other "alpha" data in general, which suggest that nonmathematical methods may provide better answers to the allocation question than mean-variance optimization.

Earlier, this chapter argued that the source of returns in hedge funds is manager skill. Above benchmark return is known as alpha for traditional asset class managers as well as skill-sector managers. In traditional long active fixed-income or equity accounts, 80 percent of the overall return is explained by asset class behavior (beta for stocks, duration for bonds), leaving 20 percent for skill or alpha. Hedge funds reverse the proportions by seeking to produce returns entirely from skill. Many hedge funds explicitly neutralize market risk or, if not fully hedged, avoid it substantially. Risk arbitrage—the purchase of an acquired company's stock in anticipation of merger consummation—is a good example of the latter, where measured betas run about .35–.40. Since there is limited market risk, 80 percent of returns in hedge funds result from skill. But the essential point is that the primary source of returns in asset class investing is from earning economic the risk premium, while in hedge funds it is from skill.

As a practical matter, it is possible to mix alpha and beta in mean-variance optimizations. And, provided the inputs for expected returns are accurate, the results will be reliable. Sponsors normally optimize only generic asset class allocations and do not input the required alpha data (return, standard deviation, correlation) for specific managers claiming the ability to exceed the applicable asset class benchmark. By way of contrast, in the hedge fund arena, there appears to be a greater willingness among sponsors to use hedge fund alphas alongside asset class betas to persuade fiduciary committees to invest in hedge funds. In such optimizations, alpha always drives out beta. As is well known, alpha is better than beta; it is usually positive, uncorrelated with most asset classes, and has lower volatility.

The theoretical issue is whether or not it is appropriate to mix alpha and beta, or to partially give effect to alpha by using it for hedge funds alone, without allowing other asset class managers the benefit of their supposed alphas in the optimizations. The reason sponsors have not optimized alphas among traditional investment managers is that alpha has proved to be very elusive, unstable, and difficult to identify. In hedge funds, as noted above, there are strong reasons to believe that alpha should be higher than in traditional active management. Some may find that logic sufficient to allow hedge fund alphas in the optimizations, while keeping other active alphas out.

On the practical side, there are several concerns about the use of hedge fund history to establish long-term expectations for mean-variance optimization. First, the required inputs for pure alpha (correlation, return, standard deviation) are unstable. Second, historic analysis on the existence of alpha in traditional managers suggest skepticism when faced with similar claims from skill-sector managers. Third, with few exceptions normal portfolios do not exist for hedge funds, making their results, at best, difficult to analyze. Fourth, there is a potentially high opportunity cost, not to mention career risk, in shifting assets from beta to alpha, should alpha prove nonexistent and capital markets deliver the expected risk premiums. Fifth, the length of the historic record is short compared to traditional asset classes and is not long enough to establish expected returns with confidence.

E. Lee Hennessee Group data for the five-year period ended September 30, 1994, shows that the hedge fund universe had a quarterly return of 4.80 percent and a quarterly standard deviation of 2.98 percent, outperforming the S&P 500 quarterly returns of 2.38 percent and standard deviation of 6.22 percent by a substantial margin. Even data as compelling as these can be misleading. For example, for the same five-year period ended September 30, 1994, Treasury bond futures leveraged 3 to 1 produced a quarterly return of 2.98 percent and a standard deviation of 6.09 percent—very impressive when compared to the equity results and competitive when compared to the hedge fund results. The leveraged bond data shows how easy it is to create compelling numbers, but it raises the important question of whether or not the hedge fund managers have skill or luck. Having shown how simple it is to create compelling returns in a short (five-year) period, practitioners should be careful to assure themselves that the hedge fund record is the result of multiple portfolio decisions and not one lucky bet on falling interest rates. Finally, recognizing how one lucky bet can result in compelling returns, would the aggressive return-oriented plan sponsor put the leveraged bond strategy in the portfolio because the optimizer liked it? Conclusion: give no more than a 20 percent weight to past performance data in funding decisions.

Investment Policy Implementation

The conclusion that mean-variance analysis is not an appropriate way to determine the allocation to hedge funds removes an important decision support system from the asset allocation policy planning process. But, we had a strong conceptual case that skill-based investing should produce higher alphas than traditional investment management, which is heavily constrained by relative performance concerns. And there were strong arguments that skill-based investing should improve the diversification of the aggregate investment portfolio.

The Rockefeller Foundation has a well-diversified investment program and as of December 31, 1993 its investment policy included 32 percent U.S. equity, 25 percent hedged foreign equity, 16 percent U.S. fixed income, 7 percent hedged foreign fixed income, 10 percent real estate, 7 percent private equity, and 3 percent junk bonds. Returns were excellent in 1993 as the above-average proportions held in international asset classes paced results. The decision to invest in hedge funds was made on the conceptual basis discussed above without using mesmerizing hedge fund return histories. Simulations of portfolio performance with and without historic hedge fund investment return simulations were not used to justify or support the recommendation. Rather, five nonquantitative judgmental considerations had the most influence on the decision.

- The allocation was to a new sector to be called the skill sector. The term skill sector was adopted to limit the role that prior biases and news reports might play in the discussion.
- Only skill-based activities with potential returns above the expected 6 percent real return of the approved asset allocation policy were eligible for inclusion in the program. Thus, the

emerging markets equity and distressed debt asset classes were
not included, since returns can be explained by the CAP-M.
Since long/short equity did not have an expected real return of
6 percent, this skill-based strategy was also not included in the
program.

- Several examples of skill-based strategies were reviewed with
the investment committee to increase familiarity and comfort
with types of activities that the managers would undertake.
The Foundation's prior experience in currency investing was
used to exemplify the types of investing that would be undertaken by skill-sector managers.

- Even though experimental, the allocation was to be of sufficient
size to mount a diversified skill-based program. At the 5 percent level, based on the Foundation's $2.1 billion asset balance,
an allocation of $105 million was approved. As a long-term
investor, there would be adequate time to examine the program
and expand or contract it as appropriate.

- The 5 percent allocation was drawn proportionately from all
other asset classes of the investment policy. Since the Foundation's long-term financial objectives are expected to be achieved
by the asset allocation policy, the investment committee concluded that the experiment should proceed only if expected skill-
sector returns were equal to the overall expected policy return of
6 percent real.

Skill-Sector Implementation

As with any strategy, sector, or investment policy, diversification is critical to
long-term success. Two dimensions of diversification should be explored
when developing multimanager hedge fund programs: (1) qualitative diversification of strategies and (2) minimum number of managers and allocation
of assets between managers. Finally, the desired risk level should be specified, including permissible leverage ratios within each portfolio. Monitoring
of securities positions and portfolio risk level is recommended to ensure that
managers are staying within guidelines and to minimize the risk exposures
that could result if several managers converge on the same trade.

Participation in multiple strategies will increase the probability that correlations between strategies will be low. The selection of strategies is ultimately arbitrary, but positively correlated strategies should be avoided (e.g.,
convertible and risk arbitrage could both decline in a rising interest rate environment). More important is the correlation between managers and the num-

ber of managers. At correlations of .2, diversification gains (risk reduction) after the tenth manager has been added become small. The higher the correlation between managers, the fewer the number of managers needed to achieve the benefits of manager diversification. More dramatic than manager diversification, however, is the risk reduction impact of selecting managers with low correlations. The reduction in monthly standard deviation between programs with 10 managers with a .6 correlation coefficient and 10 managers with zero correlation is 65 percent. Therefore, the investor's selection should seek managers and/or strategies with low correlations, which, in a portfolio of 10, will offset the high volatility of individual strategies.

The allocation of assets among managers also deserves discussion. Experience has taught us that confidence is never adequate justification for allocating more than an equal weight to each manager. Manager risk—the risk of manager collapse—is higher, as we have seen in 1994, in skill investing, since leverage and less liquid securities are tools of the trade. Because manager failure strikes unexpectedly, equal weighting among managers is the best formula for limiting damage from manager risk. This year, because of the well-publicized failures of Askin Capital and others, the best structure proved to be an equal weighted portfolio with a minimum of 10 managers. Those who were enticed by the relative stability of Askin's returns and overweighted, now regret that decision. One lesson from the hedge fund failures of 1994 is that conservative alpha targets of 3–5 percent in market neutral approaches may be difficult to justify on a risk-adjusted basis. If a manager holds 10 percent of assets and fails, the "cost" will be roughly 2 percent per year, assuming one failure every five years. If the program has focused on the market neutral hedge funds with a conservative alpha target, five-year returns will be in the range of 1–3 percent per annum, well below the level required on a risk-adjusted basis.

No essay on hedge funds can be complete without a comment on portfolio monitoring. Some hedge funds invest using illiquid positions and leverage, which, combined, can be lethal in rapidly changing markets. One critical due diligence item is to review the fund manager's risk control and monitoring system and ensure that it is properly matched to the strategy being undertaken. In addition, the sponsor should review positions and actively monitor portfolios to ensure that guidelines are being followed. Some of the better prime brokers are establishing services to help plan sponsors review risk exposures of hedge fund portfolios.

Plan sponsors who do not choose to undertake the diversification and manager selection decisions themselves or who cannot allocate sufficient assets to the strategy to achieve adequate diversification have a wide range of commingled multimanager vehicles to select from. Nevertheless, investors that select a fund of funds vehicle for investing in hedge funds should review the fund's structure, manager and strategy diversification, and risk monitoring and control systems. Although commingled vehicles have not found wide acceptance in traditional capital market sectors, such vehicles make sense in the alternative asset class arena. First, staff may be too small to properly monitor a strategy holding 5 percent of assets that engages 10–15 managers custodied at multiple clearing brokers. Second, complex legal structures, tax regulations, and partnership documents suggest that a specialist could add value in the skill sector. Third, because most institutional investors will not be experienced with hedge fund strategies, a fund of funds provides the additional oversight that fiduciary committees may need when investing in something unfamiliar.

Future Directions

From a portfolio perspective, the reduction in exposure to capital market risk (beta) is a material positive. The lack of systematic correlation in sources of return improves overall diversification of the investment program. In a real sense, the presence of the skill sector in the Foundation's investment program reduces the probability of a recurrence of the pain caused by the 1973–74 severe bear market. Over time, provided the compelling theoretical advantages are realized, my prediction is that institutional investors will expand their participation in hedge funds.

The widespread availability of derivatives introduces the opportunity to separate alpha and beta. Capital market exposure can be cheaply and easily obtained with derivatives. A critical advantage of derivatives is that little or no cash is required to maintain desired capital market exposures. This creates the opportunity to allocate capital first to high-alpha strategies and limit the use of scarce capital to purchase capital market exposures where there is limited opportunity to generate alpha. In theory, in the future, capital will be allocated to areas offering the highest alphas and capital market exposures will be managed with a derivatives overlay. Returns will, therefore, be maximized as capital will not be used to purchase capital market exposures with low alpha potential.

CHAPTER 4

Structuring a Hedge Fund Investment Portfolio

Joseph Nicholas, President
John Nicholas, Vice President
Hedge Fund Research, Inc.

This chapter outlines a process for structuring an investment portfolio of hedge funds. Constructing and managing a portfolio is a dynamic activity, and in reading this chapter it should be kept in mind that the steps described below interrelate. Also, we use the term "portfolio manager" in this chapter to describe the person who is responsible for structuring a portfolio, who may be, among others, a fund of funds manager, a commodity pool operator, a part of a bank treasury department, or the head of a brokerage operation.

The objective in structuring a portfolio of hedge funds is to access the skills of a select group of investment managers in a way that maximizes risk-adjusted return for a given level of risk. Deciding which managers to include in a portfolio involves several steps: defining the investor's portfolio objectives, establishing investment parameters for individual hedge funds and for the portfolio as a whole, and evaluating on a quantitative and quali-tative basis those hedge funds that fit within the established investment parameters. Selecting and combining managers so as to minimize the vari-ous risks associated with investing in hedge funds requires that the risks be clearly identified and then either eliminated, reduced, or ignored. Minimiz-ing risk also includes ongoing monitoring of managers selected for a portfo-lio to ensure that they meet performance expectations and stay within the investment parameters first established.

The steps in the process described in this chapter are the following:

- Defining portfolio objectives
- Establishing investment parameters
- Evaluating hedge funds

- Selecting hedge funds/constructing the portfolio
- Monitoring and managing the portfolio

Defining Portfolio Objectives

The starting point in structuring a hedge fund portfolio is defining its objectives. This may be described as "what" is sought to be accomplished in constructing the portfolio. There may be one or more objectives of differing priorities, ranging from the pursuit of pure risk-adjusted return to the desire to access specific types of financial instruments or investment strategies. Other objectives may include building business at an affiliated brokerage desk or creating a money management performance track record for use in raising investor capital. Table 4-1 illustrates examples of four portfolios with varying objectives.

While defining portfolio objectives is step one, a portfolio manager will refer back to, refine, and modify them throughout the structuring process.

Establishing Investment Parameters

"How" the portfolio objectives will be achieved is accomplished through investment parameters established by the portfolio manager. Investment parameters, as used in this chapter, mean the rules and guidelines that determine how the investment portfolio is constructed and operated, and includes requirements and limitations concerning evaluation and selection of hedge funds and forms of investment. Investment parameters may overlap with portfolio objectives. For example, a portfolio objective of having a fund using exchange-listed equities will result in an investment parameter

TABLE 4-1. Portfolio Objectives

	Portfolio A	Portfolio B	Portfolio C	Portfolio D
Portfolio Objectives:	20% net returns. Quarterly liquidity. Exchange-listed instruments only.	Generate foreign exchange deal flow at affiliated currency desk.	Attractive niche product for marketing purposes to raise investor capital.	Access spread traders and arbitrage strategies.
Portfolio Manager:	Family office	Brokerage firm	Non-U.S. bank	Specialty fund-of-funds

that limits the hedge fund universe to those that invest in such securities. Establishing well-defined investment parameters speeds the process of reviewing hedge funds for investment by narrowing, oftentimes considerably, the universe of funds eligible for consideration.

Investment parameters are used on two levels, first, with regard to individual hedge fund managers, and second, with regard to the portfolio as a whole. A portfolio manager will typically have as a parameter a certain rate of return for the portfolio and will have thresholds of acceptable volatility and drawdowns for both the individual funds comprising the portfolio and for the portfolio itself. The parameters for individual managers may differ considerably from those of the portfolio. For example, the volatility of returns of a particular hedge fund in the portfolio can be greater than the return volatility objectives of the portfolio because of the expected low level of correlation of returns among all of the hedge funds selected for the portfolio. (See Table 4-2.)

Investment parameters for individual managers are typically based on considerations such as assessment of risk and limits, types of instruments invested in or traded, length of track record, assets under management, greatest losing period or drawdown, liquidity, minimum investment, historic risk measures, and actual risk probabilities. In addition, the investor may want to include or exclude certain trading strategies or financial instruments (for example, arbitrage strategies only, leverage not exceeding 1:1, no illiquid securities, and no exotic derivatives). Other requirements may be that the funds in the portfolio invest only in U.S. securities or in specific industry sectors, or, alternatively, that the portfolio be globally diversified.

In addition, investors may prefer that selected managers have a minimum track record. Investors may also have certain liquidity needs or access to investment activities (current trades or positions) and control over invested assets, which will affect the form of the investment with a manager, as discussed below.

The portfolio manager should strive to be as objective as possible and base portfolio objectives and investment parameters on reasonable expectations and assumptions grounded in the reality of the marketplace. Reasonable investment parameters founded on reasonable portfolio objectives will

TABLE 4-2.   Investment Parameters

Portfolio	Managers
Target return: 20%	Expected returns: 15–35%
Standard deviation of returns: 8%	Standard deviation: 10–20%
Greatest loss in losing period: 10%	Greatest loss in a losing period: 10–20%

provide an investor the best chance to achieve favorable investment results. Unrealistic objectives will lead to unreasonable investment parameters which will result in no investment or a poorly constructed portfolio that will have a higher risk exposure than desired, and, therefore, a greater likelihood of failure.

Minimizing and Neutralizing Risk

A key aspect of establishing investment parameters is to manage or avoid known and perceived investment risk. The various risks must first be identified, which include, among others, the strategies and underlying investment instruments used by the hedge funds, the form of investment, credit risk, exposure to potential fraud, and government regulation. Once identified, a choice can be made on whether to avoid, ignore, or attempt to minimize or neutralize the risks. The job of controlling risk is not over once the managers have been selected and the portfolio established: the performance of the individual funds should be continually monitored and the portfolio manager must actively review the funds' activities to ensure that they are staying within the established investment parameters.

A common risk management mistake is to devote reasonable attention to obvious risks, that is, assigning proper probabilities to risk scenarios that are highly probable, but assigning probabilities of zero to those risk scenarios with lower, but not zero, probabilities of occurring. One should keep in mind that all investment strategies have flaws that can produce substantial losses of capital, and as remote as any risk may be, it should be recognized and addressed accordingly. (See Table 4-3.) In addition, remember that the objective of a portfolio is diversification, and parameters attempting to screen out risk also narrow the acceptable hedge fund universe. This may result in less diversification in the final portfolio, the portfolio manager in effect having exchanged one type of risk for another.

TABLE 4-3.   Risk Management

Risk Identified	Actions Taken
Counterparty risk	Allocate to managers investing only in instruments traded on regulated exchanges. Identify and evaluate all counterparties.
Experience of manager	Minimum five-year track record and $100 million or more under management. Prior experience.
Potential fraud	Audited track record, background check on principals.

Form of Investment

An investment manager's expertise can be accessed in two ways: by investing in an existing investment vehicle, typically a limited partnership for U.S. funds or a corporation for offshore funds, or by establishing a managed account. Each method of investment has its pros and cons, and the form of investment should be carefully weighed before proceeding with an investment with a particular manager. For example, investing in an existing fund has the benefits of limited liability, no or low organizational costs, and an investment minimum lower than that required to establish a managed account. A fund, however, generally has limited liquidity, delayed and limited position and performance reporting, and offers no control over investment structure and terms, such as fees and brokerage arrangements. Alternatively, a managed account offers flexibility in structure and investment terms, the greatest level of liquidity, and a high level of position and performance reporting. The downside of managed accounts is that they involve organizational costs, do not limit liability, and require a greater minimum investment. (See Table 4-4.)

Evaluating Hedge Funds

Evaluating a hedge fund is an imperfect process, and fully understanding, monitoring, and measuring the attendant risks of a hedge fund manager's strategy is a considerable undertaking. At a minimum, a portfolio manager, in addition to concluding that a hedge fund manager fits within various qualitative and quantitative parameters, should be able to answer yes to two basic questions before including a hedge fund in a portfolio: (1) Do I know what the

TABLE 4-4. Fund versus Managed Account

Form of Investment	Pros	Cons
Existing fund	• Limited liability • No upfront organizational costs • Lower minimum investment	• Less liquidity • No control over structure and terms
Managed account	• Immediate knowledge of managers' positions • Negotiated structure and terms • Highly liquid	• Organizational costs • Higher minimum investment • No liability limitation

hedge fund manager is doing? and (2) Does the hedge fund manager know what he or she is doing? If the portfolio manager and/or hedge fund manager does not fully grasp the pros and cons and the inherent risks of the fund manager's investment strategy, to include such a hedge fund in a portfolio would be to accept unknown risk.

While the large number and diversity of hedge funds to be analyzed may seem a daunting undertaking, using a few key parameters, such as amount of assets under management, experience of the manager, and instruments traded, quickly narrows the field to a manageable number. The short list will require a much more detailed analysis. Close inspection of managers, even those with similar self-described strategies, will reveal peculiarities and nuances in style and focus. In addition, comparing managers' performance numbers is problematic: a particular manager's performance numbers may, on closer inspection, be revealed to be an amalgam of inconsistent investment approaches implemented over time through different investment vehicles with varied amounts of capital. Promotional material and disclosure documents of a manager are helpful, but are often written in such broad terms that their usefulness is limited.

The quantitative and qualitative investment criteria described below are used as part of the evaluation process in selecting individual investment managers for the portfolio. They also are used as the basis for ongoing portfolio monitoring and performance evaluation. These criteria establish a set of reasonable expectations about future performance of the funds, upon which the construction of the portfolio is based.

Quantitative Analysis

Quantitative analysis involves a statistical evaluation of the periodic performance of a manager. In doing so we can view various measures of risk and reward and relationships between the two as represented by analysis of periodic returns. (See Table 4-5.) We can also compare these returns to those of other managers for other determinations, such as correlation of return or style analysis.

Statistical analysis of periodic performance data alone is an unreliable prognosticator of future performance. Performance is often short and across a limited range of economic cycles. As witnessed in 1994, overreliance on statistical analysis can result in poor investment recommendations. It is all too frequently used and relied upon because it is the easiest to perform. A method that will result in better fund selections going forward is to combine statistical analysis with a thorough qualitative evaluation that takes into account past and current market environments, latent risks, and the consistency of the manager's investment operation.

TABLE 4-5. Statistical Analysis

Interval: Monthly			1/1991 to 12/1994					Convertible Arbitrage Fund				
Year	Jan	Feb	Mar	Apr	May	Jun	Jul	Aug	Sep	Oct	Nov	Dec	An-nual
1991	−0.16	1.48	−0.28	2.67	−1.12	1.78	3.45	3.42	2.17	1.24	1.08	1.54	18.58
1992	3.08	1.37	0.95	0.91	1.99	0.33	0.75	0.92	1.25	1.14	0.77	0.45	14.80
1993	1.25	1.00	0.90	0.82	1.22	0.38	0.96	1.08	0.91	0.73	0.38	0.43	10.53
1994	0.62	0.20	−0.79	−2.27	−0.54	1.47	0.57	0.82	0.64	0.32	0.01	−0.55	0.45

Statistical Measures

Risk-free interest rate:	4.00
High month return:	3.45
Low month return:	−2.27
One-month average:	0.87
One-month standard deviation:	1.06
Annual average:	10.44
Annual standard deviation:	3.68
Gain months:	85.42
Average gain:	1.16
Average loss:	−0.82
Maximum drawdown:	3.57
Sharpe ratio:	1.75
Average/maximum drawdown:	3.0504
Average gain/average loss:	8.31

Qualitative Analysis

Qualitative analysis goes beyond quantitative analysis and focuses on other aspects and influences on a hedge fund, its manager, and its strategy. Unlike quantitative analysis, which gives as rough sketch of a manager, qualitative analysis fills in the detail and helps a portfolio manager see the substantive differences between managers who may appear, based on their statistical profiles, to be equals.

Qualitative analysis is critical to evaluating historic performance. For a manager's past performance to be of any use in predicting future performance, the portfolio manager should find continuity first in the manager's approach and application of his strategy, and second in the nature of the markets to which the strategy is applied. For example, the track record of a manager trading an obscure arbitrage will not be useful for forecasting performance if that market becomes more efficient or the growth of the manager's assets renders the contribution of this strategy insignificant to the manager's return. Similarly, the track record of a systematic manager provides few insights into future performance if the manager decides to invest on a discretionary basis. In addition, past performance does not tell how a manager may cope with a different market environment or whether the manager's strategy can generate similar returns with more assets under management.

Qualitative analysis may also in part be considered a due diligence review. Before investing with a manager, a portfolio manager should ask questions such as: What is the manager's regulatory history? Has the manager had less successful "past lives" as an investment manager? What do the manager's references say about him or her? Where is the manager's own money invested? What do background checks reveal about the manager? The answers to these and other questions will give a clearer picture of who the manager is and offer insight into how the manager might act in the future.

Beyond a review of performance, then, a portfolio manager will want to examine the following with respect to individual managers before investing money with them: use of leverage; diversification of portfolio and concentration of investment positions; liquidity of instruments in portfolio; length of track record; amount under management and how this has changed over time; current investment strategy and instruments used, and how these have changed, if at all, over time; percent of fund assets invested and whether the portfolio is net long or short, and how this has varied over time; fee structure assessed to the fund; brokerage costs; portfolio turnover; background of principals, including any SEC or CFTC violations; legal form of the fund; tax consequences for form of investment; redemption provisions of the fund; investment minimums; reporting and auditing procedures for the fund; which principals of the manager are responsible for a particular fund or strategy; and the amount of personal capital that principals have invested in the fund. Reviewing these considerations will help a portfolio manager better differentiate qualitatively between managers that have similar performance records.

The profile in Table 4-6 contains a number of important (though not exhaustive) areas of consideration.

Summary of Hedge Fund Strategies

In selecting a hedge fund for a portfolio, a portfolio manager needs to understand the particular investment strategy used by the fund's manager, how the manager's strategy can be expected to perform in the existing market environment, and how a combination of strategies will provide diversification and minimize volatility in a portfolio. The chart below categorizes managers according to 12 distinct strategies: convertible arbitrage, distressed securities, emerging markets, growth funds, macro funds, market neutral, market timing, merger arbitrage, multistrategies, opportunistic, sector funds, and short selling.

TABLE 4-6. Qualitative Profile—Fund Summary

Offshore Fund International

Form: British Virgin Islands company

Inception: 9/91

Assets: $30,000,000,000; (U.S.-based fund traded pari passu: $125,000,000)

Minimum: $250,000

Investment: Monthly (subscription documents must be received by Administrator at least seven days prior to month end.)

Redemptions: Quarterly upon 30 days' prior written notice.

Strategy: The Fund invests primarily long in U.S. equities (focus is on smaller cap securities) employing a bottom-up fundamental, value-oriented approach. Fund invests in predictable stocks (not cyclicals) using free cash flow analysis and own research. Managers are looking for 20% return with minimal risk. Fund also invests in risk arbitrage/distressed securities, bankruptcies (primarily in senior debt securities), and in high yield securities (together comprising about 15% of Fund assets). Short selling is used moderately (5% of assets) with a shorter-term focus than that for long positions. The Fund may invest up to 10% of its capital in unregistered securities not traded on any exchange or in the over-the-counter market (currently such investments are less than 2% of Fund assets). Cash position is usually 20–30% of Fund assets.

Leverage: Fund uses leverage, can be 2:1.

Diversification: No fixed guidelines. Current largest position constitutes 6% of Fund assets.

Concentration: Fund may at times hold a few, relatively large securities positions.

Market Risk: Fund is currently 15% net long.

Fees:
    Management Fee: 1% per annum (paid quarterly)
    Incentive Fee: 20% per annum
    Sales Load: none

Reports: Quarterly reports and annual audited report

Brokerage/execution costs: Turnover of portfolio is typically 100% annually. Brokerage costs are approximately 1–2% of net assets annually.

Principals: Principals have majority of liquid net worth in Fund. Managers do not have own accounts which they trade separately. No SEC violations.

Hedge Fund Strategies and Their Definitions

1. *Convertible Arbitrage:* Investment strategy that is long convertible securities and short the underlying equities.
2. *Distressed Securities:* Invests long (and some short) securities of companies that are in reorganizations, bankruptcies, or some other corporate restructuring.
3. *Emerging Markets:* Investment in securities of companies in developing or "emerging" countries. Primarily long.
4. *Growth Funds:* Investment in a portfolio or "core" holdings in growth stocks. Many of these portfolios are hedged by shorting and options.
5. *Macro Funds:* The investment philosophy is based on shifts in global economies. Derivatives are often used to speculate on currency and interest rate moves.
6. *Market Neutral:* Strategy that attempts to lock-out or "neutralize" market risk.
7. *Market Timing:* Allocation of assets among investments primarily switching between mutual funds and money markets.
8. *Merger Arbitrage:* Invests in event-driven situations of corporations, such as leveraged buy-outs, mergers, and hostile takeovers. Managers purchase stock in the firm being taken over and, in some situations, sell short the stock of the acquiring company.
9. *Multistrategies:* Specific portions are utilized for separate strategies, e.g., growth, convertible arbitrage, and market neutral.
10. *Opportunistic:* Investment theme is dominated by events that are seen as special situations or opportunities to capitalize from price fluctuations or imbalances.
11. *Sector Funds:* Invest in companies in sectors of the economy, e.g., financial institutions or bio-technologies. These funds invest in both long and short securities and will utilize options.
12. *Short Selling:* Short selling of securities.

The portfolio manager should be aware that the programs listed within each category vary broadly as to how the strategy is implemented, types of instruments, and degree of leverage. For example, consider convertible arbitrage. Some funds in this category may invest in U.S. issues only, others in global markets as well. Investments may be investment grade in some funds but not others. The amount of leverage used may range from none to 5 to 1. The amount of hedging may also fluctuate widely. Therefore, conducting comparative fund performance evaluation even within a specific category requires a large degree of qualitative evaluation.

Selecting Hedge Funds/Constructing the Portfolio

Constructing the portfolio involves selecting a final group of hedge funds for investment from the "short list" of funds fitting within the portfolio's investment parameters. Funds from the short list are selected across both investment strategies and instruments traded. The inclusion of each hedge fund and the size of the allocation to each are based on the expected performance forecast for each hedge fund and the expected correlation of those returns to the returns of other hedge funds in the portfolio. The portfolio manager may be following portfolio objectives and investment parameters that dictate a balanced diversified portfolio, or others that may dictate a portfolio with a market view, such as "long small-cap equities." Investment is then made by either purchasing shares or partnership interests in each hedge fund, or hiring the hedge fund manager as the investment adviser to a managed account.

The optimal number of hedge funds to include in a portfolio is debated. Opinions range from 5 to 50. The amount will partly be determined by the amount of capital available for investment. As larger and more established hedge funds have higher minimum investment requirements, fewer can be included in a portfolio than those with lower minimums. Keep in mind that it is the diversification of strategies and instruments traded that minimizes risk. A portfolio of twenty macro funds is not reducing trading risk significantly. In general, however, greater numbers of hedge funds in a portfolio will minimize risks peculiar to any one fund.

In diversifying the portfolio, having few limiting parameters allows broad diversification across instruments traded and strategies used. However, if the scope is limited, for example, to only U.S. equities, diversification across investment strategies should be sought. (See Table 4-7.)

A word about relying on statistical return correlation analysis and optimizing the portfolio—while quantitative studies should be conducted as

TABLE 4-7. Strategy Diversification

Diversified Portfolio	U.S. Equities Portfolio
risk arbitrage	risk arbitrage
convertible arbitrage	distressed
global futures	growth
macro	market neutral
emerging markets	short selling
currency	
options	

part of input into selecting hedge funds for the portfolio, the length of track record, change in assets managed, and the continuity of activity of hedge funds should be considered when evaluating the meaningfulness of the data points being compared. A portfolio manager should "stress test" the diversification benefits of the subject portfolio by answering questions such as "How will each hedge fund perform in a rising interest rate environment?" "What is the impact if there is a sharp decline in the S&P?" "Small-cap stocks?" By considering the impact of various market scenarios, the portfolio manager can develop performance expectations for each hedge fund under different conditions, can project expected correlation of returns, and therefore can better forecast portfolio performance.

Performance Expectations

The purpose of hedge fund evaluation is to develop a sense of what kind of performance can reasonably be expected in the future. The selection of hedge funds for inclusion in a portfolio is based on how each hedge fund is expected to perform on an absolute basis, and how each is expected to perform in relation to the other hedge funds in the portfolio. Performance expectations can be general or specific, and should correspond to the level of monitoring and evaluation the portfolio manager intends to conduct. Categories of evaluation include:

- Absolute performance statistics for individual hedge funds and portfolio.
- Hedge fund and portfolio performance relative to various market conditions.
- Hedge fund performance relative to peer group.
- Hedge fund and portfolio performance relative to various indices.
- Correlation of hedge fund performance to other hedge funds in the portfolio.

The performance expectations, along with the investment parameters, form the basis for ongoing monitoring of the portfolio.

Manner of Investment

The manner of investing in a hedge fund is specific to each fund, but, in general, funds accepting new investors will open on a monthly or quarterly basis. Minimum investment varies from $100,000 to $5,000,000, and normally falls within the $500,000 to $1,000,000 range.

Organizing a managed account with a money manager requires more time and effort. The minimum account size will depend on two variables: first, what is the minimum amount of capital that the manager needs in order to invest according to his or her strategy, and second, the amount of compensation a manager needs in order to make running a managed account worthwhile. For futures and interbank traders, minimum account sizes range from $500,000 to $5,000,000. For equity-based strategies, managed account minimums range from $2,000,000 to $25,000,000.

The investment can be constructed either as a fund or as a managed account. The nature of the investment vehicle for the portfolio will depend on the portfolio objective. A private investment may be in the form of an account, limited partnership, trust or corporation. If the portfolio is to be marketed or if it includes a number of investors, then a limited partnership, trust, or corporation will be used.

A portfolio manager should consult with both an attorney and an accountant that specializes in this area to assure compliance with applicable regulations as well as to understand the taxation aspects of the investment.

Monitoring and Managing the Portfolio

Monitoring Procedures

Once the portfolio allocations have been made, procedures for monitoring should be implemented. The criteria for monitoring is an extension of the investment parameters and the performance expectations discussed above. Ongoing due diligence should be conducted to assure that the requirements of the investment objectives continue to be met. In addition, actual performance should be compared to expected performance, as well as to selected benchmarks. The correlation of returns of the various hedge funds in the portfolio should also be reviewed. Divergences from expectations should trigger a re-evaluation of the selection and evaluation process.

The period of evaluation will vary depending on the managers and the type of investment. For example, while reporting may be daily for a managed account, it may be monthly for a fund.

Active Management

Portfolio rebalancing, reallocations, and manager additions and terminations are a normal consequence of ongoing management and portfolio monitoring. The performance of each manager should be regularly checked against its expected contribution to the portfolio, and should be evaluated against its historic activities, expected performance, peer group sets, and other appropriate benchmarks. This ongoing evaluation or feedback loop between the actual performance versus performance expectations will indicate how well the portfolio is achieving its objectives.

In evaluating performance, keep in mind the set of realistic performance expectations developed for each hedge fund in the portfolio, and that the selection of funds for investment is based on long-term performance information and annualized statistics. This especially applies to a portfolio manager who manages a portfolio on a week-to-week or monthly basis. As long as each hedge fund's performance and the portfolio's diversification aspects stay within expectations, performance is not a cause for alarm. Greater causes of concern are new due diligence issues, better investment alternatives, and market or personnel changes.

Conclusion

This chapter has outlined a process for structuring an investment portfolio in hedge funds. By establishing realistic objectives and well-defined investment parameters, and thoroughly evaluating and selecting hedge funds based on both qualitative and quantitative analysis, a portfolio manager can access the skills of a select group of investment managers through a portfolio that maximizes return for a given level of risk. Ongoing monitoring and evaluation of the hedge funds in the portfolio ensures that performance expectations and investment objectives are being met, and provides the basis for rebalancing the portfolio as required.

CHAPTER 5

Pros and Cons of Hedge Fund Investing for Wealthy Individuals

Mitchell A. Tanzman, Managing Director
Oppenheimer & Co., Inc.

Hedge funds. Private investment partnerships. The names even sound alluring. A hedge fund sounds secure because, presumably, it hedges. A private investment partnership has cachet. It isn't for the public, but for a limited few. Add to this the press coverage, which follows hedge funds and their managers as if they were rock stars. So now everyone wants to be in a hedge fund, which raises fundamental issues for the industry as we seek to avoid becoming like the tax shelter boom of earlier decades.

Some History

The starting point for any investor, and especially for an individual investor, is to understand what has caused the rush to hedge funds. Some of the popularity of hedge funds stems from the changing face of Wall Street.

If one looks back 20 years, the best and the brightest were not necessarily encouraged to pursue careers on Wall Street, but were focused on the professions, like doctors and lawyers. I doubt any parent told their child 20 years ago to aspire to be a hedge fund manager. However, the late 1970s and 1980s saw a rising appreciation for careers in finance, and with that change came a crop of the best and brightest. Other trends help to explain some of

The author would like to acknowledge the assistance of CME staff members Barbara Richards, David Goone, Dick McDonald, Scott Brusso, and Shweta Shyamani in the preparation of this chapter.

The opinions in this chapter are those of the author and do not necessarily represent those of Oppenheimer & Co., Inc.

the growth of the hedge fund industry. The first, and the most important, is the old adage that "water seeks its level." In the context of hedge funds, that has accounted for why so many talented individuals have pursued careers as money managers in an arena that can provide for extraordinary compensation. Not every incentive fee manager will make it, and some will fail miserably, but for those who can routinely provide above-average returns, there will always be money willing to invest.

Related to the talent pool that has come to Wall Street is the unprecedented growth of new and ever more complex instruments and trading markets. There are people who create the instruments and people who can successfully exploit them in the marketplace. The practitioners of some of the newer sectors or categories (market neutral, global derivative, and fixed-income arbitrage) have advanced degrees in science and applied engineering in order to trade the strategies employed. This is no longer only about finding cheap stocks.

Part of the explosion can be ascribed to the 1980s growth in the U.S. equity markets and in investing generally. There are now more U.S.-based mutual funds than public companies on the New York Stock Exchange. That growth has been part of the disintermediation from savings banks combined with a level of involvement in investing by the middle class that is unprecedented. And if the middle class needs thousands of mutual funds, then wealthy individuals need hundreds of hedge funds.

What Are They?

For starters, hedge funds don't necessarily hedge; in fact, some funds do not even have the ability to hedge. The title "hedge fund" is a catch-all for privately offered investment vehicles that typically have three features in common when offered in the United States:

- They charge clients a percentage of the profits (which almost always will be in addition to other expenses).
- They aim to achieve substantial absolute total returns.
- They can only take a limited number of U.S. investors.

The last point is not the case with hedge funds that are open exclusively to non-U.S. investors.

Beyond these broad commonalities lurks a host of incentive fee based "funds" that pursue excess returns in categories as diverse as distressed real estate and emerging market equity securities. There are also funds that do everything in between, depending on the manager's view of world markets.

Why Invest in Hedge Funds?

Putting aside the cachet of being in a private partnership, individual investors find hedge funds appealing for many of the right reasons. People have pursued hedge funds with ever increasing interest because many hedge fund managers have been able to provide *excellent* performance over the *long term.* Right at the start one must stop and look at the italicized words. Hedge fund investing is a long-term commitment in pursuit of superior absolute return. The first question wealthy investors should ask themselves is whether they are prepared to make a three- to five-year commitment, because that is the appropriate time frame over which to see how your investment is faring. That is not to say that one should be insensitive to how one's investments are going over shorter periods, but the standard must be longer-term.

One of the most critical considerations for investors is how much to invest and for how long. Needless to say these themes are related. You are hurting your overall performance and definitely fooling yourself if you feel that you can allocate and re-allocate and be successful. The best money managers in the world often have significant differences of opinions on which asset categories are going to work, which stock market is going to be robust, what will happen to major currencies, and the like. Do not think you can outsmart them. By investing in a hedge fund you have hired a specialist, much as you would hire a cardiologist if you had chest pains and a good tax accountant if the IRS called. Interview your specialist, understand what they do, get comfortable with it, pick an investment time horizon, decide how much capital to put in, and then leave it alone, until you have reason to believe that any of the foregoing considerations has materially changed. Do not commit capital to a long-term investment if you may need the money in six months or a year.

One question that comes up frequently with investors is the notion of being in a blind pool. Quite frankly, it causes investors a lot of anxiety. The fact is, we make many daily decisions blindly and almost all investment decisions with limited information. The mutual funds you invest in are blind pools—the limited information that is published semiannually is stale. The stocks your investment adviser has bought in your "fully disclosed" account are pretty much blind—they reflect the thinking of some analyst based on limited information from an issuer. People make a living trading around corporate earnings "surprises"—so much for you knowing about the stocks in your portfolio. Life is full of risks. So are hedge funds. You don't eliminate hedge fund risk by knowing the names of the positions. You reduce it by understanding the strategy and knowing the manager.

Another way to limit your risk is to understand the fund's use of leverage. It is very difficult to be an extraordinary stock picker and have consistently excellent long-term returns, and so many managers seek to enhance their returns by the use of leverage. Needless to say, leverage exaggerates results, whether the results are positive or negative. Moreover, there are costs associated with leverage. If you want excess returns you have to be willing to accept some risk. Leverage is just one of the risks in a portfolio. Make sure you understand how it will be utilized.

How to Select a Hedge Fund

Selecting a hedge fund is by and large about selecting a manager. The hedge fund business is about achieving excellent returns. It is not about beating an index or being in the top percentage of a peer group of funds. Its about absolute returns. Period. Relative returns are for your relatives. In order to make excess returns you are going to have to accept some risk and you need to understand where the risk is in your portfolio. Is it through exotic securities that go up or down based upon things you don't understand? Are you buying into inefficiencies, such as through convertible arbitrage strategies? Are you buying into the great unknown, for example, by investing in newly emerging markets with rapid growth but unstable capital markets? There is risk in any portfolio. Is your value stock picker leveraged? If so, you're bearing risk. Even the hedging techniques that many funds employ can be risk in the wrong hands. Ask your managers about their experience on the short side. Ask your managers about their market option strategies. Make sure you know what the fund intends to do and conclude that the manager has a reasonable chance of being able to implement the strategy. For example, do not be put off by the laundry list of tools and strategies in a hedge fund's offering documents. Ask which tools are expected to be the primary ones utilized. Ask how much margin the manager typically expects to employ; the most and the least margin that will be used under "ordinary circumstances." Then ask what are "ordinary circumstances."

Choosing a hedge fund is all about choosing a manager. It is the most important part of the due diligence process and should be the most satisfying, particularly for wealthy individuals. Wealthy individuals and families have always appreciated talent, whether it was funding artists in Europe in the Middle Ages or endowing laboratories for scientists to pursue research in the 20th century. Especially for today's entrepreneurs, getting to know a manager is an important and rewarding experience. Nobody will stop you from funding a manager without ever having a meeting, but if you can, meet the manager.

One of the most compelling aspects of hedge fund investing is to have the managers give you their vision of the world, to share their passion for investing. Particularly for self-made millionaires who are considering hedge fund investments, the entrepreneurial outlook of a hedge fund manager can be a natural fit. In almost all cases the investor will be talking to talented individuals who left the secure world of a mutual fund complex or someone else's employ because they had something to prove. Managing money for a percentage of the profits is the ultimate performance measure. There is no place to hide. When you do it successfully, it is like pitching a perfect game in the World Series. When your performance is inadequate, it's like striking out on national television with the bases loaded in the bottom of the ninth inning. In either case, it takes a certain temperament and skill set to do it successfully. In many cases, it is the same background and temperament that put the wealthy investor in the position he or she is in. They may have started a little company 20 years ago because they didn't want to work for anyone else and they have made a career and a fortune out of taking risk and seizing opportunities. That's what your hedge fund should be doing for you.

Talk to your manager. Let the manager share his or her passion. Understand the manager's perspective. Ask questions. Never feel shy to ask why something works a certain way. In fact, feel free to be a bit intrusive with your manager. Ask what he or she wants to be doing in five years; if five years is your time horizon it might as well be your manager's. Ask the manager to analyze the strengths and weaknesses of the other key personnel and what roles they play. See if you can find out whether the manager is still doing what made him or her successful in the first place. If you were recommended to a manager because of his or her great stock-picking skills, find out whether that person is still picking stocks or whether he or she has become more of a chief executive, overseeing other stock pickers. Do your homework.

Some Illusions

It is important to dispel some illusions as you consider a hedge fund investment. One is fees. You should definitely try to ascertain what the fees are in your hedge fund. Not just the management fee and incentive fee, but commission charges, miscellaneous custody fees and the like. It pays to be informed. It further pays to consider fees in the context of your investment. But if you have truly chosen a first class hedge fund manager, what matters is the absolute net return, and that is impacted much more by the strategy and the manager than by the fees. For individual investors, you must make peace with the notion of paying first-class wages for first-class service. You end up satisfied if the manager is first class, not if you can save a half a percent on fees. The fact is that good hedge funds cost a lot and you should hope to be making your manager rich. If your manager produces returns in a given year of 25 percent gross and has a standard 20 percent incentive fee, then you will "pay" 5 percent for the year, possibly on top of other fees. The issue is not the 5 percent—it's whether 25 percent gross is excellent. If it is, you should be thankful to pay the 5 percent; if it's not, you may be with the wrong manager. With incentive fee clients, the larger the fees, the happier the client. Its simple, you tend to be getting a very positive return. In fact, some clients seem better at accepting a loss of money (and not paying incentive fees but having a make-up provision) than making modest returns with relatively high absolute fees. Once the returns are double-digit, most clients think more about returns; when the returns in a given year are single-digit, the focus is on fees.

Another illusion that must be dispelled is that there are only a very few talented money managers. The fact is, there are talented people in all walks of life and many creative people have been drawn to Wall Street and will continue to be drawn to Wall Street. There is no one extraordinary heart surgeon, movie director, or lawyer; there are many talented ones.

Finding a talented money manager is especially tricky for individual clients. For individuals with less than $25 million, finding the right manager becomes a trade-off. Any hedge fund with a great five-year or more record has been "discovered" and has moved its minimum investment up into the stratosphere. Tomorrow's great discovery, however, doesn't yet have the track record and so the investment may be riskier. This is where the game called "slot arbitrage" comes into play.

Hedge funds can only have a very limited number of U.S. investors or "slots." If they took more investors in, they would have to comply with the intense regulations and restrictions under the U.S. Investment Company Act. Any smart hedge fund manager wants to gather the most assets from the permitted investors, so who gets a slot can become an interesting game. The manager ideally wants investors who can add to their capital account. Investors want to preserve the right to invest in a soon to be successful hedge fund. In a number of cases, wealthy investors invest with new hedge funds in order to assure themselves a place in the fund if the fund works. Remember, it may not.

The best advice one can give a wealthy individual (this is not a problem for big institutions for whom a slot will always be made available) is to do your homework on the fund and the manager and make a sound and informed investment decision. This new fund may be the next George Soros—it may not. If you do your homework you should feel comfortable making an investment decision without fear that the minimum on the fund may move up or that you will get shut out of the investment.

As was said earlier, one of the most compelling parts of hedge fund investing is learning about the strategy and the manager. There is an opportunity to be a pioneer, to get in on the ground floor. Do not assume that every new manager will be the next "so-and-so." Yet do not assume that you will have years to watch these managers develop. One of the nicest parts of this business is to see the relationship formed between portfolio manager and investor. That relationship is often strongest when the investor was an early backer of the manager, before the manager got "hot."

Funds of Funds

No chapter on wealthy individual investing in hedge funds can be complete without at least a mention of funds of funds (see Chapter 7). For many smaller investors, a fund of funds will provide access to managers which are otherwise inaccessible as well as providing diversification. All this at a minimum that may be much more manageable and the fees at the fund of fund level may not be that onerous.

However, two facts need to be pointed out about the fund of funds business. First, the manager of the fund of funds is *your portfolio manager*. Much like a hedge fund manager picks stock, a fund of funds manager picks managers. Do the same homework on the fund of funds manager as you would on your hedge fund manager because *they will decide your performance*.

The second fact is that it is really hard to get excellent returns in a fund of funds, and that is inherent in their structure. Though it is true that an investor gets access, diversification, and asset allocation through a fund of funds, it does so by investing with about a dozen different managers. Since it is unlikely all of those underlying hedge funds will be profitable in any given year, the return to the fund of funds will reflect the return of the winners (less 20 percent) added to the losers. To analogize, if a hedge fund manager bought stocks but the fund's winners (not losers) were all subject to an extra 20 percent tax, it would certainly drag performance down on the hedge fund. It doesn't take too many losing managers in a fund of funds to hurt overall performance, and you still have to pay 20 percent to the hedge funds that made money. Therefore, having confidence in your fund of funds manager is pivotal.

Outlook

There are a world of talented managers out there and new ones keep cropping up every day. For those with the appetite and the assets, the promise of excellent returns for years to come can be a reality. Like many other activities, it just takes some hard work.

CHAPTER 6

Assessing the Risks of Hedge Fund Investing

Michael E. Dunmire, President
Paradigm Partners, Inc.

Periodically, one reads an article that focuses on hedge funds. Too often such articles focus on spectacular returns, while very few focus on the risks being taken to achieve those returns. Often the author fails to acknowledge the strong post-selection bias that exists, and the reader concludes that achieving such spectacular returns is far easier than it is in reality. Without question, some hedge fund managers are exceptional investors, and over the years have compiled some of the most enviable track records on Wall Street. It is precisely because these individuals have demonstrated such a high level of success that the whole area of hedge fund investing has attracted so much recent attention.

This chapter discusses an evaluation process that poses questions that might enable an investor to better assess the risk actually being undertaken. But first, just to make sure we are on the same wavelength, I would like to briefly review the characteristics of hedge funds and some inherent types of investment risk.

Characteristics of Hedge Funds

Most hedge funds are housed in a limited partnership format. Furthermore, the number of limited partners is limited to 99 accredited investors, people with substantial wealth. The partnership is actually run by the general partner, most typically, an unregistered investment advisor. Since hedge funds are unregistered investment entities, the investor is not provided with the protection of the Securities Exchange Commission. Consequently, the importance of doing due diligence is heightened, and the responsibility for doing it falls directly upon the limited partner.

While there are some exceptions, hedge funds are usually relatively small in size, since most hedge funds start out as niche strategies taking advantage of some inefficiencies that occur at the fringe of the market. Often it takes many years, if ever, for these niche markets to grow to a size that would support several multibillion-dollar investment organizations. Larger hedge funds, most often, employ strategies that span many different markets and are usually more macro in scope, which enables them to deploy large assets.

One of the key differentiating factors between hedge funds and other forms of limited partnerships is that hedge funds typically deal in liquid instruments that can be marked to market on a daily basis. These instruments usually are stocks, bonds, options, and futures. Hedge funds, in the context that I will be discussing them, refer to hedge funds that operate exclusively in liquid investments that can be marked to market on a daily basis and therefore areas such as real estate, venture capital, unregistered securities, or other investments that require a multiyear commitment would be excluded.

Hedge funds are considered "alternative" investments since they employ an investment strategy that differs from conventional, long only, money management. The method of investing by hedge funds is considered nontraditional. It encompasses a greater variety of investment instruments (options and futures) and a greater variety of investment techniques (short selling, hedging, arbitrage, etc.) than conventional money management.

The risk/return diagram in Figure 6-1 demonstrates the difference in returns and risk levels that might be anticipated between conventional managers and hedge funds. The returns for the vast majority of conventional managers, all executing the same strategy (i.e., long equities), might be expected to fall within the circle thereby indicating they have risk/return coordinates close to those of the S&P 500. This is due to the conventional manager's high correlation to a broad market index such as the S&P 500, which is also only long equities. This is true even though conventional managers might have different styles such as value, momentum, earnings growth, small capitalization, etc. Styles are secondary in importance in determining risk/return expectations whereas the investment strategy is the major determinant.

By contrast, a hedge fund's risk/return coordinates (as seen in Figure 6-1) are equally likely to fall outside the circle as to fall within it. The particular investment strategy practiced by the hedge fund will be the primary determinant of the actual risk/return coordinates. Notice that the dots representing hedge fund risk/return coordinates fall in all four quadrants (above/below and right/left of the S&P 500). It is the combination of the use of a greater variety of investment instruments and investment techniques that leads to risk/return profiles that span the entire risk spectrum. It is because the risks and returns of hedge fund managers vary so dramatically that it is significantly more difficult to evaluate a hedge fund investment than an investment with a conventional manager who is more highly corre-

FIGURE 6-1. Hypothetical Capital Market Line

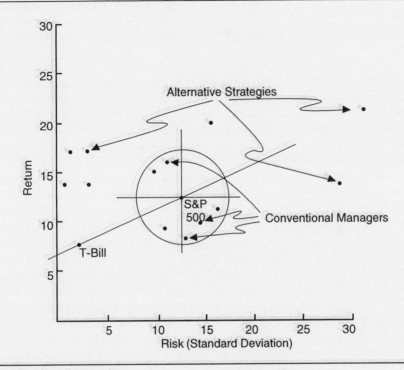

Source: Paradigm Partners, Inc.

lated to major indices. There is nothing, other than the strategy being executed, that indicates that a hedge fund is higher risk or lower risk or likely to produce higher or lower returns than the general market.

What Are the Risks of Investing in Hedge Funds?

Listed below are four categories of risk, starting with those that have the smallest and ending with those that have the largest impact on one's investment funds:

- Procedural mistakes
- Underperformance
- Severe decline in account value
- Fraud

These categories of risk apply to both conventional and nontraditional investments. However, their importance when investing in hedge funds is greater for two reasons: (1) the magnitude of mistakes can be much larger, and (2) the burden of due diligence falls more directly on the limited partner.

Procedural mistakes would include such things as investing in the wrong investment vehicle, particularly where the return/risk profile that can be anticipated is totally inappropriate for the investor. Procedural mistakes can be eliminated relatively easily if prior to making an investment a prospective limited partner would read and understand the limited partnership agreement, and then accurately evaluate if such an investment is appropriate. Typically, a confidential private placement memorandum and particularly the limited partnership agreement are dry reading. This often makes it too easy for prospective limited partners to glance through the documents, rather than to read them thoroughly to gain a greater level of understanding. A thorough reading of the partnership documents gives prospective investors the opportunity to ensure that they understand both the investment strategy and the partnership details, and offers the opportunity to surface questions that might not be addressed by the document. It also allows potential investors to understand what their legal rights would be once they became a limited partner. Not reading the offering documents and not taking the opportunity to ask questions of the general partner are the surest ways I know to risk making a procedural mistake.

Underperformance signifies performance less than a particular index or objective. It is a natural phenomenon in investing, since all investments are not going to meet or exceed expectations. While no one likes underperformance, it is a reality of investing. The risk of underperformance can be reduced through good due diligence, but the risk is real and cannot be eliminated.

A severe decline in account value, as distinguished from underperformance, signifies a sharp, significant drop in absolute value. A decline of this nature is usually due to one of three factors. First, the manager has deviated significantly from the strategy you thought he or she was executing and has taken on substantially more risk than expected; or second, you, the manager, or both, simply did not understand the risks involved; or three, you knowingly invested in a high-risk strategy and the risk was real.

Fraud is always a potential risk in any investment. By definition it is difficult, if not impossible, to detect. The best safeguard one has against fraud is to know the individuals involved in the entire investment process and to check out every possible detail. Even with the best due diligence, fraud remains a possibility. Diversification (not putting all your eggs in one basket), while not a preventative of fraud, can lessen its impact.

The purpose of listing the above types of risks when investing in hedge funds is really more to acknowledge the fact that different types of risks do exist. All types of risks can be reduced by practicing due diligence before investing and continuing close monitoring after an investment is made.

What follows in the next five sections is a review of the various stages of evaluating an investment to better understand the risks being taken. I call the process the five Ps, which stand for people, process (investment process and strategy), portfolio construction, performance, and partnership details. Taken together this framework provides a balanced approach to assessing the various types of risks when investing in hedge funds.

People

Who are the general partners of the limited partnership that you are evaluating? One must always keep in mind that these are the people to whom you are entrusting your or your clients' funds. It is sometimes difficult to imagine, but many individuals will write and mail checks for significant amounts of money—often millions of dollars—to a virtual stranger, known only by the words printed in the Confidential Offering Memorandum or the casual comments of a close friend. While this approach might possibly suffice in making a conventional investment in a managed separate account with a registered investment advisor, it simply is not adequate when investing in limited partnerships or hedge funds. If for no other reason than the fact that hedge funds are unregistered entities and therefore provide no SEC protection for their investors, it becomes more important that limited partners know who the general partner is.

It is indeed worth the time and effort to learn as much as possible about the general partner. Certainly steps such as checking out references provided by the general partner, as well as discussions with others in the investment community that know him or her, are vitally important. One simply cannot take the risk of investing with a general partner with whom you are not comfortable, either in terms of temperament, style, ethics, morals, or any other factor. It is incumbent on a potential investor to use all possible information sources to gain insight into the general partner and other key members of the investment organization. If for whatever reason at the end of this process you are not comfortable with the general partner, my advice would be to pass on the investment opportunity.

What is the general partner's background? Does he or she have the relevant skills that are required to successfully execute the investment strategy? In this area the confidential placement memorandum offers some help by providing biographies for key investment professionals. It is important to check out biographies and past job descriptions and to know how critical an individual's participation was at a previous employer, and how much of the historical success can actually be attributed to his or her efforts, skills and abilities. A few phone calls to previous employers either can result in a greater feeling of comfort with the individual being evaluated, or might result in information that could help prevent you from making a poor investment.

Assessing the relevance of the general partner's experience to the investment strategy being utilized in the limited partnership implies that you know what the strategy is, understand it, and understand what skills are required to execute it. Sometimes this is made easier by the fact that the general partner proposes utilizing an easily understood investment strategy that is exactly what he or she had been doing at prior employers. Regardless, it becomes critical (as covered in a later section) that you truly understand the investment strategy that is going to be implemented.

Has the general partner demonstrated success in implementing the same, or a similar, investment strategy? As mentioned above, if the investment strategy to be implemented is simply one that the general partner has followed for many years, the operative words in this question are "demonstrated success," and consequently evaluation of previous investment results at prior employers becomes even more important. However, if the investment strategy to be implemented is new, then the focus of analysis would shift to the match between critical skills for successful execution and the investment experience of the general partner. This would become the dominant issue and would make monitoring even more important as a means of possibly detecting a mismatch before it became a serious investment problem.

While most of the focus in evaluating the people within a hedge fund organization is directed toward the general partner as the key investment decision maker, there usually are other people involved in the investment process. To the extent that these individuals play a role in decision-making or in providing information for the decision-making process it is important to check out their investment backgrounds and past experiences in order to judge how their skills measure up to those skills needed for the successful implementation of the strategy. Due diligence on key investment professionals is an ongoing process since personnel change. As investment organizations get larger, one will find that the more successful organizations tend to bring in other top-caliber investment professionals with skills that match the requirements for the successful implementation of the investment strategy. Organizations that do not will invariably have difficulties.

Behind the investment professionals is the administrative support staff. While not the decision makers when it comes to investment policy or the implementation of investment tactics, in many instances these are the people that limited partners will be dealing with most frequently. It is easy to take administrative people for granted. Yet, the successful performance of their roles is important. They are the individuals that monitor investments, make sure the books are right, and know at all times where the assets of the partnership are and to whom they belong. More important, getting to know the administrative staff gives you a good feeling of the caliber of people that the general partner employs, as well as a better feeling for the overall organization. Over the years I have found a very high direct correlation between the caliber of the administrative staff and the quality of the investment. This is not to say that there are not exceptions, but rather when you find an administrative staff that is on top of everything, where accurate information flows quickly and freely, you are most likely to find a successful investment organization. By helping you avoid procedural mistakes and by resolving administrative hassles, good administrative people can make life a lot easier.

Investment Process and Strategy

What is the strategy? There is no way to overstate the importance of a potential limited partner truly understanding the investment strategy. It is critical that the investment strategy be understood as completely as possible. It is extremely difficult, if not impossible, to understand what investment risks are being taken without a thorough understanding of the investment strategy; moreover, without such knowledge, a determination of the resources required to successfully execute the strategy becomes virtually impossible.

Many investment strategies, when conceptualized, appear quite straightforward. They are seductively simple and easily provide an overconfidence that you do in fact understand the strategy. This is because strategies are usually conceptualized in a framework of the environment behaving normally. Given a "normal" environment most strategies should produce acceptable results. It is not the "normal" environment that is of concern, but rather what results are possible should the environment become "catiwaumpus."

In trying to understand an investment strategy, I find it useful to envision both normal and unusual operating environments. For each scenario, I try to identify those factors that make the environment unusual or non-normal and to determine both the level and the pattern of returns that might be expected. Because it is difficult for anyone to be an expert at numerous investment strategies, I find it useful to have a discussion about the investment strategy with the general partner as it provides two major benefits.

First, the general partner, being more familiar with the investment strategy, can more easily point out those factors which are most likely to create an unusual environment which will require unusual skills or some modification in the investment strategy. The general partner is also more likely to have a fair assessment as to what such an environment would mean to the investment strategy's results in terms of both return level and volatility. Second, having various scenarios and return/risk expectations makes it easier to monitor the investment results of a particular investment partnership. Sometimes returns deviating from expectations, given the particular scenario that existed, are the first indications that there are problems with the general partner adjusting to the new scenario or that resources are inadequate to deal with the changing investment framework.

One of the areas that is simpler to evaluate in a hedge fund than in a conventional investment organization is the decision-making process. Oftentimes a conventional organization's decision-making process requires several stages and is quite convoluted in nature. In contrast, the decision-making process of most hedge funds is relatively straightforward, with areas of responsibility and decision-making clearly delineated.

Having understood the strategy and the decision-making process, the potential investor is now in a position to evaluate whether the resources match the job to be done. A key component of the resources—people—has already been discussed. Other resources are involved primarily with information flow.

The investment environment is always changing and much of the change is due to highly-skilled professionals competing against each other to extract returns from the marketplace. We live in an environment where instantaneous information is often critical to investment decisions and to not have state-of-the-art resources would become an investment liability. Investment processes and investment strategies vary dramatically, and consequently will require dramatically different resources for their successful implementation. What the evaluator is interested in is seeing that the manager has access to state-of-the-art resources that match or exceed the information needs of the investment strategy. Again, understanding the strategy is paramount in determining the resources needed. For example, a manager implementing a real-time trading strategy would be better served by state-of-the-art electronic equipment than less timely information sources such as *The Wall Street Journal* or even less frequently published financial magazines. Yet a manager more oriented toward long-term value investing would likely find the value of these resources reversed.

One of the critical factors that I focus on when evaluating any investment strategy or process is to determine how risk is controlled. Risk can be controlled at several levels and each level is important. At the level of the investment process and strategy, risk controls might encompass such factors as guidelines, parameters, goals, and objectives that serve the role of keeping the general partner well-focused on the investment strategy and process. These policies provide broad guidelines whose purpose is to guard against major deviations from the investment strategy which might create unexpected return results.

Policy guidelines affecting the use of derivative instruments (options and futures) are particularly important to understand before making an investment. The use of derivatives and leverage has taken on a negative connotation because of recent press articles detailing major losses incurred because of their use. In one way this should serve as a warning that speculative use of derivatives can be very high risk. However, one should always keep in mind that it is *how* derivatives are used that determines how they influence risk, not the derivatives themselves. Just as derivatives can be used to increase potential return (and consequently risk), so too can they be used to hedge (or reduce) risk. Derivatives and leverage have the ability to "super charge" the tamest investment strategy or to tame an otherwise volatile investment strategy. *It is imperative that one understand how and to what extent derivatives and leverage will be used.*

When evaluating hedge funds, appropriate asset size for a particular strategy plays a much larger role with alternative strategies than it does with conventional investment strategies. There are several reasons for this.

First, alternative strategies, in their purest form, are niche strategies. Oftentimes these strategies take advantage of small pockets of market inefficiencies. By definition these opportunities are limited in size since as they grow they are continually arbitraged back into alignment and the inefficiencies are diminished or disappear. If the asset base is too large, successful implementation becomes impossible.

Second, alternative strategies typically employ significantly smaller asset bases. Consequently, each investment position can be high in specific risk, which would not be possible if assets were substantially greater, since too many portfolio positions would be required to invest funds without reducing liquidity.

In Figure 6-2 the bars detail the types of risk in a conventional and alternative strategy portfolio. As shown, conventional portfolios contain a high percentage of general market risk since a long equity strategy is greatly influenced by market direction. In contrast, the alternative portfolio has a significantly lower component of general market risk and a higher component of specific issue risk. The importance of having a high level of specific risk, as opposed to market risk, is that specific risk is more identifiable and more "controllable."

Consider this contrast. A small value-oriented hedge fund needs relatively few investment ideas. Each portfolio position can be a top-quality idea

FIGURE 6-2.   Portfolio Risk

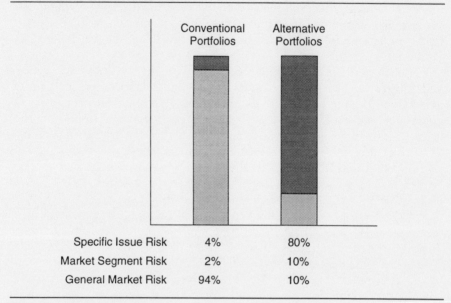

	Conventional Portfolios	Alternative Portfolios
Specific Issue Risk	4%	80%
Market Segment Risk	2%	10%
General Market Risk	94%	10%

Source: Paradigm Partners, Inc.

with solid fundamental underpinning. The investment manager has the advantage of knowing the investments in extreme depth and should be able to gauge over/under valuations more easily. This manager knows what risks are being taken and why. He or she is able to more easily interpret events and how they should impact each investment. This portfolio is heavy with specific risk.

By contrast, a large mutual fund manager needs numerous investment ideas simply to deploy a large asset base since liquidity constraints prohibit taking outsized positions in fewer issues. Obviously all ideas cannot be of the highest quality. Knowledge of specifics is less since research resources are limited. And the sheer number of issues creates a portfolio high in general market risk and low in specific risk. When unanticipated events occur it is far more difficult to interpret the most appropriate course of action.

Portfolio Construction

Evaluation of how a manager constructs the portfolio is a key ingredient in determining how risk is controlled at the portfolio level. One might view risk and return somewhat like the parts of the car, return being the accelerator and risk being the brake. Just as with a car, it is far more important to know that you can stop than you can get going. If there was only one question that I could ask the general partner of a potential partnership I was evaluating, it would be, "How do you control risk in the portfolio?" While guidelines, objectives, and goals do limit risk to some degree, most risk is controlled at the level of portfolio construction.

There are various ways to control risk within a portfolio. One of the more important and often used is the number of investment positions, but even here there are no firm rules. I have reviewed portfolios with as few as one issue and as many as several hundred. Ironically, in both situations the number of positions seemed appropriate given the investment strategy. The strategy involving only one portfolio position made an investment that had an extremely high probability of a positive payoff and utilized very close stop-loss points as a risk control parameter. The strategy with several hundred investment positions was a high-velocity, statistically-driven trading system that needed a high number of positions in order to capture the return phenomena. Nonetheless, looking at the number of investment positions can give a prospective investor insight into risk control within the portfolio. Generally, the larger the number of positions, the less volatile the overall portfolio, other factors being equal (which they rarely are).

Diversification and concentration are other methods of reducing or enhancing risk taken in a portfolio. This approach goes somewhat beyond the number of investment positions in that it considers investment positions relative to industries, sectors, or themes. While categorizing investment positions into appropriate industries, sectors, or themes can give a better indication as to the risk being taken, one must also look at whether these investments are highly correlated to one another. For example, theoretically it would seem that a $10,000,000 long position in Computer Company A and a $10,000,000 short position in Computer Company B when combined would have little general market risk or market segment risk since one would expect both companies in the same industry to rise or fall with the general market and industry tide. However, the investment takes on an entirely different characteristic if one were to say that the investment is predicated on Company A (the long position) gaining significant market share from Company B (the short position). If Company A were successful in its quest for market share then it is possible that the long position would go up, and similarly one might expect the short position to decline, resulting in a double win. Conversely, if Company A is totally unsuccessful the shares of the long position might decline while the shares of the short position might rise, compounding the loss. This same principle, two positions being highly correlated to each other because they are contingent upon the same event, holds true for investment positions whether they involve industries, sectors, themes or individual companies. It is important to know how investment positions are correlated to each other in order to understand whether they are mitigating or amplifying the risk. As a hedge fund manager once told me, "When you are long $10,000,000 of a stock and short $10,000,000 of a different stock you have $20,000,000 worth of bets regardless of what the theory says." Long/short positions that are not highly correlated is a method used by many to reduce the risk of the overall portfolio. Indeed this is the essence of hedge fund investing. Again, the lower the level of correlation, the more effective this tool is in reducing risk.

Operating with a quick "trigger finger" is another method used by some hedge fund managers as a means of controlling risk. I have reviewed several partnerships in which the primary investment strategy was actively trading investment positions. In some instances I would find that the general partner would take outsized positions, but leave him- or herself a very short leash or room to be wrong. While this would not be my personal choice as to how I would control risk within the portfolio, the important questions is, Is it appropriate for the partnership under evaluation? In some cases I have seen managers that can use quick response very effectively as a primary risk control tool.

Hard and fast rules and general guidelines, especially about the limits of acceptable losses, are tools that many general partners utilize to make certain that no one investment position accounts for an abnormally-large loss in the portfolio. Usually a loss limit of 10 to 15 percent will be established for an investment position. If the threshold is reached, the investment position is liquidated on the assumption that the original analysis was incorrect or the investment was ill-timed. Oftentimes general partners are willing to re-establish the position after some time has gone by and they have rechecked their analysis and have a fresh perspective.

In recent years the proliferation of derivative products has made the job of hedging investment positions easier. It is now possible to use derivatives, both publicly traded and customized, to hedge positions more tightly. The use of derivatives can be effective, but this can also be expensive since the manager is paying the issuer to assume risk. It is unusual for a manager to use derivatives to hedge an entire portfolio; rather, derivatives are typically employed to hedge a particular volatile investment position, or perhaps several positions. What is important is that the derivatives are used for hedging, not speculation, and that both you and the general partner understand what risks are being hedged and just how effective the hedge is likely to be under varying scenarios.

In summary, the key to evaluating portfolio risk is to focus your efforts on answering two questions: (1) Is the general partner focusing on controlling risk to a level that is acceptable? and (2) Does the general partner's approach used to control portfolio risk match the strategy being implemented? If the answers to both questions are yes, it is likely that this is a general partner with whom you can be comfortable.

Performance

Performance is a topic that receives too much focus for the wrong reason. Far too often a high return is equated with a good manager. High returns are, in many instances, caused by a favorable investing environment, not totally by skill, and consequently the general partner is given far more credit for having investment acumen than is deserved. This is not to say that performance statistics are not important in evaluating a prospective manager. Rather, I would stress that high returns must be understood in the context of the environment in which they were generated, taking into account the risk assumed to generate such returns.

The fact that a favorable investing climate can exist for a significant period of time for a particular strategy is also often overlooked. A favorable investing climate not only can create skewed high returns, but also a smoother and less volatile return pattern. Too often a series of acceptable, stable returns are viewed as an indication of skill, as opposed to the fact that the investing climate has been particularly favorable. Lack of appreciation that returns must be viewed in the full context of the environment in which they were generated, and with full regard for the risk assumed, is one of the key reasons that investors oftentimes select a manager at precisely the time that his or her investment performance is peaking.

There is no one number that will determine whether an investment is going to be a financial success or failure. That having been said, there is one tool in particular that I find helps me put returns in context with both the risk being taken and the environment that existed in the financial markets at that time. The purpose of this tool is to reduce the risk of severe underperformance by ensuring the evaluator really understands the investment strategy and its inherent risks.

Figure 6-3 is a standard risk/return diagram displaying the empirical capital market line that existed during the time period that this hypothetical equity manager is being evaluated. The empirical capital market line is constructed by connecting the points representing the risk/return characteristics of the S&P 500 and lower-risk U.S. Treasury bills. The capital market line provides a framework to evaluate return and risk generated by different investment strategies and styles in the context of the environment that existed.

Points along the capital market line represent the returns of managers who are being appropriately compensated for the assumed risk measured

FIGURE 6-3. Empirical Capital Market Line

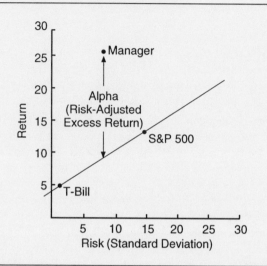

Source: Paradigm Partners, Inc.

by portfolio volatility; points below the line represent managers not being fully compensated for risk; points above the line are those managers who are being overcompensated for risk taken.

There are many different ways to gain insight into the risk/reward trade-off of a manager or investment strategy. All of the methods have their own strengths and weaknesses. However, evaluating managers relative to the capital market line is particularly useful since it contains much more information than any single ratio.

In addition to clearly displaying absolute risk and return, this diagram also provides numerous measurements relative to the environment that existed during the time period being examined. It is comparatively easy to see how numerous managers stack up against each other and to identify standout managers. The diagram makes it easy to identify the strategy that produced the highest return for an acceptable level of risk; the strategy that produced an acceptable return with the lowest risk, or the strategy that had the highest risk-adjusted excess return (alpha).

No single measure can be regarded as a comprehensive manager evaluation tool. However, we find alpha, or risk-adjusted excess return, an extremely powerful tool. Figure 6-3, the capital market line analysis, graphically displays alpha. Alpha is the vertical distance, measured in percent, between the data point representing the risk/return characteristics of a manager and the capital market line. In Figure 6-3, the manager return was 26 percent while the capital market line indicates that an 8 percent return would be appropriate for that risk level, indicating an alpha of 18 percent was generated. Over time a manager must be fully compensated for the investment risk assumed, otherwise returns will be subpar. Depending on managers who do not produce a positive alpha means the investor relies on luck or a favorable environment to produce superior returns. Avoiding managers that have historically produced negative alphas reduces the probability of underperformance.

Using the capital market line framework and the concept of alpha or risk-adjusted excess return, the potential investor can then compare expectations and actual results. This approach provides a structure for both initial evaluation and continued monitoring.

In evaluating a potential manager one of the key questions to be addressed concerning historical performance is, Does the return pattern match what you expected given the strategy as you understand it? In other words, do the historical returns that were generated match the level that you had anticipated and is the volatility similar to what you thought it should be? Affirmative answers to these questions give the perspective investor some confidence that he or she understands what the strategy is and that the manager is executing the strategy in a way similar to what he had anticipated.

If there are differences in either the level of return or the volatility of the return pattern from what was expected, it is well worth the time to investigate further. The key question to be addressed at this point then is, *Do you truly understand the strategy?* Were there unusual circumstances that contributed to the differences in return or volatility that you had not previously understood? If unusual circumstances do not answer the discrepancies then the key question becomes, Is the general partner executing the strategy as he says he is? In any event probing into these issues cannot do anything but enhance your understanding of the strategy being executed and how the general partner is executing the strategy.

One important caveat when looking at historical returns—watch out for time-specific returns. Returns that begin at a propitious point, incorporate a very favorable event, or end at an extraordinarily good point are examples of where the returns are likely to be skewed upward. Sometimes the environment for a particular strategy will be unusually favorable for a considerable period of time. This time specific distortion can often affect both the return and volatility very favorably. If returns appear to be too good, there is probably some element of time-specific results that are skewing them upwards. Remember, it is easy to make too much out of good returns by jumping to the conclusion that they are due to an element of skill as opposed to an element of luck caused by a favorable market environment. Nonetheless, serious analysis of performance returns can provide some key insights into how a particular strategy stacks up against the broad market or a custom index, as well as giving the investor a degree of confidence that the general partner is effectively executing the strategy.

In addition to establishing a capital market line framework and establishing an alpha for the manager being evaluated, there are other statistical measures that can be helpful in assessing risks that primarily relate to the risk of relative underperformance. Luckily, there are numerous statistical packages that calculate these historical statistics quickly and easily and provide graphic capabilities. Listed below are some of the more useful standard statistics:

- Sharp ratio
- Regressed alpha
- Regressed beta
- Coefficient of correlation
- Coefficient of determination
- Maximum drawdown
- Risk of ruin

Each of these measurements can be beneficial in assessing risk; depending on what strategy is being evaluated, some will be more useful than others. Over time, most analysts will develop their own favorite measurements and create their own proprietary measures.

Partnership Details

Read the document! This seems to be silly advice to give someone who is about to make an investment of $1,000,000, but if the truth were known, probably more confidential offering memorandums go unread by prospective investors than are read by those who choose to invest. Reading the document is important even if you think you understand the investment strategy and have known the general partner for your entire life.

The document can give particularly valuable insights to potential limited partners about the general partner and his or her attitude towards the partnership, as its details say a lot about what you might expect once you become a limited partner. In several instances throughout a limited partnership document, specifically those regarding fee structure, there are benefits that could go either to the limited partner or to the general partner. Noticing whether the general partner is one who tends to give him- or herself the benefit, or pass it along to the limited partners, can give some indication as to what you might expect once you are an investor. There is no reason to expect better treatment after you have invested your funds than before you have.

Another key reason why reading the partnership document is so critical is it is the only way that a limited partner will really know what his or her legal rights are, once he or she becomes an investor. Conversations between a potential investor and a general partner might be substantially different from the true legal obligations as described in the partnership document. When push comes to shove, the document will take precedence.

Another key factor that needs to be addressed regarding partnership terms involves liquidity. Most hedge funds accept partnership funds at the end of each quarter, but disburse funds to limited partners at the end of each calendar year, and then only after an audit. When making an investment in a hedge fund, one must look at the liquidity provisions quite carefully to ensure that they are consistent with one's overall investment program.

In my opinion, the most critical partnership details involve the fee structure. I have this attitude for two reasons: (1) the fee structure can tell me a lot about the general partner's character, and (2) the fees come directly out of my funds and therefore have an impact on the actual net return that I will receive. The point I would stress is that the fee structure must be understood completely. If you do not understand the fee structure, or if it is not particularly straightforward, it is not unreasonable to ask for a fuller explanation.

The follow-up question would be, Is the fee justified? Generally the fee structures that I favor are those that cause the most direct alignment between the general partner and the limited partner's investment objectives. It is easy to be in favor of a fee structure where the general partner cannot be financially successful unless the limited partners are also. Too often these days partnership fee structures are made far too generous to the general partner, in that it is possible that the general partner can do financially well while the limited partner might suffer a loss.

One of the initial reasons for the high fee structure of hedge funds, (the typical fee structure is a 1 percent management fee plus 20 percent of both realized and unrealized profits), was that hedge funds were going to limit themselves to being small in size and operating in niche markets where they felt there were significant market inefficiencies that could be exploited. Over time, hedge funds have grown from organizations thought to be limited to approximately $100,000,000 in assets to a point where some hedge funds have multiple billion-dollar investment pools. It is difficult to justify a manager with $1,000,000,000 in assets charging a fee of 1 percent plus 20 percent unless (1) you believe it truly costs $10,000,000 to operate the administrative and research functions of the partnership; and (2) that the general partner is able to deploy $1,000,000,000 in high specific risk investments where partnership results depend on his or her skill rather than the market environment. There are probably some large international partnerships that do have very expensive overhead caused by operating around the globe and around the clock, but these are the exception rather than the rule. There are even fewer large partnerships that are able to create a portfolio high in specific risk and effectively deploy $1,000,000,000. The important aspect of fee structure is to make sure that the fee structure is justified so that your investment objective is aligned as closely as possible to those of the general partner's.

Other important partnership details that can only be learned by reading the partnership documents have to do with controls on the general partner's investment latitude. Oftentimes, the general partner is given extensive latitude to invest virtually anywhere that he sees fit. Nonetheless, by reading the document you might get some indication as to what limits are placed on particular types of transactions, as well as limits placed on leverage. These two factors have a great deal to do with what the actual risk undertaken by the partnership will ultimately be. Knowing what type of leverage will be used, if any, also helps address such issues as unrelated business taxable income, and other issues only of concern with those partnerships that utilize leverage.

While it doesn't happen very often, one sometimes comes across a confidential private placement memorandum that includes some outlandish stipulations, invariably accruing to the general partner's favor. One can only conclude their purpose is to rip off limited partners. If you encounter any such documents let that be a warning about the people promoting this "opportunity." Below are a few of the outlandish stipulations I have uncovered by reading documents completely:

- *Exorbitant fixed management fees*—2 percent to 6 percent per year are sometimes encountered. One percent is more than adequate for almost any partnership.
- *General partner perks*—Including homes (needed for reflection, I assume), cars (Rolls Royces to pick up prospective investors), gyms (to stay fit), etc. Such perks are totally inappropriate.
- *Hidden fees*—Such as the general partner paying himself 1/2 percent per month to do administrative work. Such nonarm's length deals are simply a way of cheating limited partners and are never justified.
- *Very high incentive fees*—As high as 50 percent in some instances. Incentive fees this high are never justified regardless of past success.
- *Payment of past expenses*—Document creation expenses and marketing expenses fall into this category. General partners that charge these fees want limited partners to assume all risk, while they themselves take little, if any.
- *Excessive commission fee arrangements*—Fees as high as ten times normal are sometimes charged the partnership as a way to kickback commissions to brokers who bring in assets. Why should limited partners bear this additional cost anyway? All commissions should be reasonable, if not on the low side.

The point about the above examples is that such stipulations can only be discovered by reading the document thoroughly. Each example above serves only to enrich the general partner at the expense of his or her investors. Do you really want to be a partner with someone that engages in such practices?

A Point to Remember—A Word of Caution

In the early days of hedge funds, they were small entities with limited investment capacity managed by astute investment professionals exploiting particular niche markets. Such investments commanded higher fees because they were small, more expensive to operate, and provided the benefits of a direct incentive to succeed. In recent years many conventional managers have been lured by the high fees of operating a hedge fund. In many instances they have mistakenly jumped to the conclusion that they have the skills to do so, since in their minds operating a hedge fund is not dramatically different than conventional money management. At the same time investment organizations have become very marketing-oriented and the level of marketing expertise has improved exponentially. From the perspective of a potential investor, the difficulty in selecting a good hedge fund investment has increased dramatically for several reasons:

- The number of entrants into the arena has exploded.
- Lucrative fee structures have caused some general partners to be more fee-oriented than results-oriented.
- Experienced marketers know all the "buzz words" and utilize sophisticated marketing techniques to target potential clients.

These factors, combined with an environment favorable to the performance of financial assets for more than a decade and a half, make it extremely difficult to separate good hedge fund managers from the also-rans.

The purpose of this chapter has been to give a potential investor some framework in which to evaluate a hedge fund investment. While the process can seem simple and straightforward, it nonetheless is one that can give a potential investor a higher level of confidence than might otherwise be the case. It is important to go through the process and get all questions answered adequately to ensure that you truly understand the strategy—both the returns and the risks involved. The time to do the due diligence is before the investment is made. Get all your questions answered before you write the check, because *they will never love you more than when they are courting your money.*

PART II

Understanding and Evaluating Key Sectors of the Hedge Fund Universe

CHAPTER 7

Funds of Funds

Martin J. Gross

General Background—What Are Funds of Funds and Hedge Funds?

Funds of funds are limited partnerships organized under applicable state laws.[1] Since funds of funds do not, as a rule, make direct investments, but instead invest in other funds, they serve as asset allocation mechanisms. While the term fund of funds is currently used in the context of hedge funds, it need not be so limited. Technically a pension fund, endowment, or any other pool of capital is a fund of funds if it utilizes two or more submanagers, be they debt, equity, commodities, currencies, derivatives, etc., or combinations of the above. I limit my focus to U.S.-based funds of funds allocating their capital to hedge funds.

In a fund of funds, the fund of funds manager accepts capital from investing partners and allocates it to other managers, namely, hedge funds. Figure 7-1 is representative of the process.

Since a fund of funds is essentially a look-through vehicle, understanding the specific characteristics of funds of funds in general and each fund of funds in particular requires a look at the recipients of their capital, namely, the hedge funds.

---

[1] While most funds of funds are limited partnerships, some are organized as collective trusts. Offshore funds of funds are organized as either corporations or partnerships with offshore administrators.

FIGURE 7-1. Fund of Funds: Representative Structure

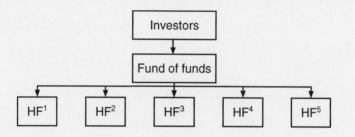

Limited Partnership and Regulatory Issues

Both funds of funds and hedge funds are limited partnerships[2] that are limited to 99 investors.[3] They usually only accept accredited investors, although technically up to 35 investors could be nonaccredited. Some general partners of hedge funds and funds of funds are registered as investment advisers, others are not.[4] As private offerings both funds of funds and hedge funds are

[2] **Securities Act of 1933:** Interests in hedge funds and funds of funds are not registered under the Securities Act of 1933 as amended, or any other securities laws, including state securities or blue sky laws. These interests are offered in reliance upon the exemption from registration provided by Section 4(2) of the Securities Act of 1933 and Regulation D promulgated thereunder. Prospective purchasers are required to represent that they are an accredited investor as defined in Regulation D and that they are acquiring the interest for investment purposes only and not for resale or distribution.

[3] **Investment Company Act of 1940:** Hedge funds and funds of funds are subject to the Investment Company Act of 1940. The number of beneficial owners of interest, for purposes of the Investment Company Act of 1940, as amended, is limited to 100 or less so as to qualify for the exemption from the provisions of the Investment Company Act. With respect to the determination of the number of such beneficial owners, the hedge funds and funds of funds obtain and rely on appropriate representations and undertakings from each limited partner in order to assure that the fund meets the conditions of the exemption on an ongoing basis.

[4] **Investment Advisers Act of 1940:** Some general partners register as investment advisers under the Investment Advisers Act of 1940. Others do not in reliance upon the exemption from the registration requirements of the Advisers Act contained in Section 203(b)(3), which exempts from registration any investment adviser who during the course of the preceding 12 months had fewer than 15 clients and who meets certain other requirements. General partners who register may be subject to both various fee restrictions contained in the Investment Advisers Act and more stringent accredited investor requirements.

prohibited from advertising and are difficult to locate. Hedge funds have high minimum investment requirements of $500,000 to $5 million. They impose performance fees of usually 20 percent of the profits over a base fee of 1 percent. Some hedge funds have hurdle rates before their performance fee applies. Most important, the general partner usually has a substantial percentage of his or her net worth invested in the fund. Unlike hedge funds, funds of funds have more modest minimums, often $250,000 to $500,000. These lower minimums allow investors to access a portfolio of hedge funds for a much smaller amount than if they were to make a direct investment.

Hedge fund and fund of funds investors should carefully read the limited partnership agreement as it contains the respective rights and obligations of the investor and the fund. The provision on withdrawal rights is critical. Hedge funds and funds of funds have either monthly, quarterly or annual redemption provisions upon the giving of appropriate notice, usually 60, 45, or 30 days. Investors are restricted to these periodic windows as concerns withdrawal of their capital. A fund of funds' withdrawal restrictions reflect those imposed by the hedge funds in which it invests. While monthly withdrawal rights with a minimal notice requirement might seem ideal, investors should be cautioned not to trade off increased liquidity from a fund of funds that, due to its need to provide it, only invests in hedge funds with monthly liquidity. Many top-quality hedge funds will be eliminated from consideration. If investors have carefully considered the selection of a hedge fund or fund of funds, quarterly or even annual liquidity should be acceptable.

Another relevant provision concerns the general partners' ability to withdraw from the hedge fund or fund of funds. The limited partnership agreement should allow the investors to immediately withdraw if the general partner withdraws or does not maintain agreed upon capital requirements. Also, if the fund's management changes the investors should have the right to withdraw since it may become unclear who is performing the investment process. This is a common problem with some large hedge funds where, as these organizations grow, more people assume responsibility for trading and investing decisions on an autonomous or semi-autonomous basis. Last, and quite important, the limited partnership agreement provides information on fees and other investment related factors. It should be carefully reviewed.

Investment Characteristics

Perhaps more important than the regulatory aspects of hedge funds are their investment characteristics. What is critical to know about hedge funds is that different hedge funds utilize very different investment strategies. The following are some representative examples.

1. *Merger arbitrage*—This strategy involves investing in announced corporate takeovers or other similar corporate restructurings. It is often referred to as event driven or special situation investing.
2. *Traditional hedge fund/long short*—These hedge funds purchase undervalued securities and sell short overvalued ones. Some of these funds limit themselves to one sector, like technology or health care, while others are more general in scope.
3. *Various market neutral strategies*—These strategies attempt to produce consistent and low volatile results often with a target annual return of 10 to 15 percent. The strategies include long/short investing (whereby equal amounts of capital are invested long and short the market), various options and futures strategies, and convertible hedging (which involves the purchase of a convertible bond or preferred stock and the shorting of the underlying common stock). One problem with "market neutral" is the label itself. Strategies using bonds are affected by the bond market. Those using equity are affected by the equity market. Investors must analyze the specific details of each strategy.
4. *Distressed securities*—This type of investing involves the purchase of securities of companies in reorganization, usually the debt, and often the active participation by the hedge fund manager in the reorganization process itself. It is also referred to as event driven or special situation investing.
5. *Commodities*—This strategy focuses on investing in commodity contracts.[5]
6. *Currencies*—This strategy attempts to profit from short-term moves in the relative prices of various currencies.
7. *Global or macro*—Global or macro investing is basically a license to do anything on a leveraged basis. The managers can, for example, be long certain stocks or stock markets, short bonds and have currency and commodity positions all at the same time. Investors are relying on these individuals to exploit opportunistic investment possibilities wherever they may be found.

---

[5] **Commodity Exchange Act:** Some hedge funds trade commodities as their main strategy and others purchase and sell futures contracts in a manner solely incidental to their securities trading activities. Those which do either must apply for registration with the Commodity Futures Trading Commission (CFTC) as a commodity pool operator, or seek an appropriate exemption.

8. *Emerging markets*—Emerging markets investing consists of purchasing sovereign or corporate debt and/or equity in countries considered to be emerging, i.e., most debt and equity markets other than North America, Western Europe, Japan, New Zealand, and Australia.

9. *Short selling*—This strategy consists of the sale of borrowed securities considered overvalued in the anticipation of purchasing them for a profit at lower prices. It is an inherently very risky strategy since the most one can make is the amount received when the securities are sold short, yet the amount one can lose is, at least in theory, infinite.

10. *Short-term trading*—This strategy consists of the short-term trading of equities and sometimes debt instruments. It is characterized by rapid portfolio turnover and is often accompanied by the use of leverage. While occasionally driven by quantitative computer models it is usually implemented by individuals trying to identify short- or intermediate-term market trends. Among various hedge fund strategies it is often the least able to accommodate large amounts of capital.

11. *Volatility investing*—With this strategy investors are betting that the markets will be volatile, regardless of direction. Volatility strategies can be extremely profitable in volatile markets but will not perform well in flat or choppy markets confined to a tight trading range.

The above sampling of hedge funds strategies evidences a very diverse approach to investing. One characteristic that hedge funds have in common is that very few of them consist of traditional buy and hold strategies the results of which have a high correlation to the U.S. equity market.[6] More important, these strategies have not only been significantly uncorrelated with the U.S. equity and debt markets but with each other. This lack of correlation among hedge fund strategies has enabled fund of funds managers to create portfolios consisting not of individual securities but of diverse and uncorrelated investment strategies. Each strategy may be represented by a small or large number of hedge funds. The result is a strategy mix capable of generating positive absolute returns over time with minimal volatility.

The above characteristics of hedge funds provide the raison d'être for funds of funds. Since hedge funds are private partnerships with large

---

[6] Since some hedge funds use a traditional buy and hold strategy with no attempt to hedge; one knowledgeable commentator has defined hedge funds as "incentive partnerships."

investment minimums, frequently in the $500,000 to $5,000,000 range, most individuals can neither spend the time trying to identify and locate hedge funds nor afford their high minimum investment requirements. Further, since many of the strategies which hedge funds utilize are quite technical, understanding them, blending the strategies and picking the best implementers of those strategies is a highly demanding task. Further, all investments, once made, must be continually monitored. Since the hedge fund world is a dynamic one where changes in a hedge fund's ability to continue providing excellent returns may occur in a very short time frame, full-time monitoring is an essential component of the investment process. It is the fund of funds manager's job to perform all of the above.

Fund of Funds Investment Approaches

General Types

Each fund of funds has an investment approach that is determined by the strategies of the underlying hedge funds to which it allocates its capital. In deciding whether to invest in a fund of funds, investors must understand these investment characteristics. There are two basic questions which investors considering a fund of funds should ask:[7]

1. What is the investment approach of the fund of funds manager?
2. How does he or she intend to implement it?

There are four basic options available to the fund of funds manager.

1. *Target return*—The fund of funds manager allocates capital to hedge funds in an attempt to generate a target return usually in the 10 to 15 percent range. Many fund of funds managers with this goal have used various "market neutral" strategies along with lower-risk distressed securities strategies.
2. *Maximal return approach*—Under this option, fund of funds managers select those hedge funds whose investment strategies they believe generate the highest return under current market conditions and are willing to accept greater volatility as a result.
3. *Dedicated strategy*—In a dedicated strategy fund, the fund of funds manager selects hedge funds that invest in a particular

---

[7] See *Lookout Mountain Hedge Fund Review* Vol. 1, No. 5 (1994) for a more extended discussion on selecting a fund of funds along with additional questions to ask.

asset class, such as emerging markets, or to event driven strategies such as distressed securities and merger arbitrage.

4. *Combinations of the above*—Under this option the fund of funds manager mixes lower risk strategies with more aggressive ones to create a fund with a more balanced risk posture. Many funds of funds, perhaps a majority, utilize diverse investment strategies along with many managers implementing each strategy. Some of these funds of funds use up to 40 or more managers. Figure 7-2 is a common example of a combined strategy fund of funds with 20 percent of its capital allocated to five strategies, each implemented by varying numbers of hedge funds.

Figure 7-3 represents a fund of funds with a dedicated strategy approach, in this case emerging markets.

FIGURE 7-2. Combined Strategy Fund of Funds

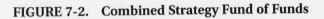
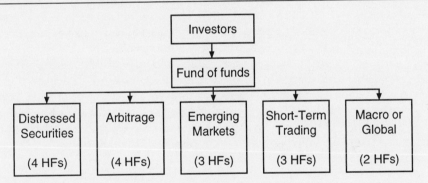

FIGURE 7-3. Dedicated Strategy Approach

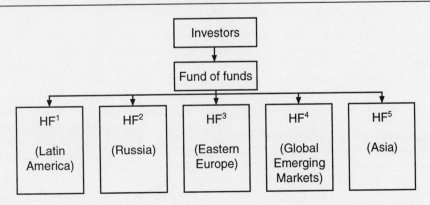

Once a fund of funds manager has formulated his or her fund's investment orientation, he or she must proceed to implement it. This leads into the strategy and manager selection process.

Strategies

There are at least three options available to a fund of funds manager.[8] These consist of:

- Attractive asset classes
- Particular strategies
- People

Attractive Asset Classes

In allocating the fund of funds capital, the fund of funds manager attempts to exploit his or her judgment concerning various market conditions. For example, the manager may conclude that Japanese small-cap stocks are very inexpensive, that Russian privatization vouchers are an extremely cheap asset or that certain Latin American or Asian markets have just experienced a severe correction and have become quite undervalued. He or she would then allocate capital to long-biased hedge funds prepared to exploit these perceived opportunities. Or, he or she may allocate more capital to high-yield U.S. bonds after a severe correction, to a short-seller if he or she thinks a given equity market is quite overvalued, or to commodities trading hedge funds if he or she discerned a macro change in a commodities cycle. Similarly, the manager may believe that the premiums in convertible bonds are at an advantageous level and therefore invest in convertible hedging. Allocating to attractive asset classes is a dynamic process to which the fund of funds manager must be continually attentive.

---

[8] A conceptual difficulty in today's hedge fund universe is terminology, starting with the term hedge fund itself. Most hedge funds don't hedge, and those that do hedge do it in different ways to different degrees. While I earlier provided a partial list of hedge fund strategies, I have now used the three categories of people, event driven strategies, and asset class since it may be more helpful from an asset allocation perspective. Asset allocations to long-biased hedge funds in distinct asset classes, be they U.S. mid- or small-cap stocks or emerging markets, are done to access those markets and will be significantly correlated to them. Allocations to event-driven strategies are also a distinct allocation due to their event-driven foundations. However, allocations to macro, long/short, or any of various trading strategies (whether involving currencies, commodities, debt or equity) are really allocations to people, and it's doubtful whether they should be deemed an asset class, as opposed to an investment in a particular individual's skills.

Particular Strategies

A second option would be to determine that the deal flow in distressed securities and/or merger arbitrage in the U.S. market presented attractive investment opportunities and to utilize managers implementing those strategies. This option is distinct from the first since its attractiveness, if not its very existence especially in the case of arbitrage, is dependent on various types of corporate activity or events. There will always be small-cap stocks whereas there may not always be much in the way of arbitrage activity.

People

The third alternative is investing in people. Most hedge funds fall into this category. While people are always a material factor in investing, in certain instances they are paramount. When investors give money to numerous large global trading hedge funds such as George Soros, Julian Robertson, or Michael Steinhardt, investors are making a bet that those managers will be able, both by themselves and through teams of people they put together, to identify and exploit the most opportunistic investment options around the world. Similarly, when one invests in hedge funds which do short-term trading or long/short investing, one is betting on a particular person since you are betting that the person is either a good trader or will be on the right side of a given stock. If a hedge fund invests long and short in technology or health care stocks, and if those sectors rise in value, you must hope that the manager was long or short specific securities at the appropriate time. Your bet is on the investment expertise of the manager, not on whether technology or health care stocks as a group go up or down.

Managers

In selecting managers to implement strategies the fund of funds manager should view each hedge fund as a business wherein its raw material is capital and its finished product, a return, is arrived at through an understandable investment process. In so doing, a fund of funds manager should focus on numerous issues including, but not limited to, people, risk, track record, capital under management, leverage, and capacity issues.

Since investing is people driven, in analyzing the track record it is critical to determine whose track record it is. Large hedge fund organizations may give money to outside managers or allocate it internally to different teams of traders. One must identify who is making the specific investment decisions on a day-to-day basis and who is monitoring them. It is important to identify whose investment skills produced the track record since if these people leave the organization the track record is less reliable. This issue frequently arises when partners split up. Each claims credit for the good investment ideas. The synergy that produced the track record is gone and so is its reliability going forward. The most reliable track records are those produced by individuals trading or investing by themselves.

Since ultimately all investment decisions are made by people, getting a clear read on the individual(s) doing the investing is critical. Many managers who rely on models often make the mistake that the model is right and the market is wrong, especially since the manager often designed the model. One should only invest with managers who are not overly reliant on fixed models but are willing to be flexible in their investment approach. Frequently superior analysts who move to managing money discover that managing portfolios and analyzing securities are not one and the same. Often superior trading skill may be required in certain instances for which the analyst may be thoroughly unprepared. There are, however, instances where fund of funds managers allocate capital to analysts who have become hedge fund managers and have no independent track records, and base their decision solely on a qualitative impression of the manager. Fund of funds managers who allocate to these "start-up" managers control the risk that the analyst may not be a successful manager by allocating smaller percentages of their capital to those start-up managers and monitoring them over time.

When interviewing hedge fund managers the fund of funds manager should ask: How have you made money in the past, and what were your markets like at those times? What are your markets like today and why should I believe you will continue to make money? A competent hedge fund manager should have a clear and concise answer to that inquiry. Remember, yesterday was yesterday, it's tomorrow's returns we are seeking.

While an excellent track record may be an excellent indicator of tomorrow's top performance, much detail work must be done to arrive at that conclusion. In reviewing a hedge fund's track record, the fund of funds manager realizes that a track record is only numbers on a piece of paper created by particular individuals, either alone or as part of a team. The key is to use the track record as a window into the hedge fund manager's investment approach and thought process. Remember, investing is the application of strategies or concepts to capital. Choosing a manager is the adoption of a thought process or approach.

Managers should always be asked how they control risk. Do they have large or small thresholds of pain, do they use derivatives, do they employ leverage? Talking to a manager about these issues should provide a good glimpse into his or her view of risk. Some managers make big bets, allocation-wise, but do not think they are taking big risks since they have conducted a very thorough fundamental analysis of their large positions or have otherwise hedged them. It's always nice to hear that managers think they control risk by buying low and selling high, but a more elaborate response is helpful.

Track records can be deceiving. In many cases a good track record merely reflects an underlying trend in the strategy or asset class in which the hedge fund invested. One obvious example is the excellent record of a short seller in a bear market. A 15 percent compound return produced by a long manager in a bear market is more impressive than a 20 percent return produced by a long manager in a bull market. Some stock or bond strategies have very long track records but do not include a period of rising interest rates. There is no magical time frame within which a track record achieves statistical significance. Obviously, the longer the better. However, shorter track records that span turbulent market conditions may be more revealing than longer track records which do not. All these factors must be considered. Quantitative data must be viewed in a qualitative context.

Careful attention must also be paid to the amount of capital under management while the track record was created. Managers with excellent 10-year records who started with $10 million 10 years ago and have $500 million under management today may be in, effectively, a new business in which their track record is not only no guarantee of future results, but may even become irrelevant, if not misleading, as to the likelihood of tomorrow's results. Fund of funds managers must, therefore, be careful when analyzing a track record and must determine that the strategy which produced the record is able to accommodate increasing levels of capital. One example of this is short-term trading. Numerous short-term traders who generate excellent returns with $25 million may be incapable of generating similar returns with $100 million in capital.

Finally, organizations change, especially as they take in more capital. The individuals who created the track record often delegate their decision making authority to others. Managers of capital can evolve into managers of people. When this happens, track records become suspect and investors must keep close tabs on what's really going on with the hedge fund.

Risk

The concept of risk is central to investments in general and to funds of funds in particular. It is a complex topic that receives much attention in academic and financial journals. According to many theoreticians, risk is synonymous with volatility, as measured by the standard deviation of investment returns. According to this model, given two investments which each produced a 15 percent return over time, the one with the least volatility would be considered to be the superior risk-adjusted investment. Others focus not on volatility in general but on down-side volatility, also referred to as drawdowns, along with the magnitude of the drawdown. A third concept of risk focuses on the possibility of permanent loss of capital. Investors who embrace this concept are not overly concerned with short-term volatility since they may be long-term investors. To these investors down-side volatility may be desirable since it provides an opportunity for them to purchase more of a security at a lower price. For example, investors wishing to continue to purchase a stock, such as Berkshire Hathaway, for the long term would welcome downside volatility, which they would consider a buying opportunity since they are convinced that what they are buying has superior long-term value. Recently, others have advanced the debate on how to understand risk by formulating "Post-Modern Portfolio Theory."[9]

Risk can be addressed by the fund of funds in a number of ways. By using multiple managers, the fund of funds has achieved manager diversity. Further, most funds of funds allocate to hedge fund managers using diverse strategies. Since these diverse strategies tend not to correlate with each other, their combination in a fund of funds portfolio produces very interesting results. The following chart is a hypothetical example of the effect of allocating capital among four diverse and significantly uncorrelated strategies, each having compound annual returns of 20 percent and standard deviations in the mid teens. Notice the effect of allocating 25 percent of a fund of funds' capital to each of the managers and rebalancing the capital each year.

As Table 7-1 shows, by investing in several hedge funds with uncorrelated strategies and different levels of volatility (as measured by their standard deviations), the fund of funds provides a relatively stable rate of return. Note the lower standard deviation and slightly higher return of the fund of funds. This can enhance risk-adjusted long-term performance when

---

[9] A comprehensive discussion of risk is beyond the scope of this chapter. Readers wanting a more detailed discussion are referred to the following articles in the *Journal of Investing*, Fall 1994:

- "Post-Modern Portfolio Theory Comes of Age," Brian M. Rom and Kathleen W. Ferguson.
- "Portfolio Theory Is Alive and Well: A Response," Brian M. Rom and Kathleen W. Ferguson.
- "Measuring Investment Risk: A Review," Leslie A Balzer.
- "Performance Measurement in a Downside Risk Framework," Frank A. Sortino and Lee N. Price.

TABLE 7-1. Hypothetical Fund of Funds Return*

Year	Manager I	Manager II	Manager III	Manager IV	Fund of Funds
Year 1	35	22	7	(8)	14
Year 2	27	(2)	29	19	18
Year 3	(10)	39	35	45	27
Year 4	19	25	35	35	28
Year 5	36	20	(1)	16	18
Compound Annual Return	20%	20%	20%	20%	21%
Standard Deviation	16.86	13.2	15.07	18.2	5.51

* Reprinted by permission of *Barron's,* © Dow Jones & Company, Inc. (February 7, 1994). All Rights Reserved.

compared with that of a fund using a single strategy that would generate returns that fluctuate more from year to year. Further, the possibility of a permanent loss of capital is also reduced since the capital is allocated over a number of managers. While a permanent loss of capital by a manager is quite uncommon, such a loss by more than one is even less likely.

Dedicated strategy funds of funds which use multiple managers do not achieve strategy diversification. These funds of funds, which allocate solely to single-strategy hedge funds such as macro or global managers, may give the appearance of a diverse manager allocation when, in fact, these macro managers are often making very similar investment bets. They do, however, allow investors to access certain dedicated strategies leaving it to the investor to create his or her own strategy diversification.

In addition to the control of risk through allocation to diverse strategies, fund of funds managers have additional ways to control risk. They can allocate their capital to hedge funds which provide low-volatility returns. Many fund of funds managers who implement target return allocations utilize hedge funds that produce consistent and nonvolatile returns. However, as early 1994 demonstrated, many "market neutral" strategies which utilized debt investments, such as mortgage-backed securities, incurred severe losses. Prior to the first quarter of 1994 these strategies had produced consistent monthly returns. Many of these strategies, which were touted as market neutral and utilized mortgage-backed securities, turned out to be extremely sensitive to both a change in the direction of interest rates and the resulting illiquidity that developed in the market. Investors in these strategies realized that many years of returns with a very low standard deviation were a poor indicator of the real risk inherent in the strategies. Risk models that equated risk with standard deviation, along with the label market neutral, lulled many investors to sleep. The existence of what statisticians refer to as an outlier event took on a whole new meaning. Understanding what one was doing from a fundamental investment perspective became more critical than filling computer screens with colored extrapolations of past results.

Another way to control risk is to avoid managers who aggressively use leverage. However, investors often mistakenly equate leverage with risk. The use of leverage may increase risk, but not necessarily. For example, an unleveraged mutual fund is long the market, usually 90 to 95 percent, with the balance in cash. Compare this to a hedge fund with $10 million in equity which borrows $10 million for a total of $20 million in investable capital. If it invests $12 million long and $8 million short, it has a net long position of $4 million, or only 40 percent of its $10 million in equity. While leveraged, it has less exposure in a serious market drop than the mutual fund. Conversely, if the hedge fund were $20 million long or $20 million short, it would be making an aggressive leveraged bet.

The amount of capital one is managing also affects risk of loss. For example, a $10 million leveraged hedge fund that is $20 million long may have less risk than an unleveraged mutual fund with $1 billion in assets in a bear market. It may only take a few days for the hedge fund to sell its positions, whereas the mutual fund, if met with redemptions, may need weeks to sell its positions with bids drying up on the way down. Thus, in assessing risk, both the size and the liquidity of one's positions is quite relevant. In late 1994 over 40 percent of Fidelity Magellan's capital was reported to be in stocks where it owned more than 5 percent of the security. Similarly, in 1994 many of the large macro hedge funds had to liquidate hundreds of millions of dollars of bonds in a falling bond market, watching prices drop along with liquidity. Those hedge funds lost a lot of money not due to bad bets, but due to the combination of bad bets and having a lot to sell.

Another option is for the fund of funds manager to take an active role in risk reduction. One way this is done is for the manager to first determine which of his or her hedge funds has unhedged long exposure to the U.S. market and then to purchase index puts. While it is always possible that the general market may not go down while a given hedge fund's positions may decline in value, in times of sustained broad market drops the puts are a good cushion. Last, as many bond investors learned in 1994, losses on bonds due to increases in interest rates can be hedged through interest rate futures. Losses due to low bids in illiquid markets, however, are not as readily hedged. Thus, before one hedges one must identify this risk with which one is concerned. Some risks are more easily hedged than others.

Advantages and Disadvantages

Advantages

Investing in a fund of funds provides investors with various portfolio construction-related advantages. A multistrategy fund of funds provides a way to participate in a unique and active asset allocation process. An investor is paying the fund of funds manager to select appropriate strategies implemented by the underlying hedge fund managers in order to further the fund of funds' overall investment orientation. Conversely, for those investors who make their own allocations, a sector fund of funds provides superior access to a specific investment option. In either case, the fund of funds manager is spending a significant amount of time and expertise identifying strategies that will yield good investment results as well as selecting the hedge funds to implement them. Given the large number of hedge funds in existence and the need to select only the best ones, it takes a lot of time and effort to go through this process. The investor is also benefiting from the substantial due diligence done by the fund of funds manager in analyzing both the strategies and the managers. This process is ongoing, complex, and challenging since the markets in which the managers invest are dynamic and changing.

Another benefit that fund of funds investors enjoy is their ability to receive consistent results with minimal volatility as well as a drastic reduction in the possibility of permanent loss of capital. For example, any individual security can be severely affected by changes in its business and therefore experience a substantial deterioration in value. Contrary to what one might think, this is by no means limited to smaller companies. Many blue-chip companies, such as General Motors, had substantial price declines in 1994. Also, if a hedge fund experiences severe deterioration in its capital, the fund of funds is insulated from meaningful loss since funds of funds allocate their capital over numerous hedge funds.

Another advantage fund of funds investors gain is their ability to access certain global markets. For example, when numerous hedge funds were created to exploit Russian privatization vouchers in mid 1994, those fund of funds managers who had existing relationships with certain emerging markets managers were in a position to take advantage of this opportunity. Most investors, unless they had spent a meaningful amount of their time focusing on the trends in emerging markets, would have missed this opportunity.

Disadvantages

As with all investments, funds of funds pose certain potential disadvantages. One obvious one is that investing in a fund of funds requires an investor to pay an additional layer of fees. Whether this additional layer of fees is worth the expense is a rather simple exercise and too much time is spent debating it. Investors in funds of funds should simply ask, *Net of all fees*, am I satisfied with my risk-adjusted results? Fund of funds managers are not going to work for free and must be paid. Fees traditionally range from 1 to 2 percent of assets with some funds of funds imposing modest performance fees.

Another disadvantage is that along with most investments, certain fund of funds managers may be either poor judges of people or inexperienced in deciphering various market cycles along with the effect of those cycles on different investment strategies. For example, some fund of funds managers may pick a few managers and spend most of their time raising money. Many, however, attempt to pick their hedge fund strategies based on their reading of various macro trends or a detailed understanding of what is happening in different markets or with different strategies.

A third disadvantage is that funds of funds are more illiquid than individual accounts where an investor can call his or her broker to sell. As a result, before investing in a fund of funds, an investor should be comfortable that he or she has made an appropriate investment decision. An investor should feel sufficiently comfortable that should markets or strategies become volatile and turbulent his managers will be able to protect his capital.

A final disadvantage of funds of funds is that they are opaque. An investor with his or her own portfolio always knows which particular securities he or she owns, whereas fund of funds investors are never provided with an immediate look through to the individual securities positions held by the hedge funds to which the fund of funds allocated its capital.

Conclusions

In constructing portfolios investors seek to increase return with minimal risk or volatility. Since many funds of funds utilize hedge funds which employ diverse and uncorrelated investment strategies, the fund of funds produces a more consistent return with lower volatility than most of its underlying hedge funds. As a result, its inclusion in a larger portfolio can reduce the larger portfolio's volatility, thereby increasing the portfolio's risk-adjusted return. It is for this reason that many pension and endowment funds are beginning to increase their allocation to nontraditional investments, whether to hedge funds directly or through funds of funds. For those investors who do their own allocations, sector funds of funds can provide excellent access to those respective sectors.

Recent studies have shown that hedge funds, as a group, outperform the broad equity market averages in all but very strong bull markets. As a result, a portfolio of select hedge funds may be a more compelling investment than an index fund or an equity mutual fund. Funds of funds serve, in effect, as diverse portfolios of hedge funds with each having its own investment characteristics based on the underlying hedge funds. By providing good absolute returns with minimal volatility, well-constructed funds of funds should continue to flourish as investment vehicles for the foreseeable future.

The global debt and equity markets are dynamic reflections of investors' perceptions of the economies of their respective countries. In navigating these financial markets, fund of funds managers are, in effect, continually making judgments as to the various opportunities which exist, at different times, in those markets. In assessing both the available strategies and their hedge fund implementers, the task of an attentive fund of funds manager remains a never ending challenge.

CHAPTER 8

Custom Hedge Funds Using Long and Short Managers

M. Kelley Price, Principal
Price Meadows Capital Management Inc.

In this chapter I hope to explain the strategy of combining conventional long managers with short-sellers to create a custom hedge fund. Topics include a little history of hedge funds and the role of short-selling, the mechanics of creating a custom hedge fund, and some thoughts on different variations and approaches. The analysis that my firm has done in this area has led to the conclusion that short-selling is such an important component of the hedge fund concept that its use should not be left up to the judgment of one's individual money managers.

The Long-Short Concept in Hedge Funds

They were originally named "hedge funds" for a reason. While today the term covers a multitude of sins, the original idea was that utilizing short-selling in tandem with a long portfolio actually could hedge some of the risk of being in the stock market. In fact, the notion that a combination portfolio of longs and shorts might have less market risk than the long portfolio alone is a fundamental justification for the use of leverage which is associated with hedge funds. A portfolio 120 percent long and 60 percent short could be described as having a 60 percent net long bet on the market and argued to have less market risk than a long-only portfolio which is 100 percent invested. And the benefit, of course, is that this hypothetical portfolio would have $1.80 of good investment ideas for every $1.00 of capital: a free lunch of leverage without increased risk.[1]

Yet, since this concept originated in the 1950s, if it were the free lunch it sounds like, why did it not grow in popularity prior to the exponential growth in recent years? Even if its apparent intrinsic superiority had not been obvious enough for the regulators to jump on board and permit hedge-style mutual funds, one might still expect that the idea would have proliferated and 30 or 40 years later there would be scores of fabulously wealthy 60- and 70-year-old hedge fund operators. Certainly, there are a few well-known names who have been at it for decades, but it is hard to name over a handful. Of the estimated 3000 funds now in existence, probably 90 percent were started in the last five years. What was it that kept hedge fund growth in check until recently?

The answer probably lies in the proposition that despite the theoretical reduction in market risk, the operation of a successful hedge fund still requires good stock selection to make it work. For any fund, it is to be expected that there will be sustained periods of time when the market will not favor even the most considered and well-researched ideas. It is possible to lose money on both sides at once, and there will be times when the leverage will produce volatility greater than a nonleveraged nonhedged portfolio, despite the theoretically reduced market risk. Furthermore, as opposed to a conventional diversified stock portfolio, the volatility in a hedge fund is relatively unpredictable—it is possible, even likely, to lose or make money quite independent of the market. Especially in rising markets, a true hedge fund is not likely to match the expectations of its investors and may test their patience. Accordingly, when the free lunch is being delivered by the market, the hedge fund manager will be tempted to feast there. Moreover, as can be seen by reviewing what is reported about the methods of the largest hedge funds today, market and sector bets are a natural response by competitive managers to perceived opportunities as well as to difficult markets. The hedging component in such times is likely to fall by the wayside, and if leverage is not decreased, one is left with serious exposure to a bear market. Several of today's best-known hedge funds were severely mauled in the 1987 crash and may have escaped far greater damage only because it was all over so quickly. There is anecdotal evidence that hedge funds were similarly

---

[1] The leverage from short-sales has one other advantage—it does not require borrowed money. In the 120 percent long 60 percent short example, the long side does require margin in the amount of 20 percent of capital. The 60 percent short is effected by the sale of borrowed shares, the proceeds of which show up in the brokerage account. While the short-sale proceeds must stay in the account as collateral, they will typically earn interest for the account at about two-thirds the broker loan rate. Accordingly, in this example, for every dollar in capital, one will be paying interest on 20 cents and be earning interest (at a lower rate) on 60 cents.

challenged 20 years ago in the 1973–74 bear market.[2] The "hedge" in hedge fund was not really there when it was needed.

The bull market move that began in 1982 has created a generational enchantment with financial assets. It has been less unusual for the extent of its rise than for the brevity of its interruptions. There have been only three calendar-year declines in the S&P 500 since 1974, and none of them greater than 7 percent, largely because bear markets have been short and the recoveries from them have been rapid. Accordingly, the lesson of the last 20 years has been "buy the dips," and it has not been lost on the hedge fund crowd. A review of today's most visible hedge funds confirms that hedging is, for many, only a side effect of having a number of bets on simultaneously. A more descriptive term might be "leverage funds," since it's unclear to what extent permanent hedges exist against unfavorable market moves. Among smaller funds, allocations short and long vary widely, often based on the premise that a bear market can be anticipated and that they can "be short when the time comes."

Some of the danger of investing in hedge funds today is the layman's assumption that to be called one, a hedge fund must be hedging something. That is not necessarily the case. Happily, however, for those uncomfortable with the idea of leveraged market-timing or leveraged sector bets, there is an alternative: using dedicated short funds in combination with long managers to create one's own hedge fund, in a proportion which can accomplish some of the risk reduction which the original hedge fund concept promised.

Hedging with a Short-Sale Portfolio

The portfolio objective of mixing asset classes within the securities markets is, of course, to diminish the market risk associated with investing in equities. The most popular mix is a so-called balanced portfolio—equities balanced by bonds. The standard asset allocations at institutions and those recommended at brokerage firms are generally among stocks, bonds, and cash. The portfolio challenge is, however, that bonds, cash, and even exotics such

[2] One alternative and perceptive theory is that many of the hedge fund crowd left for greener pastures in 1974, not because of the market, but because of ERISA and its prudence rules passed in that year. According to that theory, the businessmen and women among the hedge fund operators realized that ERISA would create a vast new market for investment management of pension funds, and short sales and incentive fees were willingly traded for balanced stock and bond portfolios and the unlimited asset growth.

FIGURE 8-1.   Short Sellers and S&P Index Mix

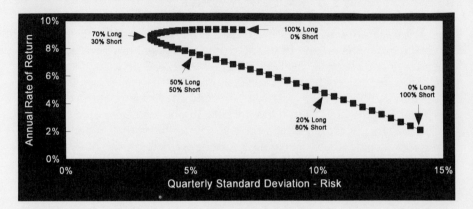

as foreign equities are generally, at best, *non*-correlated with U.S. equities over time. The effect of such balance is therefore a dilution of volatility. Over many periods, bonds and foreign stocks have had significant positive correlation with U.S. equities, which has further reduced the utility of such an approach. A more effective source of balance is something which *offsets* equity volatility, something like a short-sale portfolio, which is *negatively* correlated. On a down market day, you expect to make money in a short portfolio; the results in a bond or foreign equity account are less certain. Figure 8-1 is an efficient frontier mix of the S&P 500 and an actual multiple-manager fund of short-sellers.[3]

The efficient frontier diagram is a plot of how changing the weighting between two investments affects return and risk, as measured by the quarterly volatility of returns. The curved line shows a continuum of theoretical portfolios starting with 100 percent invested in the S&P 500 and gradually replacing the S&P 500 with the other investment—in this case the Rainier Short Fund—until there's no S&P 500 investment and it's all in the Short

---

[3] In this chapter I will use data from two sources: the Strunk Short Index and the actual results of the Rainier Short Fund. The index includes those short-sellers who report quarterly results to the index keeper; accordingly, there is probably some positive bias in the numbers due to survivorship and manager willingness to report. The Rainier Short Fund, whose numbers trail the index during most periods, is used in most of the statistical analysis in this chapter in order to make the points herein less theoretical. The Rainier Short Fund is an actual dynamic mix of short-sellers which began in 1987, and may be a more realistic record since it reflects real-time manager selections over time. It began with one manager in 1987, and as of October 1994 had four managers. During the six years seven different managers have been used.

Fund. The vertical axis plots return; the horizontal axis plots the standard deviation of quarterly returns. Most desirable are high returns and low volatility.

The period July 1987 through September 1994 is chosen for convenience (the short investment fund began then) and because it captures several up and down moves and may include one full cycle, since the dividend yield on the S&P 500 at the start point and the end point was the same—2.8 percent.

The effect of mixing this fund of short-sellers with the S&P 500 is rather dramatic. Despite the Short Fund having twice the volatility of the S&P 500, combining the two in a 70:30 ratio results in a portfolio having volatility one-half of the S&P 500, with only a slight reduction in return. The reason that a short-sale portfolio is so effective in reducing volatility is its negative correlation (although the data is not detailed here, only twice in 29 quarters did the S&P 500 and the Short Fund both show a loss). Importantly, negative correlation can also convey other advantages, if the portfolio is rebalanced periodically.

The Importance of Rebalancing

A 70:30 long:short mix means that at the end of each quarter, the profits (or losses) are rebalanced back to the starting percentages. Since a large swing in one direction will sooner or later be followed with a swing in the other direction, rebalancing assures that an investor reestablishes a full allocation to each approach before its turn comes. If there is enough volatility, this can add to returns over time. In fact, by rebalancing between negatively correlated investments it is actually possible to achieve better performance than by using either investment alone. This counterintuitive situation can be explained by use of an example: consider two investments "A" and "B." "A" increases 100 percent in year one; and decreases 50 percent in year two. One dollar turns into two dollars and then goes back to one dollar. Investment "B" does the opposite: falls 50 percent and then rises 100 percent; one dollar turns into 50 cents and rises back to a dollar. Two dollars invested passively in these negatively correlated assets is still two dollars two years later. However, something else happens if you rebalance evenly at the end of a year (when "A" is worth $2 and "B" is worth $.50) to $1.25 in each. At the end of year two, investment "A" is worth $.63, investment "B" is worth $2.50, and your portfolio is worth $3.13. The act of rebalancing gives an excess return of $1.13 over static investing.

Figure 8-2 is an efficient frontier diagram of the same multiple manager short-seller fund mixed with the NASDAQ Index (not including any dividends). Because of the higher volatility and better negative correlation,

FIGURE 8-2. Short Sellers and NASDAQ Index Mix

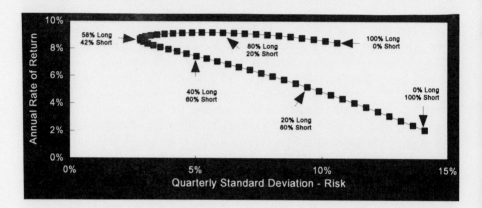

the return of the minimal volatility point is actually higher than either individual investment by itself.

This short-manager mix has had excellent negative correlation with the more speculative NASDAQ Index—for the entire 29-quarter period, any time there was a NASDAQ loss, the Short Fund had a gain. The result of combining the two in a 58:42 ratio is a 70 percent reduction in volatility over the NASDAQ alone plus a return that edged higher from 8.4 percent annualized to 8.7 percent.

To be effective, rebalancing requires negatively correlated assets, ups and downs of reasonable size and duration, and rebalancing points which catch the effect of intermediate-term trends. Theoretically, it may be possible to time the rebalancings based on the extent of market moves or manager profitability, however, arbitrary time intervals such as quarters seem to work just fine. Table 8-1 shows the relative efficacy of arbitrarily rebalancing on quarterly, semiannual, or annual periods.

TABLE 8-1. Four Rebalancing Choices and Their Effect on Returns

Annual Rate of Return	*Timing of Rebalancing*			
	Quarterly	Semiannual	Semiannual	Annual
	Qtr-end	June & Dec.	March & Sept.	Year-end
70% S&P 500/ 30% Short Mix	8.9%	8.6%	8.9%	7.9%
58% NASDAQ/ 42% Short Mix	8.7%	8.3%	8.6%	6.9%

Short-Sellers versus the Alternatives

If one wishes to protect a stock portfolio against down markets there are a number of ways to create hedges, the most obvious being put options on securities in the portfolio, or puts or futures contracts on one of several stock indices. In addition, there are several bearish mutual funds now on the block. Why go to the effort and expense of utilizing a dedicated short hedge fund?

The difficulty with a short position in index contracts is that one ends up shorting indiscriminately—hopefully something is gained by being short selective issues rather than a large basket. Secondly, since the market is known to rise over time, a market short position would be profitable over the long run only if the market never went up again or if one engaged in market-timing with excellent results. Puts have the additional characteristic of a high recurring cost, which investors grow weary of over time. A significant caveat on the bearish mutual funds is that they are unproven and probably far less than 100 percent short due to mutual fund regulations, with any bearish exposure greater than 25 percent of capital likely to be via options or index contracts—which, for reasons already discussed, may present less long-term potential.[4] Accordingly, the alternatives do not seem to provide the same potential as short-sellers.

Of course, one of the frequently voiced arguments against the use of short-sellers is that, despite all this theoretical potential, the real results have been terrible to mediocre since November 1990. Many investors who once embraced the notion of having a few short-sellers in their portfolio for balance have since concluded that the strategy as a whole is flawed. Rather than debate the point with a market timing opinion, a better argument is that short-sellers, as a group, generate alpha, which is something absent from index contracts and puts. In layman's terms, alpha is the intrinsic result a manager or investment provides once the effect of the market, beta, is subtracted.[5] The

---

[4] Also, a short-oriented fund having daily liquidity may face challenges in a volatile market. Large capital inflows may dilute the fund in a declining market as positions are difficult to add to in the absence of upticks, while sudden withdrawals could create their own short squeezes.

[5] Alpha and beta are descriptive statistics of a linear regression of a manager's quarterly or monthly results plotted versus the market. Alpha is a number which shows the expected statistical return if the market was unchanged. Beta is a multiplier which reflects the effect of the market on the manager's results [the manager result = alpha plus (beta times the market result)]. A manager having an alpha of 1 percent and a beta of 1.00 would be expected to be up 11 in a period when the market was up 10 percent. A manager having an alpha of 5 percent and a beta of –0.50 would be expected to be flat were the market down 10 percent.

TABLE 8-2. Short-Selling Alphas

	Strunk Short Index	Rainier Short Fund	S&P 500 with Dividends
Annual alpha	28.3%	20.7%	0.0%
Annual return	11.8%	2.1%	9.3%
Quarterly beta	−1.39	−1.47	1.00

S&P 500, by definition, has no alpha, even though its return may be positive, since it _is_ the market return. Conversely, an investment which has a negative return during a time period may nonetheless have a positive alpha, if its negative return has been due to an adverse impact from the market, not intrinsic weakness within the investment. Table 8-2 shows simple[6] alpha and beta calculations for the Strunk Short Index and the multiple manager short fund.

The attractiveness of an alpha of 20 percent (the Rainier result) per year is certainly diminished by the observation that real returns were only 2 percent. However, the statistics tell us that the difficulty is not a general lack of quality in the stock selection or portfolio management of short-sellers, but is due to a beta of −1.47 in a market that had a compounded return of 9.3 percent. The beta tells us that this fund, in essence, started each year about 14 percent in the hole (the beta of −1.47 times the market return of 9.3 percent), and the alpha of the short selections managed to offset that plus a little over the period.

Capturing Alpha

Of course, neither managers nor investors can spend alpha. However, what appears to be only an interesting academic statistic can actually be captured by using financial futures on the stock market indices, or with less precision, by combining short-sellers into a portfolio with long managers as we are suggesting in this chapter. Accordingly, the challenge is to neutralize the beta and be left with only the alpha effect. It is intuitive that this approach should have similar results as the combination of long and short portfolios in the efficient frontier diagrams. Table 8-3 contains statistics for an objective of zero beta effected by using S&P 500 futures contracts. This mix, however,

[6] Some calculations of alpha between investments having broadly different exposures to risk adjust alpha by some measure of the risk-free rate of return in order to make a better comparison.

TABLE 8-3.   Capturing Short-Selling Alpha by Neutralizing Negative Beta

	S&P 500 without Dividends	1.47 Units S&P 500 Futures	Short Fund	Mix
Annual Alpha	–3.4%	–5.0%	20.7%	15.2%
Quarterly Beta	1.00	1.47	–1.47	0.00
Annual Return	6.0%	8.0%	2.1%	14.1%
Qtly Std Deviation	7.0%	10.4%	14.1%	9.6%

TABLE 8-4.   Equitizing Short-Selling Alpha by Creating a Beta of +1.00

	S&P 500 without Dividends	2.47 Units S&P 500 Futures	Short Fund	Mix
Annual Alpha	–3.4%	–8.4%	20.7%	14.6%
Quarterly Beta	1.00	2.47	–1.47	1.00
Annual Return	6.0%	9.6%	2.1%	20.1%
Qtly Std Deviation	7.0%	17.3%	14.1%	11.8%

will have leverage: 100 percent short selling, plus enough futures contracts[7] to neutralize the negative beta.

Accordingly, the combination of one unit of this short fund plus 1.47 units of S&P 500 futures would theoretically create a beta of zero, a modest increase in volatility over that of the S&P 500 Index, and convert some of the alpha into a 14 percent return. This exercise can be carried one step further by now adding more index futures in order to "equitize" what has now become a zero beta portfolio. "Equitizing" nonequity investments is a common strategy among institutions when a target equity exposure is not being met, usually due to hired managers retaining too much cash or management styles not having enough equity exposure. Market-neutral hedge funds are oftentimes considered as vehicles which can be equitized in order to capture the market-neutral alpha without losing the expected benefits of equity ownership over time. Table 8-4 illustrates the effect of adding enough futures to create a net beta of 1.0.

---

[7] As futures do not pay dividends, their return lags the return of the S&P 500 Index with dividends reinvested which is used elsewhere in this chapter. The estimated futures results in these tables are the results of the S&P 500 index without dividends, including an estimate for friction. Without dividends, futures now have a negative alpha in this leveraged example.

The actual execution of such a mix would be challenging since an actual futures account is valued daily and would be subject to daily margin calls. While to my knowledge no one is doing this with short sellers, it would be possible for an investor who had sufficient collateral to absorb the volatility. The principal conclusion from this exercise is that, despite the recent record, it may be possible to tame short-selling and use it to one's advantage.

Issues in Manager Selection

The optimum mix (for minimum volatility) for a quarterly rebalanced portfolio between July 1987 through September 1994 using the multiple-manager short fund above and an index fund would be 30 to 42 percent short, depending on the long index used. As previously mentioned, this arbitrary period may include roughly one cycle, in terms of dividend yields, and therefore the analysis may be a reasonable guide. That is history. Going forward, the optimal mix will depend on where we really are in the cycle, an investor's time frame, and manager selection on both the long and the short side.

When it comes to short-sellers, to say that results have been varied is an understatement. In 1993, the performance numbers from individual managers within the Rainier Short Fund ranged from about –40 to +40 percent. Part of that difference is the varying degrees of leverage among managers as well as their individual approaches. It is intuitive that the highest alpha production will likely come from managers who are stock pickers and who have less diversification. On the other hand, managers who are correct on themes and who may have greater diversification and greater leverage may actually outperform in a real bear market.

The risk often stated about short-selling is that while what one buys can only go to zero, what one sells short can go to the moon. However, this theoretical unlimited risk is not a realistic problem in a reasonably diversified portfolio. The real problem is related to a fundamental structural difference between long and short portfolios. A conventional investor who has $100 in capital and buys $100 in stock is 100 percent invested. If the stock rises to $120, equity increases to $120; if the stock falls to $80, equity drops to $80: the investor will remain 100 percent invested in either case. The change in price of the stock creates no structural portfolio motivation to either buy or sell, and the normal effect of price on supply and demand prevails. A short sale is a very different situation. The short-seller with $100 in capital who shorts a $100 stock starts out 100 percent invested. If the stock rises to $120, a loss of $20 occurs and equity *drops* to $80, causing the short-seller to now be 150 percent invested. If the stock drops to $80, equity increases to $120 and the short-seller is 67 percent invested. Since there are portfolio motivations to avoid excessive leverage on one hand, and to remain invested on the other, a proclivity exists for the short-seller to cover (buy) positions as they go up and to sell more as they go down.

Absent new information, divergences of price in a stock which is held only by long investors will tend to be self-correcting. As prices rise, more selling would be expected to limit the rise, and conversely, falling prices stimulate demand and limit a drop. In physical terms, price oscillations tend to be self-dampening. On the other hand, the portfolio considerations of a short-seller create the opposite effect and will tend to accelerate price changes. If one is the only short-seller in a stock, the effect will be insignificant. However, if the stock is widely shorted, there is a likelihood of greater volatility. Speculators who are aware of this phenomenon can buy stocks solely for the purpose of triggering runaway short covering, or a "short squeeze." The danger to the short-seller may be less that he is wrong on his analysis than that portfolio management will force him to pare down (or eliminate) a full-size position after taking losses on the way up, and not be there in size (or perhaps at all) when the stock eventually falls.[8] Accordingly, knowing a manager's attitude toward leverage is crucial in the selection process. An investor creating a custom hedge fund with only one short-seller would probably be well served with a more conservative manager in this regard, or, if set on using a high-leverage manager, the investor might consider putting up less capital initially and keeping a cash reserve for additions during adversity.

The second major question for a prospective short-seller is where he falls on the subject of market timing. Those short-sellers who have been out of the market during even part of the last three years have probably enhanced their results by doing so. Whether a person with a bearish outlook has any advantage over a normal person when it comes to market timing is open to debate. The risk such a practice introduces, of course, is the one previously identified for all hedge funds at the start of this chapter. It does little good to have created a custom hedge fund to avoid the risk of not really being short and then choose a short-seller who market-times to any significant degree.

The final point on short-seller selection is that since it can be such a volatile enterprise, diversification among managers is a good idea, if capital permits.

---

[8] Of course, the ability to retain a position through a short squeeze may also depend on the ability of the manager to retain the "borrow" of the shares which were shorted. High volume during a stock run-up can result in shares being sold out of the "box" or margin inventory of the firm where the shares were shorted. If another source of borrowable shares is not located, short-sellers will be forced to cover or "buy in." Accordingly, one other attribute of a short-seller is his relationship with the box—where is he in the pecking order when buy-in time comes.

Regarding the long side, the two efficient frontiers can provide some guidance. An aggressive growth-stock manager with higher, NASDAQ level, volatility would likely warrant a larger allocation of short-selling. On the other hand, a Graham-and-Dodd-style manager which was regarded as more conservative might take a short-selling allocation smaller than that calculated for the S&P 500. Figures 8-3 and 8-4 are two efficient frontier diagrams for two distinctly different long manager styles: Louis Navellier (aggressive growth) and Mutual Shares (Michael Price–Graham and Dodd/special situations).

The other issue, of course, is where the market lies in the historical perspective. If we are indeed one full cycle away from the summer of 1987, it might make some sense to err on the high side in one's current asset allocations.

FIGURE 8-3.   Short Sellers and Navellier & Assoc.

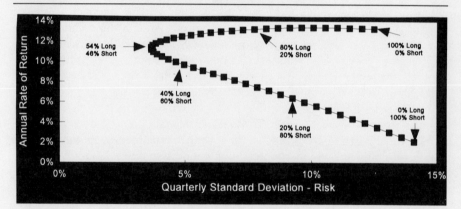

FIGURE 8-4.   Short Sellers and Mutual Shares Fund

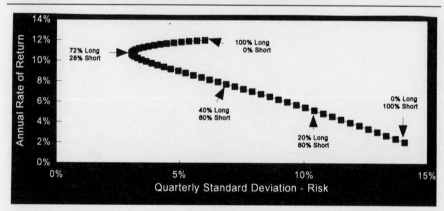

Advantages and Limitations

The advantages of a custom hedge fund go beyond the investor control over the long-short hedge and the rebalancing process. In addition, there is potential for greater selectivity on the styles of the long and short manager, as well as more potential for diversification of management.

There are some detriments however. For one thing, during a sustained strong trend, it is likely that one manager will be profitable and the other not. Accordingly, at year-ends during that trend, the investor may owe one manager incentive fees[9] and not be receiving an offset on fees from the other manager who is showing a loss for the same period. If both managers are profitable over time, this fee issue will be moot, but only if the investor does not change horses in mid-race. If one is paying a 20 percent incentive fee, shifting out of a manager when there is a loss-carry forward must be based on the assumption that the new manager will do at least 20 percent better than the old one. Accordingly, manager changes should be carefully analyzed.

A second detriment is that leverage is more difficult to establish on the portfolio as a whole. A \$1.00 invested 60:40 long:short using separate managers will mean 60 cents long and 40 cents short, unless the investor goes to the bank to borrow money for leverage.[10] In a nonseparate hedge fund, the 60:40 ratio could easily end up being \$1.20 long and 80 cents short, which may add to returns over time.

If it is apparent from this data that short-selling can add value, it is equally apparent that care is required. Establishing a custom hedge fund entails some work and should be viewed as a long-term project. Careful manager selection and matching, diversification, and a clear plan for rebalancing is essential. Care must also be taken to ensure that the introduction of short-sellers into one's repertoire does not open Pandora's box. Market timing on the long side is hazardous enough; market timing using short-sellers could be a very bad idea.

---

[9] Most hedge fund managers, including short-sellers, charge fees based on portfolio profits.

[10] This not quite as bad as it seems. The cash used to establish the short-selling account will generate income at T-bill rates. This additional source of income does not appear in a conventional hedge fund which has long positions instead of cash. A determined investor who borrowed money to establish his or her short-selling exposure would therefore have a net cost of funds equal to his or her borrowing rate less the T-bill return.

CHAPTER 9

Offshore Funds

Bryan J. MacDonald, President and Managing Director
Investment Strategies International, Inc.

Over the past decade, the rapid expansion of the global economy and a global bull market have resulted in the resurgence of offshore funds as legitimate cross-border investment vehicles. Offshore funds offer non-U.S. investors and certain U.S. investors the opportunity to invest in the world markets on a "tax advantaged" or "tax neutral" basis. The globalization of the world's capital markets has only increased the need to provide investors with commingled fund vehicles that assist in the cost effective management of assets globally, while minimizing the risks associated with potential investment strategies. This discussion will focus on the practical issues associated with investing in offshore funds. Although offshore fund structures can accommodate virtually any investment strategy, only nontraditional or hedge fund strategies offered through such offshore vehicles will be discussed. This chapter will not focus heavily on the highly complex tax and legal issues which might arise. These issues are best addressed by the legal community.

Overview

There are many similarities between offshore funds and other limited liability, commingled fund vehicles. Many hedge fund managers offer their investment expertise to U.S. investors through a U.S. limited partnership and to non-U.S. investors through an offshore fund. Like a mutual fund, most offshore funds function by providing for the purchase and redemption of shares of the offshore investment company to investors. Rather than structuring the investment company under the guise of the Investment Company Act of 1940 and related U.S. legislation, offshore funds are established under similar legislation enacted by one of the offshore jurisdictions.

Direct investment by foreign citizens in many markets around the world provides investors with numerous investment benefits. These include the opportunity to diversify their portfolio and invest in economies and companies that may offer better growth prospects than the investor's own local markets. However, investments made by investors outside their own tax jurisdiction create several potential tax issues as well. Two such issues for offshore investors are the possibility of incurring significant estate tax liability for assets held directly in foreign countries. Second, investing directly in certain types of securities or funds domiciled in a foreign country may create income tax liability in that foreign country. For instance, investing in a limited partnership or mutual fund domiciled or registered in a foreign country may create a tax liability on the income and/or gains produced from investments made by such vehicles.

Offshore funds are limited liability corporations or partnerships established in tax neutral jurisdictions to allow investors investing outside their own country to minimize tax liabilities in those foreign countries. From the perspective of countries which allow these offshore structures to exist, these vehicles help to encourage foreign investment in their own capital markets. From the perspective of the investor, these offshore structures provide a way to minimize tax liability in the market in which the assets are invested and then allow the investor to manage his or her own tax liability in the jurisdiction where he or she pays taxes.

Let's start off simply. Let's assume you are an investor who resides and pays taxes in a foreign country outside the United States and you wish to invest with a U.S.-based hedge fund manager. If you decide to invest in a U.S. limited partnership managed by this investment manager, you will incur U.S. income tax liability and may have to pay taxes on profits earned, just like a U.S. investor. If, however, you invest through an offshore fund which in turn is managed by the same investment manager, you will then only be liable for taxes on profits in the offshore jurisdiction and, if applicable, in your own country of residence. Generally, offshore jurisdictions have no such taxes on profits generated by offshore funds. While a foreign investor can establish a separate account managed by the investment manager and receive similar tax treatment, this normally requires a much greater amount of capital, is generally more expensive, and will not provide the benefits of limited liability should the investments decrease in value below the value of an investor's original investment. This is particularly important with any strategy that utilizes leverage, options, or derivatives or shorts securities, as these strategies employ techniques that expose investors to the risk of losing more than the amount invested.

While each foreign country has its own regulations concerning investments made by foreigners, the United States has the most comprehensive and detailed regulations regarding foreign investment. The United States Income Tax Regulations contain 10 requirements which a foreign partnership, trust or corporation must adhere to in order to be considered as having its principal offices outside of the United States. Along with satisfying other requirements, the foreign entity will not be considered to be conducting a trade or business in the United States. If such partnership, trust, or corporation is not considered to be conducting a trade or business in the United States and is effecting transactions in stock or securities for its own account, such offshore fund should generally not be subject to income taxes on gains made from such transactions in the United States. Certain types of dividend and interest income may be taxable in the United States and taxes on this income are typically withheld at source prior to receipt by the offshore fund or foreign investor. In most cases this withholding is small in relation to the total return generated by the particular investment strategy. Below is an excerpt from U.S. Income Tax Regulation 1.864-2(c)(2)(iii), frequently referred to as the "ten commandments:"

". . . a foreign corporation which carries on most or all of its investment activities in the United States but maintains a general business office or offices outside the United States in which its management is located will not be considered as having its principal office in the United States if all or a substantial portion of the following functions is carried on at or from an office or offices located outside the United States:

(1) Communicating with its shareholders (including the furnishing of financial reports),

(2) Communicating with the general public,

(3) Soliciting sales of its own stock,

(4) Accepting the subscriptions of new shareholders,

(5) Maintaining its principal corporate records and books of account,

(6) Auditing its books of account,

(7) Disbursing payments of dividends, legal fees, accounting fees, and officers' and directors' salaries,

(8) Publishing or furnishing the offering and redemption price of the shares of stock issued by it,

(9) Conducting meetings of its shareholders and board of directors, and

(10) Making redemptions of its own stock."

Given these "commandments" there are several structural steps that an offshore fund must take to help satisfy these requirements. The typical hedge fund utilizes a bank custodian or prime broker in the market or markets in which it invests to support the daily trading activity of the fund. An offshore fund however, additionally employs an offshore administrator to maintain the books and records of the fund which includes the valuation of fund assets, the calculation and distribution of the net asset value (NAV), the issuance and redemption of shares, the maintenance of share registers, the payment of fund expenses and other management functions. Additionally, offshore corporations are also required to establish a board of directors comprised of a majority of offshore individuals or entities who periodically review the affairs of the fund and make other management decisions for the fund. Boards are typically comprised of officers and employees of the offshore administrator or management, advisors to the fund, and as the fund grows, significant investors in the fund.

Offshore Fund Structure

In order to properly evaluate an offshore fund as a potential investment, one must distinguish between the structure of an offshore fund, and the investment strategy employed by the offshore fund. There are generally two types of structures utilized by offshore funds, namely partnerships and corporations. Both structures provide the benefits of limited liability. Both structures provide investors with certain tax advantages. While partnerships may have many advantages, the partnership structure is generally utilized for domestic hedge funds offered to U.S. investors. Also, because most partnerships are offered privately to investors, a U.S. limited partnership may only have a maximum of 100 limited partners. Most offshore funds however, are established as corporations which sell shares to investors. Offshore funds generally are not restricted as to the number of investors who can invest in a fund, even if the shares are offered privately.

There are many offshore jurisdictions in which funds may be established. Unlike countries with developed capital markets, these jurisdictions allow the formation of these funds and generally do not tax the profits earned by these funds, as long as they are not sold to the citizens and taxpayers of the particular offshore jurisdiction There are three regions where these tax havens exist, namely the Caribbean basin, Europe and the Far East. In most cases these jurisdictions are islands off the coast of the major world markets whose livelihood is based on the offshore financial business. Their proximity to these markets facilitates daily communication and management of investments made in such markets. The following is a brief review of these jurisdictions and some general comments on the types of investors they serve.

The Caribbean

There are several offshore jurisdictions located in the Caribbean basin. The major locations are Bermuda, the Cayman Islands, Curacao, the British Virgin Islands, and the Bahamas. Each jurisdiction has its own set of corporate laws which allow these tax-exempt corporations to be established. While most of the legal systems are based on British common law and maybe similar to Delaware corporate law, each jurisdiction has its own nuances. In general, the Caribbean jurisdictions are utilized for offshore funds investing in North and South America.

Bermuda is generally considered the most rigorous of the Caribbean jurisdictions with regards to establishing offshore companies. They require significant background information on those forming offshore companies and provide greater access to the shareholder registers of Bermuda-exempt companies. This tends to deter offshore investors who desire complete privacy and anonymity. Bermuda has an excellent business infrastructure including an excellent communications network, a well educated and sophisticated labor force and a large number of financial institutions domiciled on the island. More than half of the island's economy is currently involved in the financial services business. Because of its relationship to the United Kingdom, Bermuda attracts many British and Canadian investors. In fact, because of this relationship and the similarity of Bermuda's legal system to the United Kingdom, certain Bermuda domiciled funds may be submitted to the regulatory authorities in the United Kingdom for recognition and potential distribution directly in the United Kingdom. Although Bermuda has a limited amount of banking institutions on the island, there are a large number of management companies, law firms, and other service providers to chose from to manage the affairs of an offshore fund.

The Cayman Islands is the next most developed jurisdiction in the Caribbean. It is the most widely used Caribbean jurisdiction as well. It too has an excellent infrastructure and many service providers to the offshore financial community. Latin American investors utilize the Cayman Islands most actively. There are numerous banks and financial institutions either domiciled there or with branch offices. There are also numerous law firms, management companies and other service providers located in the Cayman Islands.

The British Virgin Islands (BVI) is the next most active Caribbean jurisdiction. Offshore corporations can be quickly and easily established. There are, however, only a few financial institutions, management companies, and law firms located in the BVI. Most BVI-based funds utilize offshore administrators in other offshore jurisdictions to handle their management affairs. Although certain jurisdictions require the use of local management companies and/or custodians to assist in the management of locally based funds, it is not uncommon for the actual administrative work to be performed elsewhere. Typically, domicile is chosen based on where the assets of the fund will be invested, the composition of the expected investor base, and the flexibility of the actual corporate structure, whereas the administrator and/or management company is chosen based on administrative, management, and service expertise.

The Bahamas is a growing offshore financial center. With the recent introduction of expanded corporate legislation, the Bahamas has created an attractive environment to attract offshore business. There are a growing number of financial institutions located in the Bahamas.

European Offshore Jurisdictions

The most highly developed offshore jurisdiction for funds investing in Europe and for European-based investors is Luxembourg. Luxembourg is one of the few offshore jurisdictions not physically located on an island. With the creation of the European Economic Community (EEC) Luxembourg has grown rapidly as a vibrant financial center. Luxembourg prides itself on the high quality fiduciary environment which it has created. It is used very actively as a domicile for registered funds sold to retail investors throughout the EEC. Given its focus on more regulated fund structures, Luxembourg has been used much less frequently for privately placed funds and hedge funds. Luxembourg also provides corporate trust services for other more traditional securities, such as Eurobonds, which require a corporate trustee.

Dublin, Ireland has grown very rapidly over the past decade as an offshore jurisdiction for European investors. The creation of a "zone" within Dublin to conduct offshore activities has been allowed by the EEC. Like Luxembourg, Dublin maintains rigorous fiduciary standards which include extensive disclosure and reporting requirements. The establishment of Dublin as an offshore financial center has had a very positive impact on the economy of Dublin. As a result, Dublin has aggressively moved to attract financial service providers of all types. More and more funds established in other offshore jurisdictions have sought a listing of their fund on the Dublin Stock Exchange, which despite additional disclosure and reporting, allows for broader distribution throughout the EEC. In fact, in some European countries, some form of EEC registration is being required in order to distribute any such offshore funds to qualified investors. Although Dublin registration or domicile can be complex and resource intensive, for some types of funds, Dublin offers a cost-effective alternative to Luxembourg.

Two other jurisdictions deserve mention in this discussion and they are Gibraltar and Liechtenstein. Although, these jurisdictions are used by a few offshore funds, the most significant growth has occurred in other jurisdictions.

Lastly, Switzerland has provided tax-advantaged investors with a very sophisticated and highly developed financial environment that can be extremely favorable from an investment and tax standpoint. Yet, with regards to offshore funds, Swiss regulations have not allowed for their domicile in Switzerland. The fund regulations currently in place are far too restrictive, especially for hedge funds. At the time of this writing however, Swiss authorities are actively considering allowing offshore funds to be registered and domiciled in Switzerland. This is a very positive and exciting step. Given the unique nature of Switzerland as a tax haven, a complete analysis would require much more focus than can be provided for in this overview.

Far Eastern Jurisdictions

The only jurisdiction which deserves note is the island of Mauritius in the Indian Ocean. As the Asian markets continue to develop, Mauritius is expected to blossom as an offshore domicile. As with other offshore jurisdictions, the growth of a jurisdiction is largely tied to the growth of the capital markets located near by. This allows for business days to be conducted in similar if not identical time zones, minimal language and communication barriers, and close physical proximity, which allows for easy travel to and from the offshore location.

Determination of Net Asset Values

As mentioned previously, most offshore funds are structured as corporations which sell shares to investors. Shares are typically valued on a monthly basis by the fund administrator and a net asset value per share (NAV) is determined. This NAV reflects the value of all assets and liabilities of the fund divided by the number of shares outstanding at the time of the valuation. The NAV is used as the value for all purchases and redemptions of fund shares. Unlike a domestic partnership, offshore funds must pay the expense of the fund administrator. These expenses generally range between 0.10 and 0.20 percent of total fund assets, annually. These expenses generally do not include out-of-pocket expenses incurred in managing the affairs of the fund. This may include directors' fees, communication to shareholders, share certificates, if issued, and other disbursements made by the fund. In most cases administrator fees and out-of-pocket expenses are minimal if the offshore fund is of sufficient asset size. Furthermore, given the complexity of certain investment strategies from an administrative standpoint, higher fees charged by fund administrators may be justified. Other standard operating expenses include marketing expenses, audit fees, and government registration fees. The industry generally refers to $10 million to $20 million as the "critical mass" that a fund must attain before it can properly support standard operating expenses.

Investment Management Fees

A fund's NAV also reflects the payment of management fees to the investment manager and, if applicable, incentive fees. The standard fee structure for offshore hedge funds is management fees of 1 to 1.5 percent annually and 20 percent of the profits on an annual basis, as an incentive fee. In some cases, the management and/or incentives of an offshore fund may be slightly higher than its related U.S. limited partnership, however pricing parity between offshore and onshore funds is becoming much more common. It is worth noting that some investment strategies such as commodity trading have commanded higher fees than noted above. It is strongly suggested that fees charged by any hedge fund be evaluated in terms of the potential returns *and* risks associated with a particular strategy or fund.

Most, but not all, offshore funds also have a provision known as a "high-water mark" which stipulates that if the NAV drops below its value on the last date that an incentive fee was paid or its value at the time of original issuance, any losses must be earned back before any further incentive fee is paid. Because fund shares may be sold at different times during the year, some funds also have equalization procedures which attempt to fairly allocate incentive fees to shareholders purchasing shares at different times.

Liquidity

Many offshore hedge funds provide for the purchase and redemption of shares on a monthly basis. This is somewhat different from the liquidity provided by U.S. limited partnerships, which, in many cases, only offer investors liquidity on an annual basis. Even if liquidity is offered more frequently (e.g., semiannually, quarterly), there is often a restriction on liquidity during the first year of investment. Even with offshore funds, first-year restrictions on liquidity do exist and frequently notice periods of at least 30 days are required. In several cases restrictions on liquidity offered to investors can be a function of the investment strategy or type of investments being made by the fund. If the underlying assets utilized in an offshore fund are less liquid than traditional stocks and bonds (e.g. derivative securities, distressed securities, private securities, short positions) limiting investor liquidity may be in the best interest of achieving the objectives of a particular strategy. However, in certain cases, liquidity may be restricted for other reasons.

Minimum Investments

Because most offshore hedge funds are structured for sophisticated investors with substantial assets and investment experience, the minimum investment for many such funds can be US$500,000 to US$1,000,000. These high minimums assist compliance with private placement regulations in many jurisdictions. Additionally, they emphasize the experience and financial substance that investors should have before pursuing investment strategies and structures of this type. Last, in order to obtain adequate diversification, an investor in an offshore hedge fund must be able to meet the minimum investment requirements of several funds concurrently. This reality has fostered the creation of multiadvisor funds commonly referred to as "funds of funds." Please refer below to a brief discussion of the fund of funds structure.

Other Fund Structures

One way for smaller investors to participate in offshore hedge funds is by investing in a multiadvisor fund or fund of funds. Funds of funds are simply offshore funds which invest in a variety of other single-manager offshore funds. This multiadvisor approach provides investors with greater diversification for a smaller investment of capital. Additionally, well-structured funds of funds typically diversify their portfolio by asset class, geographic exposure, and investment style. Furthermore, if the fund of funds is managed by professional investors with true expertise in hedge funds or nontraditional approaches to asset management, these professionals are typically better equipped to thoroughly evaluate each fund's investment strategy and effectively balance portfolio risk. The disadvantage of a fund of funds is that in addition to the management and incentive fees charged by each underlying fund, the fund of funds typically charges its own management and/or incentive fees and has operating expenses of its own. It is extremely important in evaluating fund of funds investments to understand these fees and expenses and to clearly understand how the fund of funds manager or sponsor is being compensated. For instance, some fund of funds managers or sponsors do share in some of the underlying fund's fees and may not disclose or pass on this savings to the fund of funds shareholders.

One of the more innovative offshore fund structures which allows for the commingling of offshore and onshore investors in the same fund vehicle is a Passive Foreign Investment Company (PFIC). Here the offshore fund can accept both offshore and onshore investors but must maintain at least a majority (50 percent) of offshore investors' assets in the fund at all times. This unique structure allows an investment manager to actually manage one single portfolio and not be concerned with allocating trades among onshore and offshore accounts. The additional focus that a single portfolio provides allows the investment manager to more effectively serve both domestic and foreign investors. While the actual workings of a PFIC are far more complicated, more and more funds may utilize this and related structures as the cross-border, global mutual fund industry develops.

Who Can Invest in an Offshore Fund?

The proper response to this question must be answered by qualified legal and tax advisors. Each tax jurisdiction in which a potential investor might reside has differing regulations on this question. In some cases, offshore hedge funds can only be offered to institutions (e.g., banks, brokerage firms, insurance companies). In other cases such funds cannot be offered at all. Even if an investor is allowed to invest in an offshore fund, it may not be to his or her advantage to do so.

How to Invest in an Offshore Fund?

Investing in an offshore hedge fund is a reasonably straightforward and simple process. In order to obtain the necessary documents required to make a proper evaluation of a particular fund, an investor must contact the fund or its administrator. Due to the fact that many such funds are offered privately, it is not always easy to obtain a contact, phone number, or address for many funds. Many investors attempt to contact the investment manager of a particular fund for information on a fund, however the investment manager will only refer you to the fund's offshore representative, placement agent and/or administrator. Two financial newspapers list the NAV's of numerous offshore funds namely, *The Financial Times* and the *International Herald Tribune*. Additionally, there are several data sources available, specific to offshore funds. Below is a list of providers which offer publications and/or computer services focused on offshore funds:

The U.S. Offshore Funds Directory
405 Park Avenue
Suite 500
New York, NY 10022
U.S.A.
Contact: Mr. Antoine Bernheim
            (212) 371-5935
            (212) 758-9032 (fax)

TASS Management Ltd.

27 Palace Street	1776 Broadway
London SW1E 5HW	New York, NY 10019
England	U.S.A.
Contact: Ms. Nicola Meaden	Ms. Karen Sampson
44-1-71-233-9797	(212) 582-9818
44-1-71-233-9159 (fax)	(212) 582-1310 (fax)

Micropal, Ltd.
Commonwealth House
2 Chalkhill Road
London W6 8DW
England
Contact: Simon Stillwell
            44-1-81-741-4100
            44-1-81-741-0839 (fax)

Micropal, Inc.
31 Milk Street
Suite 1002
Boston, MA 02109
U.S.A.
Kevin J. Thornton
(617) 451-1585
(617) 451-9565 (fax)

Hedge Fund Research, Inc.
208 S. LaSalle
Suite 774
Chicago, IL 60604
U.S.A.
Contact: Joseph G. Nicholas
            (312) 553-6458
            (312) 553-6461 (fax)

Managed Account Reports, Inc.
220 Fifth Avenue
19th floor
New York, NY 10001-7781
U.S.A.
Contact: Lois Peltz
            (212) 213-6202
            (212) 213-1870 (fax)

Once an investor has determined which offshore fund(s) meets his or her investment objectives and has obtained all the necessary documents, the process of making an investment is simple. Most offshore funds have confidential offering memorandums which outline the principal terms and investment objectives and policies of the fund. *Read this offering memorandum in its entirety.* The offering memorandum generally also provides background information of the investment manager responsible for managing the assets along with certain tax and legal information. Each fund provides subscription documents or application forms which review the qualifications of the investor and help determine if the investor is eligible to purchase fund shares. Some funds also have other legal documents which may govern the management of the affairs of the offshore fund. These generally take the form of Articles and Memorandum of Association or Incorporation. It is highly recommended to review these structural documents as well.

Below is a list of recommended steps an investor should take in actually investing in an offshore fund. Although the following steps seem cumbersome, I have found that they can help to avoid potential problems:

1. *Contact the fund* administrator to inform him or her of the incoming investment at least a week prior to the next date available for the purchase of shares. Review with the administrator the procedures required for investment in the fund. Most subscription documents include instructions for making an investment, yet some are incomplete.
2. *Complete and sign* the subscription documents for the fund. Indicate the amount of the investment and the bank from which funds will be wired. Keep a copy for your files, fax a copy directly to the fund administrator, and then mail the signed originals to the fund administrator.
3. *Contact your bank* and instruct them to transfer funds via bank wire to the fund's bank account as outlined in the subscription documents. Do not send a check. The international mail system is unreliable and the fund may require cleared funds on the purchase date in order to accept the subscription.
4. *Contact the fund* administrator on the day following the bank wire being sent, to confirm receipt. Ask the fund administrator when a purchase confirmation will be sent. Normally the fund must determine its NAV prior to issuing a confirmation.

Redemptions from offshore funds are more easily accomplished. The items to focus on are the notice period required to effect a redemption, the time one must wait before receiving the proceeds of a redemption, the amount of the redemption which one will receive prior to an audit of the funds financial records. Some funds do not provide the complete proceeds until the end of the fund's fiscal year at which time a complete audit will be performed. It is not uncommon for a fund to pay 90 percent of the redemption value within 30 days after the redemption date and the remainder within 30 after completion of the annual audit. It is therefore important to understand this before making an investment.

Investing in Offshore Funds by Tax-Exempt U.S. Investors

Participation in hedge funds by U.S. institutions has increased during recent years as these institutions seek higher risk-adjusted returns. Most U.S. institutions manage pools of capital that are generally exempt from U.S. income taxes. These pools of capital represent assets held in trust for retirees or assets of tax-exempt organizations such as educational institutions, churches, and foundations. Yet, numerous hedge funds utilize leverage in their respective strategies and as a result may generate Unrelated Business Taxable Income (UBTI). In a limited partnership, UBTI is passed through to the limited partners and can indeed create a potential tax liability for a participating tax-exempt institution. While tax-exempt institutions who have successfully employed hedge fund strategies in their asset mix are pleased with the overall investment results, they may find it difficult to justify paying taxes when they otherwise would not have to for any other traditional investment. Many times it is "politically incorrect" to justify such action to an institution's board of directors, alumni, or retirement plan participants even if the investment benefits are meaningful.

Some institutions have utilized offshore funds to avoid this problem. Because the institutions are tax-exempt, participation in an offshore fund should not generally jeopardize the offshore status of the fund. Furthermore, if the offshore fund is structured as a foreign corporation, corporations generally do not pass income through to shareholders hence, many legal experts take the position that the corporate structure "cleanses" the UBTI. While this may solve the tax problem, other fiduciary issues arise with the use of an offshore fund by a U.S. tax-exempt institution. Furthermore, many offshore funds are not structured to accept such assets. In fact, several prominent hedge fund managers do not offer their funds to any U.S. investors. This allows them to minimize the amount of regulation to which they are subject.

Investment Managers and Offshore Funds

As we have discussed, offshore funds are investment companies set up for the purpose of investing in other stocks, bonds, commodities and/or other assets. They provide a vehicle for investors to commingle their financial assets with other investors in order to more effectively manage their collective wealth. Typically, an investment manager is hired by the offshore fund to invest the assets of the fund on a day-to-day basis, based on the investment objectives and policies established by the fund. Furthermore, this investment manager may physically reside in the market in which it invests without jeopardizing the offshore status of the fund. Some investment managers have established bonafide offshore operations and in some cases have moved their entire staff to an offshore jurisdiction. This phenomenon has generally occurred in response to increasing regulatory burdens in the

United States imposed on strategies that invest in commodities and employ large amounts of leverage.

In many cases, offshore funds are originally established by investment managers to provide for an effective vehicle to attract foreign clients. The breadth and depth of investment strategies offered through offshore hedge funds are as diverse as the domestic hedge fund market including single strategy funds, multistrategy funds, and funds of funds. In most cases the offshore fund managed by a particular investment manager is managed "pari passu" or side-by-side with assets managed in the same strategy domestically. With little or no restriction on the number of investors in an offshore fund, managers who are unable to accept more domestic limited partners, can accommodate additional asset growth through the offshore fund. Furthermore, the rate of capital formation in other markets around the world is attracting more and more providers of investment management services.

While a growing number of hedge fund managers are non-U.S. based, the vast majority of managers are located in the United States. This can largely be attributed to the breadth and depth of hedging tools that exist in the U.S. capital markets and the culture associated with utilizing aggressive investment strategies. Yet, we are now seeing hedge funds established by investment managers located in Europe, the Far East, and Latin America.

Summary

The offshore fund business has become substantially larger and more legitimized with the rapid expansion of the global capital markets. Offshore jurisdictions provide "tax neutral" jurisdictions where commingling the assets of many different investors, from many different countries, each with differing tax situations seems manageable and feasible. The complexity and cost of establishing and maintaining offshore structures has historically hindered all but the wealthiest and most sophisticated investors from utilizing these structures. The use of offshore domiciles for registered funds sold to the investing public clearly requires substantial development and regulatory reform in order to properly protect and address the needs of the global retail investor. However, the advent of technology and the development of service providers skilled in providing cost-effective and high-quality service have assisted the offshore fund community in emerging as a global mutual fund industry.

The offshore hedge fund industry is clearly on a continued path of growth. This discussion has attempted to review the practical issues associated with the structure of offshore funds and the resulting impact on analyzing and investing in such funds. With a working understanding of the structure and operation of offshore funds, the most important task of evaluating the investment strategies employed and the investment managers responsible for the strategy becomes easier and more effective. While the use of offshore fund structures has been utilized extensively for hedge fund strategies, it is expected that more and more investment strategies will be delivered to investors on a global basis through offshore funds.

CHAPTER 10

Track Record Length: The Ins and Outs of Hedge Fund Size

Lois Peltz, Managing Editor
Managed Account Reports, Inc.

When one hears about hedge funds, one generally thinks of George Soros's Quantum Funds, Julian Robertson's Tiger Management, Michael Steinhardt's Steinhardt Partners or Louis Bacon's Moore Capital Management. These are among the largest hedge funds, themselves totaling about $23 billion or about one-third of the estimated hedge fund total universe, which *MAR/Hedge* currently estimates to be about $70 billion.

Based on *MAR/Hedge's* database of approximately 400 hedge funds, we find that 18 funds have over $1 billion, and 54 have between $100 million and $999 million. The bulk of the funds, 37 percent, have between $10 million and $49.9 million, and another 35 percent are smaller than $10 million (see Figure 10-1).

In this chapter, we will explore the impact of hedge fund size on performance returns, volatility and return-to-risk parameters. Not every hedge fund can be large—style of trading, leverage used, and liquidity of markets traded all have to be considered.

Asset Size Impact on Performance

Should investors have comfort or worry if their hedge fund is large? Is bigger always better? Many investors and fund of funds managers readily give assets to "core" hedge fund managers—those with large asset bases and long track records because they feel these managers represent consistency and therefore provide comfort. However, as these managers grow in size, MAR/Hedge research indicates that their performance pattern changes—returns tend to come down.[1]

---

[1] *MAR/Hedge*, "Turning point—asset size vs. performance," June 1994, p. 6.

FIGURE 10-1. Asset Size Distribution

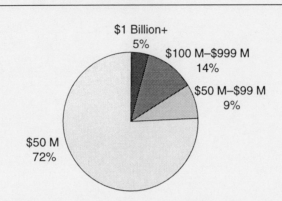

Turning Point—Between $40 Million and $80 Million

In 81 percent of the funds in the sample, we found that performance deterio-rated as assets grew (see Figures 10-2 through 10-4). Deterioration, however, was not always a steady process—in six of the 13 cases, performance was high in the early years, fell, then bounced but never attained the prior peak of annual return.

Where is the turning point? In 9 out of 13 cases, it was below $100 mil-lion. The highest frequency of occurrences was between $45 and $80 million.

FIGURE 10-2. Performance versus Assets—Example 1

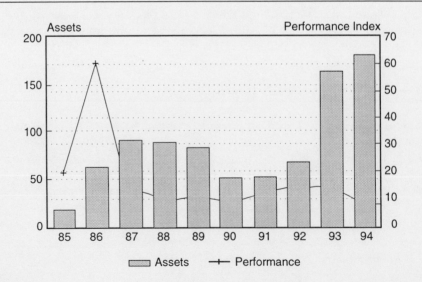

FIGURE 10-3.   Performance versus Assets—Example 2

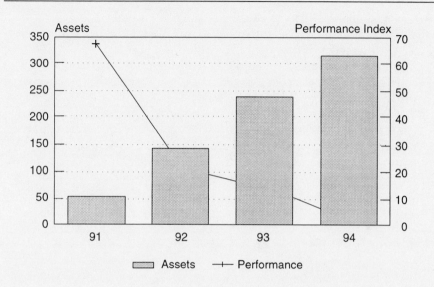

FIGURE 10-4.   Performance versus Assets—Example 3

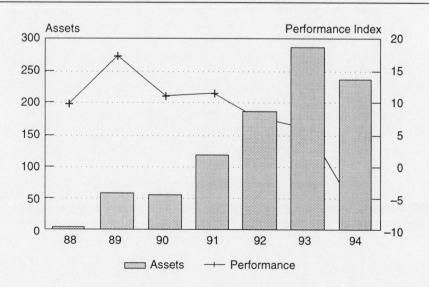

Why This Occurs

Were there similarities between the three hedge funds that bucked the general trend? The only similarity: all three were in the $500 million range in late 1994.

The differences outweighed the similarities. One was a fund of funds, while another was a market-neutral fixed-income fund and another was a global macro fund. One started in 1987, one in 1988, and the most recent in 1990. Two are based in the United States while the third is in Europe.

Why does this phenomenon occur? Some possible answers are: too large a fund cannot take advantage of small-scale opportunities, it may be difficult for directional managers to get out of trades, the quality of personnel may be difficult to maintain as the fund increases in size, more institutional assets coming in prefer lower returns with lower volatility, slippage occurs in large orders, psychological fears, and administrative inability to keep up with increasing paperwork.

Style Affects Opportunities Selected

Macro managers seem to have benefits as they take advantage of trading opportunities in global financial markets and currencies which are extremely liquid. Yet the niche manager may have an advantage over the macro managers at times since they are able to take advantage of opportunities that large macro players cannot. Their smaller size makes them more nimble. For example, if trading opportunities arise in the Netherlands or Belgium, global hedge fund managers may have to pass because the profit potential is too small relative to the total size of the fund to make it worthwhile.[2]

Another concern is that the global macro managers are more directional traders. While it may be possible for them to force the market in their desired direction at a quicker pace if the underlying fundamentals are in place, the global players may have a hard time getting out.[3]

Personnel

Personnel issues crop up as all hedge funds grow. At a certain asset level, a manager may feel the need to add additional traders or researchers in order to scout more trading opportunities. One market-neutral hedge fund, which currently has about $500 million under management with a staff of 17 including four traders and four assistant traders, said that to double its business, it will have to increase staffing to 25. "Finding qualified internal people is key, even if markets are deep enough," a representative said.

---

[2] *MAR/Hedge*, "Size as a double (h)edged sword," July 1994, p. 6.
[3] Ibid.

FIGURE 10-5.   Volatility versus Assets—Example 1

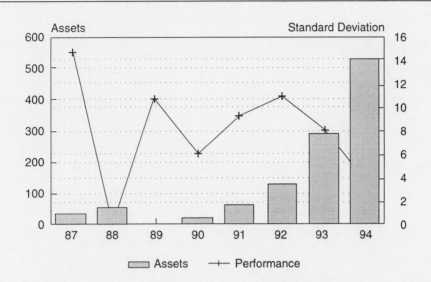

Keith Danko of Minnisink Partners also says that finding the right people and managing them is key. He adds, "Managing people may be different from managing money. . . . Indeed, the manager must decide whether he even wants to manage people."[4]

Institutional Assets

Institutional investors say hedge fund investing presents an opportunity and possible solution to add incremental return without increased portfolio risk. They often state that they are looking for volatility lower than the S&P. Institutions also primarily use macro-manager hedge funds to alleviate concerns that its assets represent such a large piece of a fund.

An analysis of the impact of asset size on volatility generally shows that as a fund's asset size increases, its volatility is lower (see Figures 10-5 through 10-7). *MAR/Hedge* looked at volatility (standard deviation) of the same $100+ million hedge funds to see if it changed as assets increased. In all but two cases, volatility generally decreased as asset size increased. In two cases, while annual volatility was lower than in earlier years, it was not at its lowest point. In other words, some type of bounce occurred.

[4] Ibid.

FIGURE 10-6.   Volatility versus Assets—Example 2

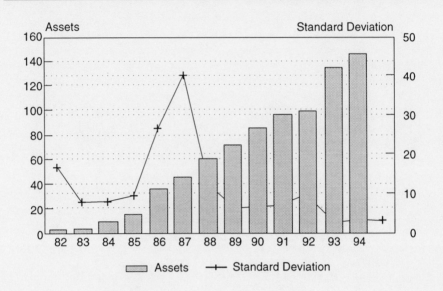

FIGURE 10-7.   Volatility versus Assets—Example 3

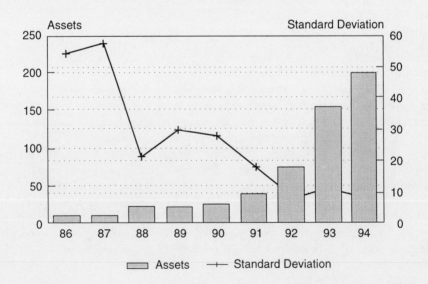

Methodology

We examined the MAR/Hedge database to find those hedge funds which contained at least $100 million on August 31, 1994. Of these 52, we eliminated 19 because historic asset size was not consistently available on a monthly basis and also eliminated another 17 because they had less than a full three-year track record. Rates of return, volatility and a return-to-risk measure were compared with year-end assets for a select number of hedge funds. The indicators were examined on an annual year-end basis except 1994, in which the latest month available, September, was used. A profile of the final sample of 16 revealed:

- Average asset base of $360 million
- Average track record length of eight years
- Five were global macro managers, four were funds of funds, three were market neutral, two were event-driven and one was global. Sixty percent were U.S. based while 40 percent were off-shore or European.

While a sample size of 16 is small, it may provide an indication of a trend. While perhaps not conclusive at this time, it is a premise which should be periodically examined as the sample base of hedge fund managers with $100 million-plus grows.

Style's Impact on Fund Asset Size and Capacity

It is wise not to compare the size of one hedge fund style against other hedge fund styles—macro managers are much more capable of handling larger sums than niche managers. The type of trading strategy or style used by a hedge fund manager is a critical factor determining optimal fund size. Use of leverage, liquidity of markets traded, performance, and personnel are factors to be considered.

Bond Arbitrage

Leverage is a tool that other styles or strategies may not have access to or cannot take advantage of as macro managers can. This inability to use leverage hinders the upside potential for some niche styles. For instance, a government bond arbitrageur can have a successful trade and only make 25 basis points. David Smith of Coast Asset Mgt. Corp., a government bond arbitrageur, says, "A macro manager can see that German bonds are cheap and buy them for 5–10 points, making a bet on the German economy. The macro manager can go out and buy a ton without moving the market and have a huge profit or loss potential since he is using lots of leverage. But for me, I can only make say 1/4 of a point."[5]

Because a government bond arbitrageur does not use leverage, he must pay close attention to profit margins. He may miss a trading opportunity if the market moves since he cannot give up 1/8 of a point to make 5 points—but a macro manager can. "I must be patient and hopefully the reward/risk dynamic will come back into play; but it may not," added Smith. Smith concludes that a government bond arbitrageur cannot handle the capacity that a macro trader does. He would not quantify what he thought the capacity limits were since other factors may come into play as well.

Convertible bond arbitrageurs feel they can handle bigger positions than the government bond arbitrageurs since they have bigger inefficiencies in the markets they deal with.

Small Caps

Those hedge funds that focus on small-cap stocks have a different problem: liquidity. If a small-cap hedge fund owns less than 1 percent of a stock and that stock is not liquid or heavily traded, the manager could get hurt either entering or exiting the trade.

Edwin Vroom, principal and founder of Roanoke Partners, estimates that a small-cap hedge fund won't have problems in the $400–500 million range but "the perfect size is between $200 and $400 million." He provides an illustration of a typical $200 million small-cap hedge fund: It will have about 50 stocks in a portfolio with each representing about 2 percent of the fund. The average position size is $4 million.

Ways exist, however, to circumvent size constraints. Vroom suggests using options to enhance liquidity of the fund or shorting a surrogate stock. The latter, however, is not a perfect solution.

Short Sellers

Those who use short-selling strategies may have a problem as they approach the $500 million area, as demonstrated by Jim Chanos's recent experience. Feshbach Brothers had trouble in the $1 billion area. Short-sell positions are fundamentally-based and only a few great opportunities occur each year—especially during bull stock markets. Ben Kopin at Lynx L.P.

---

[5] Ibid.

mentions that many of his good short-selling ideas are in the small-cap area, which many macro managers can't justify. He gives the example of having a $10 million position out of a $1 billion total on the short side, i.e., 1 percent. "To short $10 million requires a large-size small cap. . . . a $100 million market cap is hard to short." Consequently, macro managers don't do short-selling to such a large extent.[6]

Distressed Securities

Those managers focusing on distressed securities also have capacity limits. Many of the stocks they buy are a function of the high-yield bond market or the junk bond market that eventually may go bankrupt or end up in Chapter 11. Event-driven hedge fund managers such as New York–based M. D. Sass specialize in picking up the pieces and understand the process while most other managers shun these situations. Jim Chau, marketing manager, estimates, "The total junk bond market in the United States is $300 billion, of which $30–40 billion is defaulted or publicly-traded junk. The total market is about $50–60 billion and to have 10 percent of that market is not out of the question."[7] While Chau admits that having a $500 million distressed-security hedge fund is manageable, he admits that investment tactics would have to change at that size—perhaps by taking more direct positions in the company or taking control of it.

Market Neutral

Market-neutral hedge funds that trade United States financial markets tend to have relatively unlimited capacity. One told *MAR/Hedge*, "We could manage $1 billion. However, once we move outside the United States, problems may crop up. This manager added that German markets are less liquid than those in the United States, and those in France and Spain are even less liquid than those in Germany.

The bottom line remains performance, not size of the fund. "You get paid if the fund performs, not if it is big. Compensation is tied to performance, not size," Vroom concludes.[8]

---

[6] Ibid.

[7] Ibid.

[8] Ibid.

PART III

Legal, Accounting, and Operational Issues

CHAPTER 11

Critical Legal and Regulatory Issues

Paul N. Roth, Senior Partner
Schulte Roth & Zabel

I. Offering of Interests

Offering interests in a private investment partnership or fund (the terms are used interchangeably in this chapter) requires the partnership to effect a private placement under the Securities Act of 1933, as amended (the "Securities Act"), comply with applicable disclosure requirements under the Commodity Exchange Act (CEA) if the fund invests in commodity futures or interests, comply with state "blue sky" laws governing the offering and, if intermediaries are used, comply with the rules relating to the use of solicitors under the Investment Advisers Act of 1940, as amended (the "Advisers Act"). To document compliance with these rules, the investment partnership will need to receive from each investor a completed subscription document containing relevant information and representations.[1]

---

[1] Historically, funds designed for U.S. investors have been formed as limited partnerships, and this chapter assumes that investment funds are formed as limited partnerships. Now that most states have passed legislation approving the limited liability company as an entity which provides liability protection to investors, funds may be organized as limited liability companies assuming they may be structured in a manner to provide income tax treatment which is similar to that afforded investors in limited partnerships. The relative benefits and disadvantages of the two forms of organization are beyond the scope of this chapter, and, for simplicity, we discuss issues in terms of funds organized as limited partnerships.

I would like to express my appreciation to my partners, Steven J. Fredman and Stephen R. Nelson for their invaluable assistance in the preparation of this chapter, and to my other colleagues at Schulte Roth & Zabel who participated in this project.

A. Private Placement of Interests

1. Regulation D Generally

The offering of interests in a private investment partnership is an offering of securities which must be conducted as a private placement in order to avoid registration under both the Securities Act and the Investment Company Act of 1940, as amended (the "Company Act").[2] Section 4(2) of the Securities Act exempts offerings of securities by an issuer if a public offering is not involved. The Securities and Exchange Commission (SEC), its staff (the "Staff") and the courts focus on a number of factors in determining whether a public offering has occurred, including the nature of the information provided to investors, the sophistication and number of offerees and purchasers, and the manner in which solicitations of sales are made.[3]

Private placements of interests in funds are generally made pursuant to Rule 506 under Regulation D, a nonexclusive safe harbor provided to issuers relying on the Section 4(2) exemption of the Securities Act.[4] Regulation D permits sales of interests to an unlimited number of "accredited investors," but limits sales of interests to 35 non-accredited investors. As a practical matter, most private investment funds will accept only accredited investors. Rule 506 does not limit the dollar amount of securities that can be sold in reliance on the exemption. Neither Section 4(2) nor Regulation D provides an exemption for the resale of the privately placed and exempted (or "restricted") securities.

2. Accredited Investors

An accredited investor as defined in Rule 501(a) of Regulation D includes the following: specified institutional investors (such as banks, savings and loan associations, broker-dealers, insurance companies, and investment companies); employee benefit plans which have total assets in excess of $5,000,000 or have a bank, savings and loan association, insurance company, or registered investment adviser as the plan fiduciary, or if the plan is a self-directed plan, one in which investment decisions are made solely by persons

---

[2] *See infra*, Section II. Avoiding Regulation Under the Investment Company Act of 1940.

[3] For a general discussion of the securities law issues involved in private placements, *see* Hicks, *Exempted Transactions under the Securities Act of 1933*, ch. 11, Clark Boardman Callaghan Securities Law Series, vol. 7C (1994).

[4] *See generally*, Hicks, *Limited Offering Exemptions: Regulation D*, Clark Boardman Callaghan Securities Law Series (1994–95 ed.).

who are accredited investors; corporations, partnerships, or foundations (and other entities that are exempt from federal taxes under Section 501(c)(3) of the Internal Revenue Code of 1986, as amended) with total assets in excess of $5,000,000; trusts with total assets in excess of $5,000,000 not formed for the specific purpose of acquiring the securities offered and whose purchase is directed by a "sophisticated person" as defined in Rule 506(b)(2)(ii) of Regulation D; persons whose net worth (or joint net worth with that person's spouse) exceeds $1,000,000, or whose income was in excess of $200,000 in each of the two preceding years (or, together with that person's spouse, in excess of $300,000 in each of the two preceding years) and who reasonably expect to reach the same level of income in the current year; any director, executive officer, or general partner of the issuer of the securities being offered or sold, or any person holding any of those positions in a general partner of the issuer; and any entity in which all of the equity holders are accredited investors.

3. Disclosure

An issuer relying on the Section 4(2) exemption or on Regulation D must provide investors with all material information concerning the securities. An offering document is not required in an offering made only to "accredited investors," but is highly recommended and is almost always provided. A properly drafted private placement memorandum will serve both as a marketing document for the fund and, most importantly, from a legal perspective, will protect the general partner against "failure to disclose" claims.

Any purchaser who is not an "accredited investor" under Rule 506 must, in the issuer's reasonable belief, have sufficient knowledge and experience in financial and business matters, either alone or together with his purchaser representative, to be able to evaluate the merits and risks of the prospective investment. In addition, such person must receive (to the extent material to an understanding of the issuer, its business, and the securities being sold), the same disclosure that would be required had the offering been conducted as a registered offering.

4. Counting Nonaccredited Investors

Generally, any person who is not an "accredited investor" as defined above will be counted towards the permissible maximum of 35 nonaccredited investors. There are, however, certain exceptions. In Rule 506 offerings, the following purchasers are not counted: (i) any relative, spouse, or relative of the spouse, of a purchaser who has the same principal residence as the purchaser, (ii) any trust or estate in which a purchaser and any of the persons related to him (as specified in (i) or (iii)) collectively have more than 50 percent of the beneficial interest (excluding a contingent interest); and (iii) any corporation or other organization of which a purchaser and any of the persons related to him (as specified in (i) or (ii)) collectively are beneficial owners of more than 50 percent of the equity securities (excluding directors' qualifying shares) or equity interests.

5. General Solicitation

Rule 502(c) of Regulation D prohibits offers or sales of securities by any form of general solicitation or general advertising. The terms *"general solicitation"* or *"general advertising,"* however, are not defined in Regulation D. In analyzing whether general solicitation or general advertising has occurred in a particular case, the SEC's focus has been on the relationship between the offeror and offerees and the means of communication to the offerees.

A factor which has been considered in this analysis is the existence of a substantive pre-existing relationship between the investor and the general partner or person acting on the general partner's behalf. The relationship should be one that would enable the general partner (or person acting on its behalf) to be aware of the financial circumstances or sophistication of the persons with whom the relationship exists, or is otherwise one of some substance and duration. Furthermore, to avoid general solicitation or general advertising, the offer must generally be personally directed to the offeree. Nonpersonal communications have consistently been viewed as general solicitations, even when the targeted recipients of the communications could reasonably be expected to be qualified investors.[5]

In *Woodtrails-Seattle, Ltd.,* SEC No-Action Letter (pub. avail. Aug. 9, 1982), the SEC concluded that a general solicitation did not occur even though offers were made to 330 persons. Each of those persons had invested in other partnerships sponsored by the general partners during the previous three years and a determination had been made at the time of each original investment that the investor was qualified. The general partners were therefore deemed to have a substantive pre-existing relationship with the offerees and, as such, the offers to that number of persons was not a general solicitation. In comparison, the SEC did not permit use of the Regulation D safe harbor in *Kenman Corporation,* Securities Exchange Act Release No. 21962 (Apr. 19, 1985), where the entity was found to have made a general solicitation. In that case, the general partner of a real estate syndicate solicited not only past participants in its offerings, but also, among others, the CEOs of 50

---

[5] *See, e.g., Aspen Grove,* SEC No-Action Letter (pub. avail. Dec. 8, 1982); *Trust Mortgage and Loan Services, Inc.,* SEC No-Action Letter (pub. avail. Dec. 27, 1979); *A.A. Ajax Co., Inc.,* SEC No-Action Letter (pub. avail. Jan. 15, 1979); *Thoroughbred Racing Stable,* SEC No-Action Letter (pub. avail. Jan. 5, 1976).

Fortune 500 companies whose names were obtained from the companies' annual reports, and physicians whose names were obtained from a list maintained by the State of California. While the CEOs and physicians may have been "accredited" as defined in Regulation D, the absence of a pre-existing relationship with them made Regulation D unavailable.

6. *Form D*

A Notice of Sale on Form D must be filed with the SEC within 15 days after the first sale in conjunction with an offering under Regulation D. Form D requires disclosure regarding the issuer and the general partner (and certain large investors), the amount offered and sold, certain expenses of the placement, and the intended use of proceeds. Although failure to file a Form D does not affect the availability of the exemption, it can serve as a basis for the SEC to deny the issuer future reliance on Regulation D.

B. *Broker-Dealer Registration*

An issue arises for investment partnerships as to whether the partnership or the general partner is required to register as a broker or dealer under the Securities Exchange Act of 1934 (the "Exchange Act"). Most investment partnerships' activities do not sufficiently parallel those of either a "broker" or a "dealer" and thus neither broker nor dealer registration will be required. However, this is not always the case, and each situation must be addressed on its facts to determine the need for registration.

Broker registration generally will not be required in connection with the partnership's operation so long as the partnership and the general partner do not "effect transactions in securities for the account of others" and so do not come under the statutory definition of "broker" under the Exchange Act.[6] In most situations, the partnership and the general partner trade for their own accounts rather than effecting transactions for the accounts of others.

Similarly, investment partnerships generally do not register as dealers. The Exchange Act defines "dealer" as "any person engaged in the business of buying and selling securities for his own account, through a broker or otherwise, but does not include a bank, or any person insofar as he buys or sells securities for his own account, either individually or in some fiduciary capacity, but not as a part of a regular business."[7] Arguably, the partnership, or the general partner on behalf of the partnership, is buying and selling securities for its own account as part of its regular business. However, in a

---

[6] Exchange Act §3(a)(4).

[7] Exchange Act §3(a)(5).

series of no-action letters, the SEC has identified several indicia of acting as a dealer, including (i) acting as an underwriter or participating in a selling group in any distribution of securities; (ii) carrying a dealer inventory in securities; (iii) quoting a market in any security; (iv) advertising or otherwise holding itself out to the public as a dealer or as being willing to buy or sell any security on a continuous basis; (v) extending or arranging for the extension of credit on securities; and (vi) lending securities.[8] Investment partnerships generally do not have these indicia of a dealer to the extent that would bring them within the definition of "dealer" and, hence, generally do not need to register as such.

A partner, employee, or independent solicitor whose primary function is to place interests in the partnership, (i.e., to raise money from investors), may be subject to registration as a broker. In particular, general partners should review carefully the provisions of Rule 3a4-1 under the Exchange Act to determine whether they or any of their personnel are potentially subject to registration as a broker as a result of placing interests in the fund. Registration would ordinarily be required of an independent solicitor engaged by the partnership to place interests in the partnership.

If registration as a broker-dealer is required, the investment partnership and/or its general partner must comply with various fiduciary and disclosure rules and regulations of the SEC and self regulatory organizations.

C. Use of Solicitors under the Investment Advisers Act of 1940

Rule 206(4)-3 under the Advisers Act regulates the use of solicitors and the payment of cash fees to such solicitors with respect to their solicitation activities. The rule, which is designed to disclose the amount that is paid by the adviser for the solicitation activities (and thus the conflict of interest that the solicitor has in recommending the adviser), by its terms applies only to registered advisers. Unregistered advisers are not covered by this rule because the SEC inferred that any adviser using a solicitor must be "holding itself out" as an adviser and therefore cannot take advantage of the exemption from registration as an adviser under Section 203(b)(3) of the Advisers Act.[9] Despite the SEC's view, it should be possible to structure a solicitation arrangement where the solicitation is conducted in a sufficiently discreet manner to avoid a "holding out." Assuming the solicitation activities are so

---

[8] *See, e.g., Davenport Management, Inc.*, SEC No-Action Letter (pub. avail. Apr. 13, 1993). *See generally*, Lipton, *Broker-Dealer Regulation*, Clark Boardman Callaghan Securities Law Series, vol. 15, ch. 1 (1994).

[9] *See* Advisers Act Release No. 688 (July 12, 1979) (adopting release).

structured, the conflict of interest would exist in a scenario involving an unregistered adviser to the same degree as a registered adviser. For this reason, it is advisable for the unregistered adviser to comply with the rule as well.

Under the rule, referral fees may be paid by an adviser only pursuant to a written agreement between the solicitor and the adviser, and in the case of referral fees paid to unrelated third parties (as opposed to employees of the adviser), the client must acknowledge in writing its receipt of the adviser's brochure (pursuant to Rule 204-3) and a separate disclosure document describing the relationship between the solicitor and the adviser, the nature and amount of the compensation to be paid, and the impact, if any, of such compensation on the advisory fees to be charged to the client.

D. Subscription Documents

A private investment partnership should provide all prospective investors with subscription documents. The completed subscription documents permit the general partner to determine and document that an investor is appropriate for the fund, thus addressing the suitability concern that the SEC believes exists in every advisory relationship, i.e., is this a suitable investment product for the particular investor.

In a subscription agreement, the investor should represent that: it can financially withstand the loss of its investment in the fund; it is purchasing the interest for investment and not for distribution; it meets the minimum net worth or income tests to be an "accredited investor" under Regulation D; it has sufficient knowledge and experience in financial and business matters to be capable of evaluating the merits and risks of the investment; it is an "eligible client" under Rule 205-3 under the Advisers Act (if the general partner is a registered investment adviser and is receiving an incentive allocation or if the partnership will directly or indirectly pay incentive compensation to another registered investment adviser); and (for certain investment partnerships investing in commodities) it is a "qualified eligible participant" pursuant to Rule 4.7 under the CEA. To verify the suitability of the investment for the investor, information should be elicited regarding the investor's past investment history. Appropriate information also should be elicited so that the general partner can determine how to count the investor for purposes of the 100 person limit under Section 3(c)(1) of the Company Act.[10] If employee benefit plans subject to the Employee Retirement Income Security Act of 1974, as amended (ERISA) are permitted to invest in the fund, representa-

---

[10] *See infra*, Section II. Avoiding Regulation Under the Investment Company Act of 1940.

tions addressing particular ERISA issues should be included.[11] If the partnership intends to invest in "hot issues," as defined by the National Association of Securities Dealers (NASD), the subscription agreement should include a section designed to elicit information from the investor as to its status as a "restricted person" under the NASD's Free Rider and Withholding Interpretation relating to "hot issues."

E. State Laws Governing Offerings

In addition to the federal law discussed above, each state has its own statutes and regulations ("blue sky laws"), governing the offer and sale of securities into or from such states or to residents of such states. In many states, filings must be made to qualify for an exemption from registration. While the majority of states have adopted in some form the Uniform Securities Act of 1956, and several states have adopted in some form the Revised Uniform Securities Act of 1985 (collectively the "Uniform Securities Act"), the particular laws of each state differ, and compliance with a state's blue sky laws must be determined before any offer is made into, from or to a resident of such state.[12]

1. Method of Offering

Depending on the version of the Uniform Securities Act adopted, any offer (or, in some states, any sale) made to 10 or fewer (or, in some states, 25 or fewer) persons in the state within any 12 consecutive months, generally excluding institutional investors, will qualify as a private placement exempt from state registration requirements. An "institutional investor" typically includes banks, thrifts, insurance companies, and pension or profit sharing trusts. In some jurisdictions, entities such as corporations with a certain level of assets or universities may be considered institutional investors as well. A few states expand their definition of institutional investors to include accredited investors, even those who are natural persons, thereby excluding accredited investors from the numerical limitations of the private placement exemption.

The purchaser must be acquiring an interest in the partnership for investment, and no commission or other remuneration may be paid, directly or indirectly, to any person for soliciting buyers (except generally to locally

---

[11] *See infra* Section IV. ERISA.

[12] *See generally*, Long, *Blue Sky Law*, Clark Boardman Callaghan Securities Law Series, vols. 12 and 12A (1985); *see also*, Moriarty & McNeily, *Regulation of Financial Planners*, Clark Boardman Callaghan Securities Law Series, vol. 19 (1994).

registered broker-dealers). Although general advertising or solicitation is not expressly prohibited, many states have further conditioned this exemption by including this limitation. Noncompliance with any element of the state exemption may result in the requirement that the investment partnership rescind its sales to investors.

Many states have adopted some form of the Uniform Limited Offering Exemption (ULOE), comparable to Regulation D. The ULOE has no limitation on the number of offerees and, like Regulation D, the exemption permits sales to an unlimited number of "accredited investors." Under the ULOE exemption, the issuer may not make a general solicitation, sales may not be made to more than 35 nonaccredited investors[13] and no commissions, finder's fees or other remuneration may be paid other than to locally registered broker-dealers. Issuers generally may not rely on ULOE if the issuer is the subject of certain statutory disqualifications within five years prior to commencement of the offering.[14] The ULOE is not self-executing; the issuer must file a Form D (or the state's equivalent form) typically within 15 days after the first sale in the state.[15]

2. State Broker-Dealer Registration

Under the Uniform Securities Act, any person engaged in the business of effecting transactions in securities for the account of others or for his own account is a broker-dealer. Although specific exclusions from the definition of broker-dealer vary from state to state, generally (i) agents[16], issuers, banks, thrifts, trust companies, and (ii) persons with no place of business in the state (a) who deal only with institutional investors, or (b) who make 15

---

[13] The issuer must reasonably believe that the investment is suitable for a nonaccredited investor (suitability may be presumed if the investment does not exceed 10 percent of the purchaser's net worth) or that the investor has sufficient knowledge and experience in financial and business matters to be able to evaluate the merits and risks of the investment. Some states have additional suitability requirements for all investors, accredited and nonaccredited.

[14] States vary in their disqualification provisions (i.e., Alaska requires disclosure of certain convictions occurring within a 10-year period prior to commencement of the offering).

[15] In some states, the Form D or equivalent must be filed no later than 10 days prior to the first sale, and in some instances, prior to the first offer being made in such state.

[16] Agents are generally defined as individuals representing the issuer in connection with the purchase or sale of a security. Agents have a separate state registration requirement, and some states may require "agent" registration for exempt transactions.

or fewer offers within a state to noninstitutions during any 12-month period, will not come within the broker-dealer definition. However, New York specifically includes as a "dealer" any person selling or offering its own securities to the public within or from the state and requires such issuers to register with the state. In a recent decision, the New York Court of Appeals held that sales of securities to 12 individuals constituted a "public offering" requiring the issuer to register as a dealer where the purchasers did not have "sufficient knowledge or access to information of defendant's background and experience to substitute for what could have been learned about defendant from a state registration, or what could have been learned about the securities under the requirements of Federal law."[17]

II. Avoiding Regulation under the Investment Company Act of 1940

A private investment partnership generally falls within the definition of an "investment company" under Section 3(a)(1) of the Company Act, since it is an entity that "proposes to engage primarily in the business of investing, reinvesting, or trading in securities." However, registration under the Company Act would severely impair the operation of an investment partnership. The Company Act requires registered investment companies to have a board of directors, in the case of partnerships at least 60 percent of whom must be "independent," and the board must approve the investment advisory contract, custodial arrangements, and other matters affecting the fund's operations. Registration under the Company Act would mean that certain affiliated transactions, which otherwise might be permissible with disclosure and consent, would be proscribed by statute. Limitations on the amount of "leverage" that the partnership could use would apply, effectively limiting short sales, futures, forwards, and margin transactions.

For all of the above reasons, a private investment partnership should attempt to come under the "private" investment company exclusion from the definition of investment company found in Section 3(c)(1) of the Company Act.[18] In order to rely on Section 3(c)(1), the fund must meet the following two requirements: (i) it must have no more than 100 beneficial owners of its securities or interests (the "100 investor test"), and (ii) it must not be mak-

---

[17] *New York v. Landes*, 645 N.E. 2d 716 (NY 1994).

[18] Section 3(c) of the Company Act excludes from the definition of "investment company," and therefore from regulation under the Company Act, a number of entities that otherwise would come within the definition.

ing or proposing to make a "public offering" of its securities or interests under Section 3(c)(1) of the Company Act. With respect to the latter criterion, the SEC has stated that a private offering under Section 4(2) or Rule 506 of Regulation D would not be a public offering.[19]

A. Section 3(c)(1) and Counting Investors

An issuer relying on Section 3(c)(1) must continuously monitor the number of beneficial owners of its securities to ensure that it meets the 100 investor test. It is not always easy to determine whether an entity investor (as contrasted to an individual investor) counts as a single beneficial owner for the purposes of the 100 investor test.[20] Under the statutory provision, a two part test is used to determine whether it is necessary to "look-through" an entity investor and count the holders of securities issued by the entity investor as beneficial owners of interests in the investment partnership. The first part of the test asks whether the entity investor owns 10 percent or more of the outstanding voting securities of the issuer. This part of the test must be performed on an ongoing basis and thus, the test can be failed at any point in time, even if the investor reaches the 10 percent level as a result of withdrawals by other investors.

A threshold issue always exists as to whether limited partnership interests are voting securities. If, as is often the case with investment partnerships, the sole matters put to a limited partner vote are amendments to the partnership agreement proposed by the general partners or various matters in the event of dissolution of the limited partnership, the securities may not be considered voting securities.[21] However, while limited partnership interests in an investment partnership arguably may not always constitute voting securities, if the position held by an investor is sufficiently large, the SEC may view the investor as being able to exert sufficient commercial influence on partnership matters such that the interests are akin to voting securities.[22] The SEC has also determined, as a policy matter, that it will treat limited partnership interests as voting securities where an entity investor acquiring more than 10 percent of the interests in the limited partnership is itself relying on the Section 3(c)(1)

---

[19] *See Oppenheimer Arbitrage Partners, L.P.*, SEC No-Action Letter (pub. avail. Dec. 26, 1985); *C&S Investment Funds*, SEC No-Action Letter (pub. avail. July 18, 1977).

[20] Lemke & Lins, *Private Investment Companies Under Section 3(c)(1) of the Investment Company Act of 1940*, 44 Bus. Law. 401 (1989).

[21] *Kohlberg Kravis Roberts & Co.*, SEC No-Action Letter (pub. avail. Sep. 9, 1985).

[22] *Devonshire Capital Corp.*, SEC No-Action Letter (pub. avail. Feb. 15, 1976).

exclusion from the definition of investment company.[23] If the limited partnership interests are not deemed to be voting securities, no look-through is required even if an entity investor holds 10 percent or more of the interests. However, as may often be the case, if the limited partnership interests are deemed to be voting securities, a look-through is required if an entity investor holds 10 percent or more of the interests, but only if the second part of the look-through test is also met.

Under the second part of the Section 3(c)(1) test (which is only applied if the first part of the test is met), if more than 10 percent of the entity investor's assets are invested in securities of entities that are themselves excluded from the definition of investment company by Section 3(c)(1), a look-through is required. This test is conducted only at the time of each investment by the entity investor.[24] This second test was adopted to permit large, widely held entities to make investments in private funds without look-through in circumstances where such investments are small in relation to the size of the investor, but large in relation to the fund. The SEC was concerned, however, that if such investments represented a significant portion of the entity investor's assets, all of the investor's beneficial owners should count as beneficial owners of the fund; hence the 10 percent limit.

In addition to the statutory "look-through" under Section 3(c)(1), "look-through" situations can arise if an entity investor has been formed for the purpose of investing in the fund or if the owners of such entity are able to opt in or out of particular investments. The statutory authority for this look-through policy is found in Section 48(a) of the Company Act which forbids doing indirectly what may not be done directly. Generally, if less than 40 percent of the entity investor's assets are invested in the fund and investment decisions are made centrally, without the ability of the beneficial owners of the entity investor to opt in or opt out of particular investments, no look-through will be required.[25]

Under Section 3(c)(1), if a "look-through" is required, it is the security-holders of the entity investor that must be counted to determine whether the investment partnership meets the 100 investor test, and in certain circumstances the securityholders of entities holding interests in the entity investor. However, certain entities may not have securityholders. For example, the SEC has said that interests in an employee benefit plan would not be securities for purposes of the 100 investor test if the plan was involuntary (i.e., an employee made no decision to invest in the plan, which was automatic upon

[23] Id.; *Weiss, Peck, & Greer Venture Associates II, L.P.*, SEC No-Action Letter (pub. avail. Apr. 10, 1990).

[24] *Weiss Global Hedged Investment Limited Partnership*, SEC No-Action Letter (pub. avail. Nov. 1, 1990); Lemke & Lin's, *supra* note 20.

[25] *Six Pack*, SEC No-Action Letter (pub. avail. Nov. 13, 1989); *Handy Place Investment Partnership*, SEC No-Action Letter (pub. avail. Jul. 19, 1989).

employment) or noncontributory (i.e., assets were not contributed to the plan by the employee), generally defined benefit plans.[26] Under such circumstances, the beneficiaries of the plan are not making any investment decisions and, hence, cannot be deemed to be securityholders. The absence of securityholders should also allow most charities, academic institutions, and foundations to acquire more than 10 percent of the interests in an investment partnership.

The application of the look-through rules can become quite technical, and can require look-through of the chain of ownership in the case of entity investors which themselves hav' significant entity ownership.

B. Integration under Section 3(c)(1)

When an investment manager serving as a general partner to a private investment partnership wishes to start a second fund, the manager must consider whether, for purposes of determining compliance with the 100 investor test of Section 3(c)(1), the two funds must be integrated. Again, the statutory basis for integration is Section 48(a) of the Company Act, which forbids indirect conduct which is forbidden directly. The test developed by the SEC, which is based on the test for integration used by the SEC in determining whether ostensibly private offerings should be integrated for purposes of registration under the Securities Act,[27] is whether a reasonable investor qualified to invest in both funds would view the two funds as being the same in economic reality.[28] In analyzing the issue, the focus has been on the differences between the funds' investment programs, portfolio holdings, and risk/return profiles, with emphasis on the latter factors.[29]

[26] *Kodak Retirement Income Plan*, SEC No-Action Letter (pub. avail. Feb. 29, 1988). *Compare, The Panagora Group Trust*, SEC No-Action Letter (pub. avail. Apr. 29, 1994).

[27] Rule 502(a) of Regulation D; *see generally*, Hicks, *supra* note 3, vol. 7A, sch. 7.

[28] *PBT Covered Option Fund*, SEC No-Action Letter (pub. avail. Feb. 17, 1979), *Oppenheimer Arbitrage Partners, L.P.*, SEC No-Action Letter (pub. avail. Dec. 26, 1985).

[29] The integration analysis for Company Act purposes has its origin in the five factor test used by the SEC in determining whether private placements should be integrated into a public offering. These factors are whether the offerings (i) are part of a single plan of financing; (ii) involve the issuance of the same class of securities; (iii) are made at about the same time; (iv) involve receipt of the same type of consideration; and (v) are made for the same general purpose. While the test enunciated in *PBT Covered Option Fund, supra* note 28, is still the prevalent analysis used by the Staff, the Staff has stated that it is not the exclusive test and that, in appropriate circumstances, the Securities Act test can be used. *See Equitable Capital Management Corp.*, SEC No-Action Letter (pub. avail. Dec. 16, 1991), which involved three asset-backed securities products that had similar investment objectives, portfolio securities, and risk/return characteristics and the Staff nevertheless concluded that integration was not necessary.

An analysis of the no-action letters in this area indicates that, at least in terms of its public statements, the SEC will take the position that integration is required where there is sufficient overlap in the investment portfolios of the funds. Thus, for example, the SEC agreed to issue a no-action letter to the manager of an arbitrage fund and a general equity fund only when the manager agreed to limit the overlap of the securities held by the two funds to 10 percent.[30] In situations involving the integration of small capitalization, large capitalization, and balanced funds, and the integration of two funds where, with respect to one, the manager served as general partner and, with respect to the other, served as the primary portfolio manager pursuant to an investment management agreement, the SEC refused to grant no-action relief.[31]

Where the SEC has been more forthcoming is where two funds have been structured to accommodate the needs of two different types of investors.

In *Oppenheimer Arbitrage Partners, L.P.*, SEC No-Action Letter (pub. avail. Dec. 26, 1985) the Staff concluded that two domestic limited partnerships managed by the same general partner were not subject to integration even though both invested in arbitrage strategies. The primary difference between the funds was that one was designed for taxable investors that wished to participate in a trading program that would utilize leverage and short sales. The other was designed for tax-exempt investors that wished to avoid incurring unrelated business taxable income through an arbitrage program that did not utilize leverage or short sales. The difference was that the investment programs for these two groups of investors was believed to yield materially different risk/reward profiles for the two funds.

Similarly, the general view is that a domestic partnership with U.S. investors and a parallel non-U.S. fund with non-U.S. investors will not be integrated, even though advised by the same investment adviser, as the result of the tax differences to the two types of investors. Further, in *Shoreline Fund, L.P.*, SEC No-Action Letter (pub. avail. Apr. 11, 1994), the Staff granted no-action relief where two investment funds, one domestic and one non-U.S., were managed by the same individuals and had substantially identical investment strategies and securities portfolios. In determining that the two funds need not be integrated for the purposes of the 100 investor test of Section 3(c)(1), the SEC focused on the fact that the two funds would be viewed as "materially different" to investors. One fund, a U.S. limited partnership, proposed to limit its private offering of limited partnership interests exclu-

---

[30] *Meadow Lane Associates, L.P.*, SEC No-Action Letter (pub. avail. May 24, 1989).

[31] *Frontier Capital Management, Incorporated*, SEC No-Action Letter (pub. avail. July 13, 1988), *Monument Capital Management, Incorporated*, SEC No-Action Letter (pub. avail. July 12, 1990).

sively to residents of the United States that were subject to federal income tax. The other fund, an off-shore corporation, proposed to offer its common shares only to non-U.S. persons or, in the United States, exclusively to U.S. tax-exempt investors on a private placement basis. Since the non-U.S. and U.S. tax exempt investors in the offshore corporation were both not subject to U.S. income tax on their investments, and investors in the U.S. limited partnership were subject to such tax, the SEC concluded that: "We are satisfied that the tax treatment of investments in offshore corporations as compared to domestic limited partnerships create materially different investments for taxable and exempt investors." In order to rely on this structuring approach, which permits up to 100 U.S. investors in a domestic fund and up to 100 U.S. tax-exempt investors in a similar or parallel offshore fund, the adviser should ensure that there is no overlap of one type of investor in both funds.

III. Operation of the Fund

A. Registration of General Partner as an Investment Adviser

1. Federal Law

Any person "who, for compensation, engages in the business of advising others . . . as to the advisability of investing in, purchasing or selling securities . . ." is an investment adviser under the Advisers Act.[32] A general partner of an investment partnership who controls the partnership's trading activities or is actively engaged in selecting managers that trade on behalf of the partnership is providing just such ongoing investment advice. Under Section 203 of the Advisers Act, an investment adviser must register with the SEC as such, unless an exemption from registration is available.

The exemption from registration most frequently relied upon is that contained in Section 203(b)(3) of the Advisers Act. Under Section 203(b)(3), so long as the adviser does not hold himself out to the public as an investment adviser,[33] has had fewer than 15 clients in the past 12 months, and does

---

[32] Advisers Act Section 202(a)(11). This section excludes from the definition of investment adviser certain banks, broker-dealers, accountants, lawyers, publishers, and others not directly, or incidentally, involved in providing investment advice.

[33] Advertising, telephone listings, business cards, and letterhead indicating the entity is an investment adviser have all been cited as indicia of "holding oneself out." *See, e.g., George J. Dippold*, SEC No-Action Letter (pub. avail. May 7, 1990). Use of the words "Asset Management" or "Investment Management" in the name of the adviser could also be deemed a "holding out."

not serve as an adviser to a registered investment company or a business development company, an exemption from registration is available. The limited partnership itself will be counted as one client under Rule 203(b)(3)-1 generally, so long as the general partner provides advice to the partnership based on the partnership's objectives rather than tailoring its advice to the needs of particular limited partners.

Registration under the Advisers Act is accomplished by filing with the SEC an application on Form ADV. A Form ADV must contain information regarding the investment adviser's owners and business practices, including but not limited to, compensation schedule, types of accounts, affiliate relationships, brokerage practices, solicitation arrangements, and scope of authority with respect to clients' funds and accounts. In addition, information regarding an investment adviser's personnel (including educational and employment background) and their disciplinary history must be provided on Form ADV. Each investment adviser must keep current the information disclosed in the Form ADV, which must generally be updated once a year.

Under Advisers Act Rule 204-3, a registered adviser must deliver to each advisory client or prospective advisory client a written disclosure statement, which may be either a copy of Part II of the adviser's Form ADV or a written document that includes the information contained in Part II of the adviser's Form ADV. In light of the fact that a general partner cannot meaningfully deliver its Form ADV to itself on behalf of the partnership, Part II of the general partner's Form ADV should be delivered to each prospective investor. An adviser must deliver its written disclosure statement to an advisory client or investor (i) at least 48 hours prior to entering into an advisory contract with such client, or (ii) at the time of entering into an advisory contract or investing in a partnership, if such client has the right to terminate the advisory contract without penalty within five business days after entering into the contract. An adviser must also deliver, or offer in writing to deliver, its written disclosure statement to each advisory client at least annually.

2. State Law

Under the Uniform Securities Act, an "investment adviser" is any person who, for compensation, engages in the business of advising others, either directly or through publications or writings, as to the value of securities or as to the advisability of investing in, purchasing, or selling securities or who, for compensation and as part of a regular business, issues or promulgates analyses or reports concerning securities. The definition of "investment adviser" under the Uniform Securities Act does not include, among other things, a person who has no place of business in the state and (i) whose only clients in the state are other investment advisers, broker-dealers, banks, savings institutions, trust companies, insurance companies, investment companies registered under the Company Act, pension or profit-sharing trusts, or other financial institutions or institutional buyers, whether acting for themselves or as trustees, or (ii) who during any period of 12 consecutive months does not direct business communications into the state in any manner to more than five non-institutional clients, whether or not the adviser or any of the persons to whom communications are directed are then present in the state.

Most states have not formally determined, by statute or regulation, whether an investment partnership is counted as one client of the adviser or whether the state will look through the partnership to determine how many of its residents are investors and also clients of the adviser. Several states have informally advised that they will not look through an investment partnership and have informally taken the position that, in the absence of contrary interpretation of their statutes or regulations, Rule 203(b)(3)-1 under the Advisers Act would apply. Others, however, may take a contrary position and look through an investment partnership to determine who is a client of the general partner. The issue should be reviewed on a state-by-state basis.

B. Incentive Compensation

1. Federal Law

The Advisers Act restricts the ability of registered investment advisers to receive performance-based compensation. Performance-based compensation is generally prohibited under Section 205(a), which provides that a registered investment adviser may not enter into an investment advisory contract where compensation is based on a share of the capital gains or capital appreciation of the funds of a client.

An important exception to Section 205(a) is contained in Rule 205-3, which allows an investment adviser to enter into performance compensation agreements with certain eligible investors. Under Rule 205-3(b), an "eligible investor" includes a natural person or company that has a net worth at the time the contract is entered into of more than $1,000,000 or that immediately after entering into the advisory arrangement has at least $500,000 under the management of the investment adviser. An important qualification to the definition of an "eligible investor" relates to investor entities that are themselves investment funds.

Each beneficial owner of an entity investor must itself be an "eligible investor" under Rule 205-3 if (i) the entity investor would itself be defined as an investment company under Section 3(a) of the Company Act but for the exclusion provided by Section 3(c)(1) of the Company Act (e.g., a fund of funds, family partnership, or any other private investment fund); or (ii) the entity investor is an investment company registered under the Company Act.

Another requirement of Rule 205-3 is that performance-based compensation must be calculated based upon the performance of the client's account for a period of not less than one year. The calculation must include, in the case of securities for which market quotations are readily available, the realized and unrealized capital losses over the period and, in the case of securities for which market quotations are not readily available, at least the realized capital losses of the securities over the period, but if the unrealized capital appreciation of the securities over the period is included the unrealized capital depreciation of the securities over the period must also be included.

Mandatory disclosure under Rule 205-3 includes: (i) the fact that the fee arrangement may create an incentive for the adviser to make investments that are riskier or more speculative than would be the case in the absence of a performance fee; (ii) where relevant, the fact that the investment adviser may receive increased compensation with regard to unrealized appreciation as well as realized gains in the client's account; (iii) the periods which will be used to measure investment performance throughout the contract and their significance in the computation of the fee; (iv) the nature of any index which will be used as a comparative measure of investment performance, the significance of the index, and the reason the investment adviser believes the index is appropriate; and (v) where an investment adviser's compensation is based in part on the unrealized appreciation of securities for which market quotations are not readily available, how the securities will be valued, and the extent to which the valuation will be independently determined. Rule 205-3 also requires that the investment adviser (and any person acting on its behalf) reasonably believe, immediately prior to entering into the contract, that the contract represents an arm's length arrangement between the parties and that the client alone or together with the client's independent agent, understands the proposed method of compensation and its risks.

In the investment partnership context, performance-based compensation generally is either paid as a fee to a management company which serves as the investment adviser or to the general partner as a special allocation of a percentage (frequently 10 to 20 percent) of the fund's investment profits. However, performance compensation is frequently offset by prior unrecouped losses (a "loss carryforward") and/or only taken on profits which exceed a minimum rate of return (a "hurdle rate"). If the general partner is a registered investment adviser (or is affiliated with a registered adviser), this allocation must be calculated in a manner that conforms to Rule 205-3. If limited partners are admitted to the partnership on an interim-year basis, the general partner must usually wait until the limited partner has been an investor in the partnership for at least one year before the performance allocation with respect to that partner is made. Similarly, if limited partners are permitted to withdraw on an interim-year basis, the performance fee or allocation is usually calculated based on performance measured over a period of at least 12 months ending with the interim-year withdrawal date and adjusted so that the fee is not paid for any portion of the period that was already subject to a performance fee calculation.

2. State Law

State regulation of fee arrangements vary from state to state. Several states have statutory or regulatory provisions which prohibit, as a fraudulent practice, the acceptance of performance-based fees as compensation by any investment adviser. Both registered and unregistered investment advisers are subject to these provisions. The restriction is generally modified to allow compensation based on the total value of a fund averaged over a definite period of time. Others states qualify their restrictions on acceptance of performance-based fees by investment advisers, either by statute or by regulation. These qualifications generally serve to bring the state law into compliance with Rule 205-3 of the Advisers Act, by reference or by describing the conditions to Rule 205-3. In general, the conditions to qualify acceptance of performance-based fees are based on the "eligible client" test of all investors in the investment partnership.

C. Registration as a Commodity Pool Operator

1. Basic Requirements

A Commodity Pool Operator (CPO) is defined under the CEA as a person who solicits, accepts, or receives from others funds, securities, or other property (either directly or through capital contributions, the sale of securities or otherwise) for the purpose of trading commodity futures contracts (including financial futures contracts such as stock index futures contracts) or commodity option contracts. The Commodity Futures Trading Commission (CFTC) generally takes the position that any transactions in commodity futures contracts or commodity options by an investment fund, no matter how infrequent or small, will cause the fund to be considered a commodity pool, and the manager/sponsor of the fund to be a CPO.

A CPO registered with the CFTC must also become a member of the National Futures Association (NFA), the self-regulatory organization for the futures industry. Any individual who solicits funds for a commodity pool (or who supervises persons soliciting funds for a commodity pool) must register as an associated person of the CPO (subject to certain exemptions for persons already registered in certain capacities). In addition, subject to a narrow exemption for persons who are not in fact engaged in any solicitation or supervisory activities, any principal of the CPO who is in the "supervisory chain of command," such as the president of a corporation, must register as an associated person even if he or she is not involved in solicitation activities.

Absent an exemption from the CFTC (discussed below), a registered CPO is required to provide a detailed disclosure document (a "Disclosure Document") regarding each commodity pool to each prospective participant in the pool prior to soliciting, accepting, or receiving assets from such prospective participant. The information contained in the Disclosure Document must include, among other items, information about the CPO and its principals, commodity trading advisors (CTAs), futures commission merchants (FCMs), and introducing brokers; the types of commodity interests to be traded; conflicts of interest; the performance record of the CPO and its principals; expenses incurred and to be incurred by the pool; minimum investment amounts; restrictions upon transferability, and redemption of interests; material administrative, civil, or criminal action against a CPO, CTA, FCM, introducing broker, and their principals; and risk disclosure.

The CPO must file the Disclosure Document with the CFTC and with the NFA not less than 21 calendar days prior to the date the CPO first intends to deliver the Disclosure Document to a prospective participant in the pool. Subsequent amendments to the Disclosure Document must be filed with the CFTC and with the NFA within 21 calendar days of the date on which the CPO knows or has reason to know of the defect requiring the amendment. The 21-day waiting period may be waived in the case of a pool exempt from the registration requirements of the Securities Act pursuant to Regulation D, and only sold to "accredited investors," but the Disclosure Document must still be provided to participants and filed with the CFTC and the NFA, and the CFTC may (and in all likelihood will) review and comment on the Disclosure Document.[34] The waiting period may also be waived with respect to offerings under Regulation D for pools that qualify for the Rule 4.12(b) exemption discussed below.

The Disclosure Document must contain information which is current

---

[34] A CPO that conducts its offering under Regulation D and that opts to solicit investors prior to receiving comments on its offering memorandum from the CFTC runs a risk of receiving comments after the offering has commenced, being required to revise the fund's offering materials, and sending them to the prospective investors a second time.

as of the date of the Document, except that performance data may be current as of a date not more than three months preceding the date of the Document. A Disclosure Document may not be used more than six months after it was last updated and filed with the CFTC. A CPO must receive a written acknowledgment from each participant confirming receipt of a Disclosure Document prior to accepting that participant's contribution.

Any type of promotional activity undertaken by a CPO must be in accordance with the relevant NFA compliance guidelines. The CPO must also adopt and enforce written supervisory procedures for promotional material which, at a minimum, require all promotional material to be reviewed and approved by a responsible officer or supervisor prior to its use. Copies of all promotional material, together with a record of the review and approval of the promotional material, must be kept on file by the CPO.

2. Exclusions and Exemptions

a. Rule 4.5. CFTC Rule 4.5 excludes certain persons acting with respect to "qualifying entities" from the definition of a CPO. Such persons must file a notice of eligibility with the CFTC, and do not have to register as CPOs, so long as such qualifying entities only use commodity futures and commodity options for bona fide hedging purposes, or aggregate initial margin and premiums for commodity futures and commodity options do not exceed 5 percent of the value of the qualifying entity's portfolio. However, the definition of qualifying entity is quite restrictive and only includes registered investment companies, insurance company separate accounts, trust and custodial accounts for which a bank or trust company is acting as a fiduciary and for which it is vested with investment authority, and ERISA plans (many of which do not even have to file a notice). Rule 4.5 is thus not available to investment partnerships.

The CFTC has determined in interpretive letters that it will not take action against managers of certain types of group trusts in which participants are certain employee benefit plans, or are other pension plans subject to Title I of ERISA, if such managers do not register as CPOs (provided that, if the group trust will include pension plans other than four types of plans which CFTC Rule 4.5 enumerates as being deemed not to be commodity pools, the operator of the group trust files with the CFTC a notice of eligibility under Rule 4.5).[35] As a result, Rule 4.5 may be available to a fund which is organized as a group trust solely for ERISA plans.

b. Rule 4.12(b). CFTC Rule 4.12(b) permits a registered CPO to obtain relief from certain of the disclosure, reporting, and recordkeeping require-

---

[35] *See, e.g.,* CFTC Interpretative Letter No. 94-52, Comm. Fut. L. Rep. (CCH) ¶26,116 (June 1, 1994); CFTC Interpretative Letter No. 93-91, Comm. Fut. L. Rep. (CCH) ¶25,857 (Sept. 7, 1993).

ments discussed above by filing a claim of exemption with the CFTC. The relief is available to an investment partnership which:

1. Will be offered and sold pursuant to a registration statement filed under the Securities Act, or pursuant to an exemption from registration under the Securities Act;
2. Will generally and routinely trade in securities;
3. Will commit no more than 10 percent of the fair market value of the fund's assets as initial margin or premiums for commodity interest trading; and
4. Will trade in commodity interests in a manner "solely incidental" to its securities trading activities.

The CFTC indicated in the release adopting Rule 4.12(b) that trading in commodity interest transactions will be "solely incidental" to securities trading activities if such trading is not an "integral part" of the fund's trading strategy and the trading strategy can be accomplished without the use of commodity interests.[36] Each existing or prospective participant in the fund must be informed in writing of the Rule 4.12(b) restrictions prior to the date that the fund commences trading commodity interests.

A CPO satisfying these criteria must claim relief under Rule 4.12(b) by filing a claim of exemption with the CFTC, with a copy to the NFA. While a CPO claiming relief under Rule 4.12(b) is not required to comply with all of the disclosure requirements applicable to a pool, it still must provide to its investors, and pre-clear with the CFTC, an offering memorandum complying with many of the disclosure requirements described previously. In addition, while the pool's financial statements and annual reports need not contain all of the information that would be required of a full-fledged commodity pool, financial statements are still required, with annual financial statements being filed with the CFTC and NFA.

c. Rule 4.7. CFTC Rule 4.7 exempts a registered CPO from most of the disclosure and reporting requirements of Part 4 of the CFTC's regulations where investors in the pool are limited to investors that qualify as "Qualified Eligible Participants" (QEPs). The rule defines QEPs to include generally:

1. Registered FCMs, registered broker-dealers, registered CPOs managing pools with more than $5,000,000 in assets, registered CTAs managing commodity accounts with more than $5,000,000 in assets, and the CPO and CTA of the pool being offered;

---

[36] 52 *Federal Register* 41975 (Nov. 2, 1987).

2. Natural persons and entities falling within certain categories similar to those for an "accredited investor" under Regulation D under the Securities Act, who have at least a $2,000,000 investment portfolio, have deposits of at least $200,000 in initial margin and option premiums for commodity interest trading, or have a portfolio satisfying a combined securities and commodity interest threshold. Persons comparable to "accredited investors" for purposes of Rule 4.7 include certain investment companies, banks, insurance companies, employee benefit plans, private business development companies, tax-exempt organizations, corporations, business trusts, partnerships (each generally with total assets in excess of $5,000,000) and high-net worth individuals. Also included in this category are other funds, pools, trusts, insurance company separate accounts or bank collective trusts with total assets in excess of $5,000,000, not formed for the specific purpose of participating in the exempt pool, and whose participation in the exempt pool is directed by a QEP, provided that (except where the entity would be a QEP because all of its equity owners are QEPs) no more than 10 percent of the fair market value of the assets of such entity are used to purchase units in exempt pools;
3. Entities in which all of the equity owners are QEPs; and
4. Non-U.S. persons, as defined in Rule 4.7.

A commodity pool which has made a claim for exemption pursuant to CFTC Rule 4.7 does not have to provide to pool participants a Disclosure Document, or have to file a CEA Disclosure Document with the CFTC or NFA. However, if a Disclosure Document or other form of offering memorandum is provided to participants, the document must include all disclosure necessary to make the information contained therein not misleading.

3. Position Limits

For the purpose of preventing excessive speculation in any commodity futures contract, futures exchanges are required to adopt position limits which limit the maximum net long and net short position which any one person may hold or control in each commodity futures contract, and each put and call option on futures, traded on the exchanges. Such contract market limits, however, are not applicable to "bona fide hedging positions" as defined in CFTC Rule 1.3(z). Certain other exemptions from the position limits for stock index futures are available from the exchanges on which such futures are traded upon application to the exchanges.

The CFTC requires persons holding or controlling positions for future delivery exceeding a specified amount to file reports (CFTC Rule 15.01(c)). Every trader who holds a reportable position must file a Form 40 with the CFTC within 10 business days after assuming reportable status (CFTC Rule 18.04). Form 40 provides the CFTC with biographical information about the trader, identification of other accounts owned or controlled by the trader or in which the trader has a financial interest and identification of all brokers through whom the trader deals at the time the form is filed. Additional information must be provided, depending upon whether the trader is an individual, partnership, or corporation. Form 40 must be filed annually by the reporting trader so long as it continues to hold a reportable position. It must be updated whenever material changes occur in the information it contains.

A trader who holds or controls a reportable position in financial futures is required to keep books and records detailing all positions and transactions in commodity interests on all contract markets and must also furnish additional information regarding such transactions to the CFTC upon request (CFTC Rule 18.05).

D. Marketing

1. Advertising

The SEC regulates marketing and advertising material used by investment advisers, including general partners of private investment partnerships, through Section 206 of the Advisers Act which is the general anti-fraud provision of the Advisers Act. Under Rule 206(4)-1, which applies to registered and unregistered advisers, an "advertisement" includes, among other things: any letter or written communication addressed to more than one person which offers any of the following: (i) any analysis, report, or publication concerning securities or which can be used to determine when to buy or sell securities or which securities to buy or sell; (ii) any graph, chart, formula, or other device which can be used to determine when to buy or sell securities or which securities to buy or sell; or (iii) any other investment advisory service. This definition is broad enough to cover marketing brochures for investment management services and confidential memoranda for private investment funds.

Certain prohibitions under Rule 206(4)-1 have particular relevance to private investment funds. Among other things, the rule prohibits any type of testimonial concerning the adviser or concerning any advice, report, or any other service rendered by the adviser. The term "testimonial" is not defined in the Advisers Act or Rule 206(4)-1. The SEC has characterized a testimonial as "a statement of a customer's experience or endorsement."[37] Testimonials are prohibited because they may give rise to a fraudulent or deceptive implication, or mistaken inference, that the experience of the person giving the testimonial is typical of the experience of the adviser's clients.

Kurtz Capital Management SEC No-Action Letter (pub. avail. Feb. 16, 1988) illustrates an important exception to the ban on testimonials: the use of bona-fide, unbiased, third-party reports in a newspaper or magazine. Under *Kurtz*, an adviser may include in its marketing materials a reprint of an article in a business publication that discusses an adviser's strategy or outlook without running afoul of the ban on testimonials. However, such reprints cannot be used if they fail to disclose additional facts which, if disclosed, would imply different results than those set forth in the article.

In addition to prohibiting testimonials, Rule 206(4)-1 prevents the disclosure of past recommendations by the adviser which were or would have been profitable to any person unless *a list of all recommendations* made by the adviser over at least the past year is provided or offered to be provided. The first page of any brochure containing or describing the recommendations must include a statement that:

IT SHOULD NOT BE ASSUMED THAT RECOMMENDATIONS MADE IN THE FUTURE WILL BE PROFITABLE OR WILL EQUAL THE PERFORMANCE OF THE SECURITIES ON THIS LIST.

Rule 206(4)-1 also prohibits any direct or indirect representation by an adviser to the effect that a particular investment program or strategy can, in and of itself, be used to determine which securities to buy or sell or when to buy or sell them without prominently disclosing all of the limitations and difficulties associated with such a device. This rule is designed to prevent unwarranted claims with respect to "black box" investment strategies, where investment decisions are claimed to be made on the basis of objective factors.

In addition to specifically prohibited advertising practices mentioned above, Paragraph (a)(5) of Rule 206(4)-1 prohibits any advertisement which contains "any untrue statement of a material fact or which is otherwise false or misleading."

---

[37] *See, e.g., J. Y. Barry Arbitrage Management Inc.*, SEC No-Action Letter (pub. avail. Oct. 18, 1989). In *John Anthony*, SEC No-Action Letter (pub. avail. Apr. 18, 1975), the Staff dealt with necessary disclosures for a psychic medium who used ESP to make stock selections. In addition to reminding Mr. Anthony that he had to prominently disclose that the predictive value of extrasensory perception has not been scientifically established, the Staff took the position that the word "recognized" in an advertisement referring to the adviser as a "recognized powerful psychic medium" would constitute an indirect testimonial under Rule 206(4)-1.

2. Presentation of Performance

In a number of no-action letters, the Staff has provided guidance on the presentation of performance information by investment advisers, both registered and unregistered[38]. In presenting a fund's track record, the following principles should be observed:

(i) Advisory fees, brokerage or other commissions, and any other client expenses should be deducted from performance.

(ii) The effect of any material market or economic conditions on the results should be disclosed. If the fund and the market moved in lockstep, this may be relevant information to an investor.

(iii) It may be relevant to disclose how the market performed during the period through the presentation of an appropriate index. Of course, any facts bearing on the fairness of the comparison must be disclosed (e.g., nature of the index, whether the figures for the index assume reinvestment of dividends).

(iv) All material differences between the fund's results and any index used for comparison must be disclosed (e.g., if the volatility of the index is greater than that of the fund's portfolio, this should be disclosed).

(v) The possibility of loss must be disclosed.

(vi) Material conditions, objectives, or investment strategies used to obtain the fund's results (e.g., specific types of equity securities, hedging techniques).

(vii) The size of the fund during the periods presented should be disclosed. Disclosing that the fund appreciated 50 percent for the year without saying whether the fund consisted of $100,000 in assets or $100 million in assets fails to provide material information to an investor.

While generally, performance must be shown net of advisory and other fees, the Staff has permitted written performance material used in one-on-one presentations made to sophisticated persons in a private and confidential manner and not made to the public to show performance on a "gross basis" so long as certain guidelines are followed.[39] The guidelines

---

[38] *Clover Capital Management, Inc.*, SEC No-Action Letter (pub. avail. Oct. 28, 1986).

[39] *Clover Capital Management, Inc.*, SEC No-Action Letter (pub. avail. July 19, 1991).

are: (i) that written disclosure be made that the performance figures do not reflect the deduction of advisory fees and that the client's return will be reduced by such fees and expenses; (ii) the client must be advised that the adviser's fees are described in Part II of the adviser's Form ADV, or an equivalent disclosure document; and (iii) an example must be provided to the prospective investor that shows the effect an advisory fee would have on the total value of the client's account, compounded over a period of years. The utility of this approach is questionable in the private fund area since one-on-one presentations are not always made. Alternatively, some investment advisers show both gross and net performance in the same table.

An issue that frequently must be confronted in presenting performance for a newly organized fund is whether the manager's performance at another employer or for another account may be shown. Here, the guiding principles are that the manager must have been primarily responsible for achieving the results presented and that the account presented must be sufficiently similar to the fund to make comparison to the fund meaningful and relevant to an investor.[40] Performance of an account other than the fund should not be presented once the fund is up and running for a year.

E. Allocations among Client Accounts and Transactions among Advisers and Client Accounts

1. Allocations among Client Accounts

Investment advisers servicing multiple clients should have well defined procedures for allocating among those clients securities purchased in blocks, or during a trading day, rather than merely waiting until a convenient time to allocate the results of their trading activity. The need for such procedures stems from the fiduciary duties that the adviser owes to each of its clients to treat them fairly and act in their best interests.

In *Kemper Financial Services, Inc.*,[41] a portfolio manager of Kemper did not allocate trades in S&P futures contracts at the time the trades were executed but, rather, waited until he could observe the performance of the trades. The better trades went into an in-house benefit plan account and the weaker trades went to client accounts. The SEC made clear that allocations of trades among client accounts should be made prior to the actual trades being made or through an "established proper allocation system."

---

[40] *Growth Stock Outlook*, SEC No-Action Letter (pub. avail. Apr. 7, 1988).

[41] *In the Matter of Kemper Financial Services, Inc.*, Advisers Act Release No. 1387 (Oct. 20, 1993).

Similarly, in *Michael L. Smirlock*,[42] the head of the fixed-income desk of a registered investment advisory firm failed to allocate purchases of mortgage-backed securities to particular client accounts for a period of between two and nine business days. The individual was fined, even though these late allocations did not cause the firm's clients any loss. The trader failed to promptly prepare order tickets allocating the trades, and instead waited until the securities were sold to write both the purchase and sale tickets. The SEC found this conduct violative of various record-keeping requirements under Rule 204-2 of the Advisers Act. While the language in *Smirlock* used the vague requirement of "promptly" preparing allocated tickets, it indicates that recordkeeping violations would exist during virtually any period that the adviser's records do not reflect the precise interest of each client.

One can conclude from the SEC's positions in these administrative proceedings that, whenever possible, pre-execution allocation of trades is the appropriate manner in which to make allocations among client accounts. However, in the event that pre-execution allocation is not practicable, the next safest course of action would be to have in place an allocation system which operates on a fair and equitable basis and which is promptly reflected in written orders.

2. Principal and Agency-Cross Transactions

Section 206(3) of the Advisers Act prohibits an adviser, when acting as principal for its own account, from knowingly selling any security to or purchasing any security from a client, without prior written disclosure to, and prior written consent from, the client. It also generally prohibits an adviser, when acting as a broker for a person other than its client, from knowingly effecting any sale or purchase of any security for the account of the client, without prior written disclosure and consent. It is unclear whether "acting as a broker" means acting as a registered broker-dealer.[43]

Under Section 206(3), written consent to principal and agency-cross transactions generally must be obtained on a trade-by-trade basis before the trade. However, the SEC has adopted Rule 206(3)-2 which permits a registered investment adviser to make agency-cross transactions through an affiliate registered broker-dealer if adequate disclosure is provided to the client and advance consent is obtained, although written confirmations of each transaction and annual reports on such transactions must be provided to each client, and certain other requirements must be met.

---

[42] *In the Matter of Michael L. Smirlock*, Advisers Act Release No. 1393 (Nov. 29, 1993).

[43] *Compare In the Matter of Dimitri Balatsos*, Advisers Act Release No. 1324 (Aug. 18, 1992), with *Smirlock, supra*, in note 42.

In the investment partnership context, obtaining consent to principal and agency-cross transactions is a cumbersome, and perhaps impracticable process. Because the general partner has a conflict of interest and may be deemed a principal, the effectiveness of its consent on behalf of the partnership is questionable. For the provision to be meaningful in the partnership context, consent would have to be sought from the limited partners of the partnership. A general partner of a partnership should either avoid all principal and agency-cross transactions or, perhaps, consideration should be given to including a provision in the limited partnership agreement whereby a majority-in-interest of the limited partners not affiliated with the general partner could consent to agency cross or principal transactions.

F. Personal Trading and Compliance

Investment advisers should address whether, and if so the manner in which, they and their employees may invest or trade in securities for their own account. Although personal trading by investment advisers and their employees is not prohibited or explicitly limited by statute or regulation (other than restrictions on "insider trading" under the Exchange Act), personal trading in various circumstances may constitute a breach of fiduciary duty and fraudulent conduct prohibited by Section 206 of the Advisers Act, may violate various provisions of the Company Act and ERISA and may, if not adequately disclosed, constitute a material omission giving rise to rescission claims under the Securities Act in the context of offerings of investment fund securities.

The SEC has made clear over the years its concern that investment advisers should not benefit from personal investments which are timed to benefit from client investments, such as "front-running." Similarly, the SEC has made clear that investment advisers and their employees cannot appropriate to themselves investment opportunities that should belong to their clients or use client investments to generate personal investment opportunities.[44] These concerns apply whether or not the investment adviser is advising registered or unregistered investment funds, and, because they give rise to anti-fraud concerns under the Advisers Act, logically apply equally to both registered and unregistered investment advisers.

In order to comply with their fiduciary responsibilities regarding their and their employee's personal trading, investment advisers should adopt a compliance manual, also called a Code of Ethics, to set out guidelines on permissible personal trading, as well as other compliance matters generally.

---

[44] *In the Matter of Joan Conan*, Advisers Act Release 1446 (Sept. 30, 1994); *U.S. v. Ostrander*, 999 F.2d 27 (2d Cir. 1993).

In fact, the Advisers Act and the Company Act contain various provisions which suggest, if not always explicitly require, the adoption of a compliance manual and code of ethics to govern investment advisory firms and employees.

First, Section 203(e)(5) of the Advisers Act authorizes the SEC to censure, limit the activities, functions or operations, suspend, or revoke the registration of any investment adviser if it finds that such action is in the public interest and that such investment adviser, or any person associated with such investment adviser,

> *has failed reasonably to supervise, with a view to preventing violations of the provisions of [the Securities Act, the Exchange Act, the Company Act, the Advisers Act, the CEA, the rules and regulations under any of such statutes, or the rules of the Municipal Securities Rulemaking Board], another person who commits such a violation, if such other person is subject to his supervision. For the purposes of this paragraph (5) no person shall be deemed to have failed reasonably to supervise any person, if—*
>
> *(A) There have been established procedures, and a system for applying such procedures, which would reasonably be expected to prevent and detect, insofar as practicable, any such violation by such other person, and*
>
> *(B) Such person has reasonably discharged the duties and obligations incumbent upon him by reason of such procedures and system without reasonable cause to believe that such procedures and system were not being complied with.*

In fact, the failure of an investment advisory firm to supervise one of its partners in order to prevent securities fraud violations has resulted in censure of the firm by the SEC. *In the Matter of Shearson Lehman Brothers, Inc., In the Matter of Stein Roe & Farnham*[45], (the investment firm agreed, without admitting or denying the allegations, to engage an independent consultant to examine the manner in which it administered its investment advisory operations).

Second, Section 204A of the Advisers Act requires every investment adviser to establish, maintain, and enforce written policies and procedures reasonably designed, taking into consideration the nature of such investment adviser's business, to prevent the misuse in violation of this Act of the

---

[45] Advisers Act Release No. 1038 (Sept. 24, 1986).

Securities Exchange Act of 1934, or the rules and regulations thereunder, of material, nonpublic information by such investment adviser or any person associated with such investment adviser. Section 204A thus requires investment advisory firms to establish written policies and procedures to prevent insider trading.[46]

In addition, Rule 204-2(a)(12) under the Advisers Act, discussed in Section III-J-5 below, requires every investment adviser to keep true, accurate, and current records of transactions in securities by the adviser and its employees. Rule 204-2(a)(12) further provides that "[a]n investment adviser shall not be deemed to have violated the provisions of subparagraph (12) because of his failure to record securities transactions of any advisory representative if he establishes that he instituted adequate procedures and used reasonable diligence to obtain promptly reports of all transactions required to be recorded."

Although an investment adviser may not be subject to the requirements of the Company Act unless it acts as an adviser to a registered investment company, Rule 17j-1(b)(1) of the Company Act specifically requires every registered investment company, and each investment adviser of or principal underwriter for such investment company, to "adopt a written code of ethics containing provisions reasonably necessary to prevent its access persons from engaging in any act, practice, or course of business prohibited by paragraph (a) of this section and . . . use reasonable diligence, and institute procedures reasonably necessary, to prevent violations of such code." Rather than outline uniform procedures, the SEC adopted rule 17j-1 without express guidelines to allow each investment company to design codes of ethics suited to its particular practices.[47]

Neither the CEA nor regulations adopted by the CFTC require a commodity trading advisor to adopt a compliance manual. However, each member of the NFA has a continuing responsibility to "diligently supervise its employees and agents in the conduct of their commodity futures activities for or on behalf of the Member" under NFA Compliance Rule 2-9. Other NFA Compliance Rules impose more specific supervisory responsibility on members and require members to adopt written procedures to ensure compliance with various NFA rules. Rule 2-8(b) provides detailed requirements for supervision of discretionary accounts. Rule 2-29(d) governing communications with the public and promotional material also directs members to adopt and enforce written supervisory procedures to ensure that any communication with the public and any promotional material comply with the

---

[46] *In the Matter of Gabelli & Company, Inc.*, Adviser's Act Release 1457 (Dec. 8, 1994).

[47] Company Act Release No. 11421 (Oct. 31, 1980).

NFA's rules. Rule 2-30(h), governing customer information and disclosure, also requires members to establish and enforce "adequate procedures" to review all records made of information obtained from customers and to supervise activities of their Associates, as defined in Rule 1-1, in obtaining customer information and providing risk disclosure. Rule 2-30(h) does not expressly require written procedures, but rather affords each member flexibility to tailor the procedures to its particular practice.

ERISA does not impose any specific requirement on investment advisers who act as fiduciaries of accounts subject to ERISA to adopt compliance procedures. However, Section 502(l), which gives the Secretary of Labor discretion to impose a 20 percent penalty in addition to directing recovery of losses sustained for a breach of fiduciary duty, provides that the Secretary may waive or reduce the penalty if the Secretary determines that the fiduciary has acted "reasonably and in good faith." The adoption and enforcement of a compliance manual and code of ethics may indicate a fiduciary's reasonableness and good faith, which could contribute to a reduction of liability for ERISA violations.

G. Custody of Client Assets

Under the Advisers Act, an investment adviser who has or who is deemed to have custody of its clients' assets must comply with the provisions of Rules 204-2(b) and 206(4)-2 under the Advisers Act.

An investment adviser may be deemed to have custody of client assets where it has access to the assets of a partnership for its own account — for example, by withdrawing funds to pay itself a management fee, by allocating to itself an incentive allocation, or by withdrawing its own capital. Moreover, the SEC has made it clear that an adviser who has general access to client funds, which is inherent in the authority generally held by a general partner, will be deemed to have custody of those assets.

Rule 206(4)-2 imposes substantive requirements on investment advisers, including that client funds must be maintained at a bank, securities must be segregated, marked to identify the particular client who owns them and held in safekeeping, statements must be sent to the client at least quarterly and an independent public accountant must conduct an annual surprise audit to monitor compliance with the Rule. These requirements are intended, among other things, to protect investors against an investment adviser utilizing client funds or securities for its own benefit.

Most advisers serving as general partners to partnerships prefer to avoid having custody of client assets, if only to avoid the cost and inconvenience of a surprise audit. To this end, an arrangement, approved by the SEC in a series of no-action letters, has been developed whereby an independent bank or broker-dealer holds the assets of the fund and an independent representative—an attorney or certified public accountant—reviews and "authorizes" any transfers to the adviser.[48]

Under these types of arrangements, the independent bank or broker-dealer acting as custodian should receive capital contributions directly from the limited partners. The funds or securities should be held in the name of the partnership, and the partnership must maintain records regarding the location of all funds and securities and all transactions. The partnership should receive from the custodian, at least quarterly, statements detailing all transactions in the account for the period. In addition, the partnership should instruct the custodian to furnish copies of the statements to the independent representative. The books and records of the partnership should be audited annually by an independent certified public accounting firm.

Specific instructions should be given to the custodian regarding when funds can be transferred to the general partner. In general, this will be permitted only in certain, limited instances which are provided for in the limited partnership agreement. These instances could include: payment of a management fee or making an incentive allocation, both of which are calculated using formulae specified in the agreement, withdrawal of capital by the general partner from its capital account, or any annual or periodic distributions.

When the general partner is entitled to receive funds from the partnership, it must notify the custodian and the independent representative and provide information regarding the amount to be transferred and the manner in which the amount was calculated. The request should include the value of the partnership's assets on which the requested fee, withdrawal, or distribution is based. The custodian should be instructed not to transfer any funds or securities to the investment adviser except upon written confirmation of the independent representative that the transfer is calculated in accordance with the partnership agreement.

Most independent representatives will seek to state to the custodian that nothing has come to the their attention that would lead them to believe that the requested transfers are not in accordance with the terms of the partnership agreement, but not that they have independently verified assets. The confirmation should state, however, that it is based on the representative's review of the adviser's calculations, the partnership agreement, and the other documents, if any, that it believes are necessary to provide the con-

[48] *See Blum Shapiro Financial Services, Inc.*, SEC No-Action Letter (pub. avail. Apr. 16, 1993); *Clifford Associates*, SEC No-Action Letter (pub. avail. Sept. 22, 1992); *Daniel H. Renberg & Assoc.*, SEC No-Action Letter (pub. avail. Jan. 3, 1983).

firmation. An audit or other formal testing procedure is not required in connection with the confirmation procedure.

Transfers of funds or securities other than those for the benefit of the general partner may be effected upon direction from a designated officer or employee of the general partner, so long as such transfers are limited to the following circumstances:

1. transfers for the account of the partnership to brokers, banks, or trust companies that, to the best of the custodian's knowledge, are independent of the adviser;
2. transfers to partners of the partnership other than affiliates of the adviser;
3. transfers to other third parties that, to the best of the custodian's knowledge, are independent of the adviser (e.g., attorneys and accountants) in payment for fees or other charges;
4. transfers to independent third parties for any other purpose that, to the best of the custodian's knowledge, are legitimately associated with the management of the partnership (e.g., acceptance of a tender offer or a subscription in connection with a rights offering); or
5. transfers with brokers in connection with purchases and sales on a payment versus delivery basis.

A written agreement setting out the terms of the arrangement with the custodian should be prepared.

H. Use of Soft Dollars

1. General

A soft dollar arrangement generally refers to an arrangement between an investment manager and a broker whereby a portion of the commissions generated by the investment manager through the purchase and sale of securities on behalf of investors is used to purchase goods or services that will be utilized by the investment manager.

These arrangements often give rise to a conflict of interest. In situations where the goods and services would have been paid for by the investment manager absent the soft dollar arrangement or where the commissions generated by the investment manager exceed the lowest commissions available, the resulting conflict should be of concern to every investment manager.

In 1975, Congress amended the Exchange Act to add Section 28(e). Section 28(e) provides a safe harbor to an investment adviser for the use of soft dollars where all of its elements are present.[49] In general, Section 28(e) provides a safe harbor to an investment adviser who exercises discretion over an account with respect to the use of commissions in connection with effecting transactions in equity securities to acquire brokerage and research services provided by the broker if the investment adviser determines in good faith that the amount of the commission paid is reasonable in relation to the value of such services, subject to the adviser's general duty to obtain best execution.

Brokerage services include execution, clearance, settlement, and custody. Research services are those services that provide lawful and appropriate assistance to the investment manager in carrying out his investment decision-making responsibilities. The broker should either generate the research services itself or have entered into a direct contractual relationship with a third-party provider whereby the broker incurs the obligation to pay the provider.

Notwithstanding the protections of Section 28(e), it is well established that an investment manager must exercise its fiduciary discretion to direct brokerage to benefit its clients and must generally seek to obtain "best execution." In particular, an investment adviser should not commit, through a contract or understanding, to direct a specified level of brokerage to a broker in a set period because doing so may not be in the best interest of the adviser's clients and as a result would be a breach of its fiduciary duty.[50]

Registered investment managers must comply with the disclosure requirements of Form ADV and provide clients with material information about the investment manager's brokerage allocation policies and practices, and describe the factors it considers in choosing a broker-dealer and in determining whether a commission rate is reasonable. The investment manager must describe (if research or other services are relevant to brokerage allocation): (i) the products, research, and services received; (ii) whether clients may pay commissions higher than those obtainable from other bro-

---

[49] Investment managers, from time to time, engage in soft dollar practices outside of Section 28(e)'s safe harbor. Practices outside of the safe harbor must be given careful consideration. Such practices must be clearly contemplated by the fund's governing documents and disclosure of the practices should be made and client consent should be obtained. The non-Section 28(e) services acquired should be used solely for the benefit of the fund generating the soft dollars. It would be advisable to set out the dollar amount of soft dollars used for non-Section 28(e) services in the fund's financial statements. Where the SEC has found inadequate disclosure and client consent, it has not hesitated to censure and fine investment managers.

[50] *See generally, In the Matter of Stein Roe & Farnham Incorporated*, Advisers Act Release No. 1217; Company Act Release No. 17316 (Jan. 22, 1990).

kers for those products and services; (iii) whether the research received benefits all of the investment manager's clients or only those who pay for it; and (iv) any procedures the investment manager used during its last fiscal year to direct client securities transactions to a particular broker in return for the products and research services received. Form ADV also requires disclosure of arrangements whereby the investment manager receives economic benefits from any nonclient (including commissions, equipment, or nonresearch services) in connection with providing investment management services to clients (e.g., includes all benefits not within Section 28(e)).

2. ERISA and Section 28(e)

Where an investment manager is a fiduciary to an employee benefit plan subject to ERISA, the investment manager must meet the fiduciary responsibility standards of ERISA.

In general, a plan's assets must be held for the exclusive purposes of providing benefits to the plan participants and defraying reasonable expenses of administering the plan. The investment manager must act prudently and solely in the interest of the plan participants. The investment manager cannot cause the plan to engage in a transaction if it would result in the transfer of plan assets to the fiduciary or to any other party-in-interest (i.e., a broker for the investment manager). Finally, the investment manager cannot engage in self-dealing transactions and cannot receive consideration from a party dealing with the plan.

In Technical Release 86-1 (the "Release"), the Department of Labor (DOL) acknowledged that soft dollar arrangements coming within Section 28(e) do not violate ERISA. The Release contains an example of a situation where an investment manager retained by a plan acquires research in return for brokerage. Although the research related to tax-exempt securities which would not be a suitable investment for the plan, such research was useful to the investment manager's accounts as a whole. The DOL indicated that this arrangement falls within Section 28(e) and does not violate ERISA.

Where investment management responsibility has been properly delegated by a plan trustee to an investment manager, the investment manager has fiduciary responsibility for trading decisions. The plan trustee has oversight responsibility to periodically review the investment manager's performance. Oversight responsibility exists even when the investment manager has entered into a Section 28(e) soft dollar arrangement. The plan trustee must monitor the investment manager to assure that the investment manager is seeking best execution and that the commissions paid are reasonable in light of the services received. If the plan trustee invests in a fund which is not "ERISA Plan Assets"[51] the plan trustee, as a fiduciary, has the responsibility to determine on an ongoing basis that the plan's investment in the fund is prudent. This evaluation should include the general trading practices of the fund. However, the plan's trustee would not be required to monitor on a regular basis whether the fund is seeking and receiving best execution.

3. Directed Brokerage Arrangements

Directed brokerage refers to an arrangement whereby a client, generally a plan sponsor, requests its investment manager, subject to best execution, to direct commissions to a particular broker who will provide services, pay obligations, or make cash rebates to the client. Such arrangements are outside of Section 28(e) because Section 28(e) is only available to persons who are exercising investment discretion. The client who instructs an investment manager to use a particular broker is not exercising "investment discretion" over the account managed by the adviser.

Such arrangements generally pose few issues with respect to most clients. However, under ERISA, such an arrangement must be for the exclusive benefit of the plan and cannot benefit the plan trustee or any other party. The plan documents should be reviewed to determine that any expenses being paid through commission dollars are, in fact, plan expenses. Representations from the plan trustee to this effect should also be obtained. In fulfilling its fiduciary obligations to the plan, the plan trustee who instructs the investment manager to use a particular broker must initially determine that the broker is capable of providing best execution and evaluate whether the commissions are reasonable in light of the services provided and periodically monitor the broker's execution of transactions for the plan.

I. Reporting Requirements under the Exchange Act

A fund's investment activities may subject it and its investment manager to certain reporting obligations and investment restrictions under the Exchange Act. These obligations and restrictions may be triggered by the size of the fund's investment in a particular company, the size of the fund itself, or the fund's level or program of trading activity.

1. Section 13(d) and Section 13(g)

Section 13(d) of the Exchange Act requires any person or group of persons that has acquired direct or indirect beneficial ownership of more than 5 per-

---

[51] *See* Section IV-A below.

cent of a class of voting equity securities registered under the Exchange Act to file a statement with the SEC. The statement may be filed on Schedule 13D or, if the investor and the transaction are appropriately qualified, on Schedule 13G.

Subject to the availability of Schedule 13G, a Schedule 13D must be filed with the SEC, and a copy must be sent to the issuer and to each exchange on which the securities are traded, within 10 days following the acquisition that makes the investor a 5 percent beneficial owner. For purposes of Section 13(d), the beneficial owner of securities is the person (or group of persons acting in concert) who has or shares voting and/or investment power over the securities.[52] A person who has the right to acquire securities within 60 days, due to the exercise of options, warrants, or other derivative securities or the conversion of convertible securities, is deemed to be the beneficial owner of the underlying securities. Schedule 13D contains information regarding (i) the identity of the investor, (ii) the source of the funds used to make the acquisition, (iii) the purpose of the investment, (iv) the number and percentage of securities owned, (v) the nature of the ownership interest in the securities, (vi) voting power with respect to the securities, and (vii) material contracts or arrangements with respect to the securities. In addition, all written arrangements relating to, among other things, the financing of the acquisition and any proposed acquisition of control of, or extraordinary transaction with respect to, the issuer must be filed as exhibits to Schedule 13D. In the context of an investment partnership, the information requested on Schedule 13D must be provided with respect to the partnership itself, each general partner, and any person controlling a general partner.

Schedule 13D must be amended periodically to reflect any material changes to the facts set forth therein. Acquisitions or dispositions of securities constituting 1 percent or more of the class of securities with respect to which the Schedule 13D has been filed are considered to be "material" changes, and smaller acquisitions or dispositions may be deemed to be material as well, depending on the facts and circumstances.

Schedule 13G is available to, among others, registered investment advisers and registered broker-dealers, provided that such persons have acquired the securities in the ordinary course of business and not with the purpose or effect of changing or influencing the control of the issuer. Schedule 13G must be filed with the SEC, and must be sent to the issuer and to the principal national securities exchange on which such securities are traded, within 45 days of the end of the calendar year in which a person held in excess of 5 percent of a class of voting equity securities registered under the

---

[52] Rule 13d-3.

Exchange Act as of the end of such calendar year. Schedule 13G is a short form version of Schedule 13D, requiring information regarding only (i) the identity of the investor, (ii) the nature of the ownership interests in the securities, and (iii) voting power with respect to the securities. Schedule 13G must also disclose any other person that the filing person knows to have the power to receive or direct the receipt of dividends from, or the proceeds from the sale of, 5 percent of the class of securities with respect to which the Schedule 13G is being filed.[53]

In addition, a qualified investor must file a Schedule 13G within 10 days after the end of the first month in which such investor's beneficial ownership interest in a class of registered equity securities as of the end of such month exceeds 10 percent of such class, and such investor must file a Schedule 13G within 10 days after the end of any month thereafter in which such investor's beneficial ownership of such class of securities increases or decreases by more than 5 percent of such class of securities as of the last day of such month.[54] Once the investor reports that its beneficial ownership interest has fallen below 5 percent of the class of registered equity securities, Schedule 13G filings no longer need to be made unless beneficial ownership again exceeds 5 percent.

Schedule 13G must be amended within 45 days after the end of each calendar year to reflect any changes from the previous filing, except that no filing is required if the only changes resulted from a change in the number of the issuer's securities outstanding.[55]

Those required to file Schedule 13D and 13G must do so electronically via the SEC's Electronic Data Gathering, Analysis, and Retrieval System (EDGAR) if the registrant to which the statement relates is an electronic filer.[56] The phase-in of all registrants to the EDGAR system is underway and is scheduled to be completed by May 1996.[57] If a Schedule 13D or 13G relates to a phased-in registrant, the filer must obtain its own EDGAR access codes from the SEC. The filer may make the filing under the SEC's electronic filing software (EDGARLink) or choose a law firm or financial printer to act as its filing agent. If a Schedule 13D or 13G has been filed previously in paper, the first amendment required to be filed electronically must be a complete restatement of the Schedule 13D or 13G.[58]

---

[53] Item 6 of Schedule 13G.

[54] Rule 13d-1(b)(2).

[55] Rule 13d-2(b).

[56] Rule 101(a) of Regulation S-T.

[57] *See* Securities Act Release No. 33-7122 (Dec. 20, 1994).

[58] Rule 101(a)(2)(ii) of Regulation S-T.

2. Section 13(f)

Section 13(f) imposes a quarterly reporting requirement on institutional investment managers with investment discretion over accounts holding "Section 13(f) securities" with a fair market value of at least $100,000,000 as of the end of any month during the calendar year.[59] Section 13(f) securities are voting equity securities traded on a national securities exchange or quoted on an automated quotation system of a registered securities association, a list of which is published by the SEC. A Form 13F must be filed within 45 days of the end of the first calendar year in which such threshold is passed and within 45 days after the last day of each calendar quarter of subsequent calendar years. Form 13F contains information regarding the securities managed by the investment manager (including their fair market value), the nature of the investment discretion held by the manager with respect to such securities and the voting power held by the manager with respect to such securities.[60] Short positions in Section 13(f) securities are not required to be reported on Form 13F, and the SEC takes the position that short sales "against the box" are not offset against the long position to be reported on Form 13F.

3. Section 16

By virtue of owning in excess of 10 percent of a class of voting equity securities registered under the Exchange Act,[61] an investment partnership may become subject to the restrictions of Section 16, which requires that insiders (i) disclose all trades in the equity securities of the issuer, (ii) disgorge short-swing profits derived from any purchase and sale of the issuer's securities taking place within a six-month period, and (iii) generally not engage in short sales of the issuer's securities.

For purposes of determining whether a person is a 10 percent beneficial owner for Section 16 purposes, the definition of beneficial ownership used under Section 13(d) applies; however, certain investors (including registered broker-dealers and registered investment advisers) are not deemed

---

[59] Section 13(f)(1) and Rule 13f-1(a).

[60] Holdings of fewer than 10,000 shares (or less than $200,000 principal amount in the case of convertible debt securities) and less than $200,000 aggregate fair market value (and option holdings to purchase only such amounts) need not be reported on Form 13F. *See* Special Instruction (iii) to Form 13F.

[61] Persons may also become subject to the restrictions of Section 16 by virtue of being officers or directors of an issuer. Investment partnerships may become subject to Section 16 if a general partner is "deputized" to represent the fund as a director of an issuer, even if the fund holds less than 10 percent of a class of voting equity securities.

beneficial owners of securities held for the benefit of third parties or in customer or fiduciary accounts in the ordinary course of business.[62] Within 10 days after becoming a 10 percent owner, a person must file a Form 3 with the SEC, and send copies to the issuer and to the principal national securities exchange on which the security is traded, disclosing its interests in any equity securities (and certain convertible or derivative securities) of the issuer. Thereafter, any transactions (except for certain transactions exempted by rule) in the issuer's securities by such person must be reported on Form 4 within 10 days of the end of the month in which they occur.[63] In addition, a Form 5 filing may be required annually within 45 days of the end of the issuer's fiscal year to report certain transactions not required to be reported on Form 4 or to report delinquent trades that were not previously reported on Form 3 or Form 4.[64] General partners of an investment partnership which is a 10 percent holder may be deemed the beneficial owner of all or a portion of the investment partnership's holdings and may also be subject to Section 16's reporting and liability provisions.[65]

Section 16(b) requires that any profit derived from a purchase and sale, or sale and purchase, of the issuer's securities occurring within any six-month period during which a person is a corporate insider must be disgorged to the issuer. Profits for Section 16(b) purposes may exceed actual profits realized, since Section 16(b) profits are determined by matching the highest priced sales with the lowest priced purchases during the six-month period in order that the provisions of Section 16 will have the maximum deterrent effect. The purchase which brings a shareholder above the 10 percent threshold is not considered a purchase transaction for purposes of determining whether there have been purchases and sales within a six-month period.[66]

Section 16(c) further restricts the ability of a 10 percent holder to trade in the securities of an issuer by preventing short sales unless the insider owns an amount of securities at least equal to the amount being sold short (a

---

[62] Rule 16a-1(a)(1).

[63] Section 16(a); Rule 16a-3(a).

[64] Rule 16a-3(f). Examples of transactions that need not be reported on Form 4 but should be reported on Form 5 include (i) the exercise of certain options granted under employee benefit plans exempt from the short-swing profit prohibition of Section 16(b) pursuant to Rule 16b-3 and (ii) certain small acquisitions of equity securities that, under Rule 16a-6, would not have to be reported on Form 4 unless a Form 4 would otherwise have to be filed.

[65] Rule 16a-1(a)(2)(ii)(B).

[66] Rule 16a-2(c).

"short sale against the box") and delivers the securities within 20 days of the sale or places them in the mail within 5 days of the sale.[67]

J. Record Keeping

Registered investment advisers are subject to extensive record-keeping requirements under the Advisers Act. Most of these requirements are set forth in Advisers Act Rule 204-2. Unregistered investment advisers are generally not subject to the record-keeping requirements of the Advisers Act. In light of their fiduciary obligations to their clients, however, unregistered advisers should comply with the record-keeping requirements of the Advisers Act to the extent practicable.

Books and records required under the Advisers Act must generally be kept in an office of the adviser for a period of two years, and in an easily accessible place for a period of three additional years. Organizational documents relating to a registered adviser's business (such as articles of incorporation, minute books, stock records, and partnership articles) must be maintained in the principal office of the adviser and must be preserved until three years after termination of the adviser's business. Books and records may be kept in electronic form provided that appropriate access and safekeeping procedures are established and maintained.

1. Advisory and Other Agreements

Under Advisers Act Rule 204-2(a)(10), a registered adviser must keep a copy of all written agreements entered into by the adviser with any client or otherwise relating to the business of the adviser, such as investment management agreements for managed accounts and limited partnership agreements. Other agreements relating to an adviser's business may include brokerage, soft dollar, solicitation, custody, credit, and operating agreements.

2. Investor Communications

Under Advisers Act Rule 204-2(a)(7), a registered adviser must keep originals of all written communications received and copies of all written communications sent by the adviser relating to (i) any recommendation or other investment advice made or given to any advisory client, (ii) any receipt, disbursement or delivery of funds or securities, and (iii) the placing or execution of any order to purchase or sell any security.

---

[67] *See* Exchange Act Release No. 34-18114 (Oct. 1, 1981) at n.30.

3. *Brokerage Records*

Under Advisers Act Rule 204-2(a)(3), a registered adviser must keep a memorandum of (i) each order given by the adviser for the purchase or sale of any security and (ii) any instruction received from a client concerning the purchase, sale, receipt or delivery of any security. Such memorandum must (i) show the terms and conditions of the order or instruction, (ii) identify the person associated with the adviser who recommended the transaction and the person who placed the order, (iii) show the client account for which entered, the date of entry, and the bank, broker or dealer through whom executed, and (iv) indicate whether the order was executed pursuant to the exercise of discretionary power.

Trade tickets or daily trade blotters will generally satisfy the memoranda requirements of Rule 204-2(a)(3) and should be time stamped.

4. *Advertisements*

Under Advisers Act Rule 204-2(a)(11), a registered adviser must keep a copy of each notice, circular, advertisement, newspaper article, investment letter, bulletin or other communication that the adviser circulates or distributes to 10 or more persons (other than persons connected with the adviser). Under Advisers Act Rule 204-2(a)(16), a registered adviser must keep all accounts, books, internal working papers, and other records or documents that form the basis for or demonstrate the calculation of the performance or rate of return of any or all managed accounts or securities recommendations of the adviser in any notice, circular, advertisement, newspaper article, investment letter, bulletin, or other communication that the investment adviser circulates or distributes to 10 or more persons (other than persons connected with the adviser).

5. *Personal Trading*

Under Advisers Act Rule 204-2(a)(12), a registered adviser must keep a record of every transaction in a security in which the adviser or any advisory representative of such adviser has or by reason of such transaction acquires a beneficial ownership (except transactions effected in accounts over which neither the adviser nor the advisory representatives of the adviser has any influence or control and transactions in obligations of the United States). Such record must show the title and amount of the security involved, the date and nature of the transaction, the price at which the transaction was effected, and the name of the broker or dealer through whom the transaction was effected. The "advisory representatives" of an adviser will generally include any partner, officer, director, portfolio manager, trader, or research analyst of the adviser, and any other employee or affiliate of the adviser who obtains information regarding which securities are being recommended by the adviser before the effective dissemination of such information by the adviser.

Each advisory representative should also provide the adviser with copies of all personal brokerage statements which should be reviewed by the adviser to ensure that the employee has not engaged in any inappropriate trading.

6. Form ADV Delivery Requirements

Under Advisers Act Rule 204-2(a)(14), a registered adviser must (i) keep a copy of each written disclosure statement delivered to an advisory client or prospective advisory client pursuant to Advisers Act Rule 204-3, and (ii) keep a record of the dates that each written disclosure statement was given, or offered to be given, to each advisory client or prospective advisory client.

7. Solicitation

Under Advisers Act Rule 204-2(a)(15), a registered adviser must keep a copy of (i) all written disclosure statements delivered by solicitors to advisory clients pursuant to Advisers Act Rule 206(4)-3, and (ii) all written acknowledgments received by the adviser from advisory clients pursuant to Advisers Act Rule 206(4)-3.

8. Accounting Records

Under Advisers Act Rule 204-2(a)(1),(2),(4),(5) and (6), a registered adviser is required to keep certain accounting records relating to its advisory business. Such records include (i) all journals (including cash receipts and cash disbursements journals) that form the basis of entries in any ledger, (ii) general (and auxiliary) ledgers reflecting all asset, liability, reserve, capital, income, and expense accounts, (iii) all check books, canceled checks, bank statements, and bank reconciliations of the adviser, (iv) all trial balances, financial statements, and internal audit work papers relating to the business of the adviser, and (v) copies of all bills and statements, both paid and unpaid, relating to the business of the adviser. Registered advisers must also keep such accounting records for each investment partnership in which the adviser serves as general partner.

9. Records Kept by Commodity Pool Operators

CFTC Rule 1.31 requires a registered CPO to maintain certain books and records for at least five years, during the first two years of which the books and records must be readily accessible. The books and records shall be open to inspection by any representative of the CFTC or the Department of Justice. At the request of the CFTC, a registered CPO is required to furnish the name and address of each pool participant and to submit copies of all reports, letters, circulars, memoranda, publications, writings, or other literature or advice distributed to participants or prospective participants.

CFTC Rule 4.23 requires certain of the books and records to be kept at the main business office of the CPO. Such books and records must be made available to participants for inspection and copying during normal business hours. If the main business office of the CPO is outside the United States, the CFTC may require the CPO to provide the books and records at a designated location inside the United States within 72 hours after receipt of the request.

K. Reports and Audit

General partners of partnerships and advisers to funds generally provide for an annual independent audit of the financial statements of the partnership or fund, and either monthly or quarterly unaudited reports to investors. The Advisers Act does not require audits of financial statements or periodic reports other than with respect to custody or the Form ADV.

A CPO, however, must comply with the CFTC financial reporting requirements (CFTC Rule 4.22) with respect to each commodity pool it operates. Absent an exemption from the CFTC, reports to commodity pool participants in the form of account statements must be made by CPOs at least monthly if the pool has net assets of $500,000 or more at the beginning of the pool's fiscal year and otherwise at least quarterly. Account statements must be distributed within 30 calendar days after the last day of the reporting period. An account statement for a pool's last reporting period need not be distributed if the annual report (discussed below) is sent to participants within 45 days after the end of the fiscal year. These reports need not be filed with the NFA. The account statement must include (i) a statement of income (or loss) and (ii) a statement of changes in net asset value for the period involved. Absent an exemption from the CFTC, an annual report must be distributed to each commodity pool participant within 90 days after the end of the pool's fiscal year. Two copies of the annual report must be filed with the CFTC and one copy must be filed with the NFA. The information required to be contained in the annual report is similar to the information currently contained in annual reports distributed to investors in most private investment partnerships, but certain additional items are required.

IV. ERISA

A. _Plan Asset Rule_

If an employee benefit plan invests in a fund, does the plan's assets include the investment in the fund (e.g., a limited partnership interest) or does it include the underlying investments of the fund? The answer to the question has broad implications to the management of the fund, including (i) who is the fiduciary managing the assets, (ii) whether any of the underlying transactions of the fund are prohibited transactions, (iii) how the manager may be compensated (i.e., the use of incentive compensation), (iv) whether the persons managing investments of the fund must be bonded, and (v) whether, in the case of investment of foreign securities, special arrangements must be made.

The Plan Asset Regulations[68] generally provide that when an employee benefit plan subject to ERISA acquires an _equity_ interest in an entity such as an investment partnership, that is neither a U.S. publicly offered security nor a security issued by an investment company registered under the Company Act, the plan's assets include both the equity interest and an undivided interest in each of the underlying assets of the fund unless it is established that (i) the fund is an "operating company," (ii) equity participation in the fund by plan investors (as defined below) is not significant, or (iii) the fund satisfies the special grandfather rule. Should the plan be deemed to have an interest in the underlying assets of the fund, the fund will be deemed to have ERISA Plan Assets ("Plan Assets") and both the entity and the investment manager will be subject to the various restrictions imposed by ERISA and discussed below.

1. _Debt or Equity_

The threshold inquiry in plan asset analysis is whether the interest which a plan has acquired in an entity is an equity interest. The Plan Asset Regulation defines an "equity interest" as "any interest in an entity other than an instrument that is treated as indebtedness under applicable local law and which has no substantial equity features." Under the Plan Asset Regulations a "profit interest in a partnership, an undivided interest in property, and beneficial interest in a trust" are all equity interests.

2. _Operating Company Exception_

The plan will not be deemed to have an interest in the underlying assets of a fund, if the fund is considered an "operating company" (including a "ven-

---

[68] DOL Regulation, 29 C.F.R. § 2510.3-101, 51 Fed. Reg. 41262 (Nov. 13, 1986).

ture capital operating company" (VCOC) or a "real estate operating company" (REOC). The Plan Asset Regulations define operating company as an "entity that is primarily engaged, directly or through a majority-owned subsidiary, in the production or sale of a product or service other than the investment of capital." The distinction between an operating company, which is excluded from the application of the Plan Asset Regulations, and a nonoperating company primarily engaged in making investments which would fall within the regulation's scope should generally be relatively clear. However, there are two types of entities that can have the characteristics of both operating and investment companies included within the definition of operating company. These are the VCOC and the REOC.

a. Venture Capital Operating Company. A VCOC is an entity of which 50 percent or more of the assets are invested in venture capital investments (i.e., operating companies as to which the VCOC has management rights) and which actually exercises such rights in the ordinary course of its business. The Plan Asset Regulations do not define what particular kinds of conduct constitute management activities. Although an entity that qualifies as a VCOC is treated as an operating company for purposes of the exclusionary rule, investments in VCOCs are not treated as venture capital investments. Accordingly, for purposes of determining the amount of assets invested in operating companies (i.e., the 50 percent test), investments of an entity in VCOCs are non-operating company investments. The Plan Asset Regulations also contain various rules regarding the timing for testing compliance with the above VCOC exclusion.

b. Real Estate Operating Company. A REOC is an entity of which 50 percent or more of the assets are invested in real estate which is managed and developed and with respect to which such entity has the right to substantially participate directly in the management or development activities. As with the VCOC definition, the Plan Asset Regulations do not define what particular kinds of conduct constitute management or development activities. However, the DOL has indicated that an entity may carry out its management or development activities through an independent contractor. Therefore, merely assuming the risks of ownership or financing the acquisition of real estate, would not qualify an entity as a REOC. Similar to the VCOC rules, the Plan Asset Regulations contain various rules regarding the timing for testing compliance with the REOC exclusion.

c. Insignificant Participation by Plan Investors. Plan investors are considered to hold less than a "significant" amount of equity interests if they hold, in the aggregate, less than 25 percent of the value of any class of equity interest of the entity. Plan investors include employee benefit plans, whether or not subject to ERISA, church plans, government plans, individual retirement accounts, Keogh plans, and entities whose assets are considered to be plan assets. For purposes of determining the percentage of plan ownership, the value of equity interests held by certain parties related to the entity, such as the general partner, are disregarded. Under the Plan Asset Regulations these related parties are: "a person (other than a benefit plan investor) who has discretionary authority with respect to assets of the entity or any person who provides investment advice for a fee (direct or indirect), or any affiliate of such person."

The 25 percent test must be met each time an acquisition of any equity interest is made in the entity. For example, a plan holding a limited partnership interest will be deemed to have acquired an additional interest if another partner's interest is redeemed.[69] Thus, reliance on this exemption requires continual monitoring, forming, and imposing restrictions on resales.

d. Grandfather Rule. In general, a fund will satisfy the grandfather exception if the fund was in existence on March 13, 1987 and no plan has acquired any equity interests in the fund since March 13, 1987.

B. Fiduciary Duty

An important consequence of a fund's assets being considered Plan Assets is that such status imposes new obligations, responsibilities, and restrictions on the "fiduciaries" of the fund (i.e., the investment manager or general partner, as the case may be). In general, a "fiduciary" of a fund under ERISA includes any person who either exercises discretionary authority or discretionary control over the fund's assets or renders, for a fee or other compensation, investment advice to the fund. Accordingly, the investment manager or general partner is considered a fiduciary under ERISA.

As a fiduciary under ERISA, the investment manager is required to (i) act solely in the interest of the participants and beneficiaries of each plan investor, (ii) act prudently, (iii) diversify the investments of the fund to minimize the risk of large losses, (iv) act in accordance with the documents and instruments governing each plan investor to the extent such documents and instruments are consistent with ERISA, and (v) maintain the indicia of ownership of the fund's assets within the jurisdiction of the U.S. District Courts.

C. Prohibited Transactions Generally

If a fund does not meet one of the exceptions to the Plan Asset Rules discussed above, and the fund's assets are considered ERISA Plan Assets, then, in addition to the investment manager's duties and responsibilities as a fiduciary discussed above, the investment manager must not be involved in

---

[69] DOL Advisory Opinion 89-05A (Apr. 5, 1989).

prohibited transactions with the fund. The investment manager cannot engage in acts of self-dealing involving the fund's assets and cannot cause the fund to engage in certain transactions with a "party in interest." The term "party in interest"[70] includes plan fiduciaries (i.e., the investment manager), persons providing services to the plan and the fund (i.e., the accountant for the fund), sponsoring employers of each plan, and other parties having relationships to such persons. Among the transactions which are prohibited are sales or leasing of property, extensions of credit, and the furnishing of services between the fund and a party in interest.

A statutory exemption permits a party in interest (other than a fiduciary) to provide necessary and appropriate services to the fund if no more than "reasonable compensation" is paid for such services. This exemption permits service provides (i.e., lawyers and accountants) to a plan to be compensated for their services.

A fiduciary (i.e., the investment manager) is permitted to provide services to the fund only if (i) the services are necessary and appropriate, (ii) no more than "reasonable compensation" is paid by the fund for such services, and (iii) the fiduciary either (a) does not use the authority, control, or responsibility that makes it a fiduciary to select itself or an affiliate to provide the service or (b) provides such service for no compensation from the fund other than reimbursement of direct expenses. The investment manager should ensure that the services to be provided to the fund comply with the provisions of the statutory exemptions provided under ERISA.

The DOL has promulgated an important exemption from the prohibited transactions rules for investment managers who qualify as a Qualified Professional Asset Manager (QPAM). To qualify as a QPAM, the investment manager must, among other things, be an investment adviser registered under the Advisers Act, have client assets under its management in excess of $50 million, and have equity in excess of $750,000. Accordingly, if a fund does not meet one of the exemptions to the Plan Asset Rules, the QPAM exemption is likely to be the most significant exemption applicable to the day-to-day operations of a fund manager.

D. *Incentive Compensation*

If a fund does not meet one of the exceptions to the Plan Asset Rules discussed above, and the fund's assets are considered Plan Assets, then, as a fiduciary, the investment manager is generally not permitted to deal with

---

[70] For purposes of this discussion, the term "party in interest," as used in ERISA, will include the substantially similar term "disqualified person," as used in the Code.

the fund's assets in his own interest or act on behalf of a party whose interests are adverse to those of the fund. Thus, the investment manager may not cause the fund to pay a fee (i.e., an incentive fee), the amount of which the investment manager can impact by its actions.

However, according to applicable DOL advisory opinions,[71] the investment manager may be compensated through an incentive fee if the following requirements are met:

(i) the investment manager is registered under the Advisers Act;

(ii) the decision to retain the investment manager and to pay the incentive fee is made by an independent plan fiduciary;

(iii) each plan has total assets of at least $50 million;

(iv) no more than 10 percent of each plan's total assets are placed in the fund (i.e., under the control of the investment manager);

(v) the investment manager generally invests the fund's assets in securities for which market quotations are readily available, and if market quotations are not readily available (e.g., illiquid securities that are not regularly traded), the securities are valued by a qualified party who is independent of the investment manager and who is selected by the plan;

(vi) the investment manager's services may be terminated on reasonably short notice under the circumstances;

(vii) the incentive fee arrangement complies with the terms and conditions of Advisers Act Rule 205-3;

(viii) the total fees paid to the investment manager do not exceed reasonable compensation for services performed by the investment manager;

(viv) securities purchased or sold by the investment manager on behalf of the fund are not securities for which the investment manager (or an affiliate) is a market-maker;

(x) the incentive fee is based on annual performance, taking into account both realized and unrealized gains and losses and where the investment manager's services are terminated on a date other than an anniversary date, net profit is determined for the period from the commencement of the preceding full year through the termination date; and

(xi) each independent plan fiduciary represents that it fully understands the formula for calculating the incentive fee and the risks associated with such an arrangement.

---

[71] *See* Adv. Op. 86-20A (BDN Advisers, Inc.); Adv. Op. 86-21A (Batterymarch Financial Management); and Adv. Op. 86-31A (Alliance Capital Management L.P.).

E. Foreign Security Custody Rules

If a fund's assets are considered Plan Assets, then, the ERISA custody regulations apply. Generally, no ERISA fiduciary may maintain the "indicia of ownership" of any assets of plan outside the jurisdiction of the U.S. District Courts. It should be noted that the requirement to maintain the indicia of ownership of the fund's assets within the jurisdiction of the U.S. District Courts does not strictly prohibit or restrict foreign investments. Rather, it relates to the conditions under which the "indicia of ownership" may be maintained. The phrase "indicia of ownership" refers to the evidence of ownership of the fund's assets (e.g., stock certificates). If the fund has a U.S. custodian, then assets maintained by that custodian are within the jurisdiction of the U.S. District Courts.

The DOL has promulgated regulations (the "Custody Regulations")[72] which provide exceptions to the foregoing requirement that permits a "foreign security" (e.g., a security issued by a corporation which is not organized under the laws of the United States and which does not have its principal place of business within the United States) to be held outside the jurisdiction of the U.S. District Courts. Under the Custody Regulations, the indicia of ownership of foreign securities may be held abroad under three alternative custody arrangements: "The Asset Manager Alternative," "The Custodian Alternative," and the "The Foreign Entity Alternative." The Asset Manager Alternative requires that the custodian be an asset manager (i.e., a fiduciary) which is a substantial U.S. bank, insurance company, or registered investment adviser. The Custodian Alternative requires that the holder of the assets be a *custodian* which is a substantial U.S. bank (including foreign branches of such bank), or a U.S. broker or dealer. The Foreign Entity Alternative requires that a substantial U.S. bank or broker or dealer be responsible for custody of securities held by certain other persons or entities.

F. ERISA Bonding Requirements

To protect employee benefit plans against loss as a result of fiduciary misconduct, ERISA requires that certain plan fiduciaries be bonded in an amount equal to the lesser of 10 percent of the funds handled by such fiduciaries or $500,000. Typically, such bonds cover losses resulting from fraud or other types of misappropriations. In addition, if an investment manager is handling plan assets it is recommended that such investment manager also obtain fiduciary liability insurance to cover potential claims against the

---

[72] 29 CFR Section 2550.404b-1.

investment manager relating to other possible breaches of ERISA's fiduciary requirements.

G. *Penalties under ERISA*

If the investment manager is found to have breached its fiduciary duties under ERISA, the investment manager, including each employee or officer thereof that is involved in the breach, may be personally liable for (i) any damages resulting from the breach, (ii) a 20 percent penalty based on any amount recovered by the DOL with respect to such breach, and (iii) any other equitable relief that a court may consider appropriate under the circumstances.

V. **Dissolution and Termination**

The final distribution of the assets of an investment partnership to investors and creditors is governed by those provisions of the partnership agreement and of the state law under which the partnership was formed[73] relating to dissolution. Once a partnership is dissolved, its business continues only for the purpose of winding up its affairs. The winding up of a partnership's affairs is usually administered by the general partner, and the period during which the affairs of the partnership must be wound up is generally not provided for under state law and may be specified in the partnership agreement. A certificate of cancellation is generally filed to terminate the existence of the limited partnership.

Under state law, dissolution generally takes place under the following conditions: (i) at a time or upon the occurrence of an event specified in the partnership agreement, (ii) upon the action of the partners, (iii) upon the withdrawal of the general partner, or (iv) upon the entry of a judicial decree. Depending on the state in which the partnership is formed, provisions may be added to the partnership agreement specifying the actions that may be taken by general or limited partners to dissolve the partnership and the circumstances under which the withdrawal of a general or limited partner will cause a dissolution of the partnership.

In winding up a partnership, assets are typically distributed in the following order of priority: (i) to creditors (including partners who are creditors) of the partnership, (ii) to partners and former partners in satisfaction of

---

[73] The conditions under which dissolution occurs will vary from state to state. The discussion below is generally based on the Revised Uniform Limited Partnership Act (1976) with the 1985 Amendments (as amended, RULPA).

liabilities for distributions, and then (iii) to partners for the return of their contributions and then with respect to their partnership interests. While state law generally mandates that assets first be distributed to creditors of the partnership, the manner in which assets are then distributed among the partners may be varied by the terms of the partnership agreement. With respect to distributions to creditors, reasonable provision should be made for all contingent, conditional, and unmatured claims known to the partnership. What constitutes reasonable provision may vary depending on the nature of the claim. In determining the assets available to the partnership to pay creditors, limited partners, depending on state law, may be liable to the partnership for improper distributions previously received, i.e., distributions received when the liabilities of the partnership exceeded the fair market value of its assets. The terms of the partnership agreement may also expand the circumstances under which a limited partner may be liable for improper distributions, and bankruptcy and fraudulent transfer laws may impact the liability of limited partners with respect to previously received distributions.

In making distributions, assets may be distributed in cash or in kind. Generally, a partner does not have a right to demand a distribution in a form other than cash. But, if a distribution in kind is made, such distribution must be in proportion to the percentage in which the partner receiving such an in kind distribution shares in cash distributions, unless the partnership agreement provides otherwise.

CHAPTER 12

Critical Accounting, Tax, and Systems Issues

Joel Press, Senior Partner
Ernst & Young LLP

An investment partnership, or hedge fund, is basically a vehicle through which high net worth individuals, tax-exempt organizations and other institutions can invest their capital with a group of unique individuals. The terms *investment partnership* and *hedge fund* are used interchangeably in this chapter as both terms are commonly used throughout the industry. In fact, the term hedge fund is a misnomer, as many funds do not always employee hedging strategies. Investing in an investment partnership requires a great deal of acumen, patience, and hard work. There are many choices to review and problems to avoid in selecting an investment partnership. The issues concerning the appropriate selection of investment vehicles include: investment strategy, tax efficiency, compensations to the general partner, adequacy of supporting systems, and the financial strengths of the prime broker utilized by the investment manager as well as various other issues.

This chapter addresses these issues along with several others to provide stimulus to ask the right questions in selecting the appropriate hedge fund.

Business Considerations and Accounting

Raising Capital and Marketing

The confidential offering document is one of the principal vehicles through which the hedge fund is introduced to potential investors. This document

The author wishes to thank Salvatore DiFranco, senior partner; Jeffrey R. Hoops; Rich Barry, principal; John Perna, manager; and Mary Traer, senior partner at Ernst & Young LLP for their invaluable contributions to the creation of this chapter.

presents a general overview of the fund including its investment objectives, fees and expenses, risk factors, method of allocating profits and losses, minimum investment, withdrawal policy, tax status, as well as the biographies and additional information about the key investment-making individuals. The offering document is an overview designed to provide potential investors with a summary of the key elements needed to make an investment decision. The partnership agreement is drafted concurrently and is the governing legal document.

A term sheet, which is an outline of the economic terms of the venture, is generally the first piece of marketing data that is presented to lead investors. Subsequent tranches of investors are generally furnished with the offering memorandum first, and from a legal perspective, no valid offering can be made without a complete confidential offering memorandum. The term sheet at one point is very tentative and gives the initial large investors the opportunity to negotiate the terms of the deal.

Available to investors are numerous professional money raisers and consultants. Some of these consultants are paid for by the hedge fund and some are retained by the investor. It is obvious that the investor should determine what condition exists in order to place any comments or discussion into appropriate perspective.

It is generally a good idea from the fund's marketing standpoint and from an investor's viewpoint that the general partner(s) has a significant amount of personal capital invested in the partnership.

Structure

The basic types of investment vehicles are:

- Investment partnerships
- Funds of funds
- Separate managed accounts
- Offshore corporations

Investment Partnerships

The traditional hedge fund structure is in the form of a limited partnership with fewer than 100 limited partners. As a limited partnership, the taxable character of all items of income and expenses are passed through to the individual partners at their pro-rata share. A fund with fewer than 100 limited partners generally operates without regulation by the Securities and Exchange Commission (SEC). It might be well to note that there are also limitations as to the amount of ERISA money that can be included in the total assets of a hedge fund. In general, a limited partnership will not accept more than 25 percent of its invested capital in the form of pension plan assets, since it would be subject to onerous reporting requirements and legal exposure. A common solution to this problem is a separate managed account for the pension fund.

The limited partnership has a general partner(s) which can be either individuals or some form of legal entity, e.g., a Limited Liability Company (LLC) or a corporation. The general partner typically receives an incentive allocation of profits which retains the same tax character as those of the partnership. In addition, management fees, which are generally 1 percent per annum of assets under management are normally paid by the partnership, either to the general partners or to an entity controlled by the general partners.

Funds of Funds

There are all kinds of partnerships today, such as classical value investing, small cap, large cap, convertible arbitrage, sector funds such as media and entertainment, health care, energy, and gold.

In recent times there has been a proliferation of funds of funds, which are a variation of the traditional hedge fund. Simply stated, a fund of funds is a hedge fund which invests in other hedge funds. The principal advantage for an investor in a fund of funds is that it enables the investor to utilize several investment disciplines within one investment vehicle. A fund of funds also allows an investor to gain access to popular fund managers whose funds are no longer accepting investors or have large minimum investment requirements. A fund of funds differs from the traditional hedge fund in the structure of the management fees and the incentive allocations paid to the general partners. Fund of funds fees charged by general partners are typically a percentage of net assets under management, and, while older funds of funds did not utilize an incentive allocation to the general partner, the newer ones are using some sort of incentive fee.

Separate Managed Accounts

A separate managed account is a securities account which is managed by the money manager (typically the same person as the general partner(s) of the hedge fund) on a discretionary basis. It is managed pursuant to the terms and conditions of an investment management agreement. Copies of all transactions and brokerage statements are sent to the client or beneficial owner, who then has the responsibility of incorporating that data into its books and records. This is one of the significant differences between an individual managed account and investment in a limited partnership, as the former is responsible for all of its own bookkeeping and tax return preparation.

There are many reasons for an investor to place money with a fund manager outside of the hedge fund as well as reasons for the fund manager to manage money outside of the hedge fund. An investor may be unwilling or unable to invest in a hedge fund because the fund has reached the maximum number of investors, or the investor's organization prohibits investments in hedge funds. A fund manager may be unwilling to accept large pension fund investments because of the 25 percent limitation on pension fund assets, and likewise may be unable to accept large contributions from fund of funds because of certain SEC rules related to the counting of investors. Investment advisors typically are compensated through a fee based upon the performance of the portfolio under management. However, unlike an incentive allocation normally made to a general partner in an investment partnership, the fee to an investment advisor, an expense of the investor, is ordinary income to the advisor and does not retain the taxable characteristics of the underlying income. If the investor is an individual, this structure could be disadvantageous from an income tax standpoint since the fee could be subject to a 2 percent ceiling limitation and therefore not deductible, whereas an allocation of profits, instead of a fee would reduce taxable income to the investor with no limitation.

Offshore Funds

Domestic hedge funds normally are not marketed to foreign investors because they expose foreign investors to U.S. income tax rules and regulations. To remedy this, many investment managers create offshore funds. Offshore funds provide an excellent mechanism for organizing pools of money in a tax-efficient basis in an unencumbered regulatory environment. Offshore funds, which are typically corporations (similar to mutual funds), can essentially make the same investments as domestic funds, and indeed their portfolios often are a mirror image of the domestic fund's.

The Internal Revenue Service (IRS) has determined that an offshore fund can be exempt from U.S. income taxes provided it adheres to a list of rules commonly known as the "ten commandments." These rules require that certain activities of the fund be performed offshore. These rules specify that all communications with shareholders and the general public originate from an offshore location, generally from the fund's administrator. In addition, all marketing, soliciting of shares, and accepting of subscriptions must be performed offshore. Although investment transactions can be originated from the United States, the maintenance of the corporate books and records, the payment of redemptions, and the disbursements of dividends, fees, and salaries must be performed offshore. Finally the annual audit and share-holders' and directors' meetings must be performed offshore. Any violation of these rules may taint the offshore fund status thereby subjecting the fund to U.S. income taxes.

The first step in forming an offshore fund is selecting a domicile. There are many factors involved when selecting a domicile and sound legal advice is critical. The location of the domicile is important. Is the location easy to reach? Does the offshore administrator speak the same language? Also important is the economic and political environment of the domicile as well as the infrastructure. A politically unstable environment will be a detriment to raising capital for the offshore fund. The system of taxation and the regulatory environment are also equally important. Finally, the reputation of the administrators in the domicile, their facilities, and the communication systems are critical.

Based upon the above factors, the domiciles of choice have been the Bahamas, Bermuda, the Cayman Islands, and Curacao. Most recently, Toronto has also been viewed as a favored domicile.

After selecting a domicile, the capabilities of the offshore administrators should be evaluated. There are multiple factors involved in selecting an offshore administrator. The startup costs as well as the ongoing fee structure, including the billing of expenses can be of extreme importance. The computer capabilities of the offshore administrator can have the largest impact on the timeliness of generating reports to shareholders. Similar to a mutual fund, the offshore fund must calculate a net asset value (NAV) per share in order to accept new subscriptions as well as keep current investors apprised of their performance. The capability of the offshore administrator's computer systems to send and receive information from the prime broker and the investment manager are of the utmost importance. Finally the administrator's reputation and ability to handle shareholder communications and marketing are as important as the fund's performance because these activities are expressly prohibited in the United States by the investment manager.

An investment manager's earnings are generated in a fashion identical with that of a separate managed account which, in fact, the corporation is viewed as. Because the incentive fee is charged to the corporation, and not directly to each individual shareholder, an equalization factor is often used and is charged to or allocated from investors subscribing to shares during the year. Equalization is a method of ensuring investor parity when the net asset value of the offshore funds has fluctuated between the beginning of the year and the subscription date by temporarily adjusting the subscription price by the amount of the incentive fee until the year-end when all values are finalized and it can be determined whether or not a fee has been earned.

Participants in a Typical Investment Partnership

A traditional hedge fund, operated as an investment partnership, is a legal structure group effort consisting of various elements. The following is a summary of those elements:

General Partner

The general partner interest is the fund manager's participation of his or her capital in the hedge fund. The general partner is typically an individual, limited partnership, S corporation, or an LLC. An attractive element to many investors in a limited partnership is the fact that the fund manager has an amount of capital at risk along with the limited partners. In fact, partnership agreements typically specify a minimum amount of capital that the general partner must maintain in the fund. Additional financial incentive for general partners to manage the partnership comes in the form of a reallocation of gains from the limited partners to the general partner.

General partners are rewarded with an incentive allocation of capital appreciation (as defined in the individual agreements) of between 15 and 25 percent. The use of "loss carryforwards," "clawbacks," and "high-water marks" are common in the structuring of partnerships since they generally enable the investor to either be made whole or receive a preferential rate of return before allowing any incentive allocation to the general partner. However, these techniques are beyond the scope of this chapter.

Limited Partners

Investors who wish to enter an investment partnership as limited partners must qualify as "accredited investors" as defined by SEC rules. In essence, this definition is one utilizing a minimum net worth or a minimum annual income test. SEC rules mandate that the fund limit the number of limited partners (including general partners) to 100. If the number of limited partners exceeds 100, the fund would become regulated by the SEC under the Investment Company Act of 1940 (the "Act") rather than a private partnership. As such, the fund would be subjected to onerous reporting requirements and very restrictive trading and finance rules. Therefore it is of vital importance that the partnership keep an accurate count of the number of its partners. There are several common pitfalls to avoid when counting the number of investors. A joint investment made by a husband and wife also counts as two investors. More importantly, if a fund of funds' limited partnership interest in the fund exceeds 10 percent of the fund's capital, the "look-through" rules may apply. If the "look-through" rules apply, the partnership will be required to count each of the investors in the fund of funds as if they were individual investors in the partnership. It should also be noted that a fund manager is precluded from establishing a "sister" fund with identical strategies for the principal objective of creating a second group of investor slots.

Another pitfall faced when admitting new limited partners are limitations on employee benefit plan assets. If 25 percent or more of a funds' partnership interests are comprised of employee benefit plans, the fund would be subjected to the provisions of the Employee Retirement Income Security Act of 1974 (ERISA). As in the case of a fund regulated under the act, the fund's investment strategies may be limited as well as the fund would be subjected to onerous reporting requirements.

The prospective limited partner should be cognizant as to the percentage of the partnership assets his or her capital represents from the standpoint of risk as well as from the standpoint of regulatory issues (e.g., ERISA).

Management Company

The hedge fund normally does not have any employees or assets other than those which are investment related. It is the management company that provides the administrative resources for the hedge fund. The management company, which is typically owned by the same individuals who are the general partners of the fund, is compensated for these services in the form of a management fee based upon the net assets of the fund. This fee, which is computed and paid quarterly, has traditionally been in the range of .75 to 2 percent of the funds' net assets (committed funds, not discussed in the chapter have different fee and incentive relationships). However, there are many variations on this percentage, including a sliding scale percentage dependent upon the total capital raised or the capital invested by each partner.

The management company is usually a corporation or LLC that provides the investment administration and back office support to the hedge fund. The management company's operations vary depending upon the size of the fund and the amount of services required. Services provided by management companies may include portfolio and general ledger accounting, operations (trading and back office), cash management, performance calculation, risk management, legal and compliance, systems, tax, and administration.

The partnership agreement and the confidential offering document should specify the expenses that will be borne by the partnership. In many cases legal and accounting fees are paid by and expensed by the limited partnership (not the management company). In addition the organizational expenses incurred are typically charged to the hedge fund. From a marketing prospective, the management company can limit the actual amount of expenses the partnership will be charged.

As discussed later, the management company also provides services to manage the offshore activities, and can directly manage individual managed accounts. The management company can also be registered with the SEC as an investment advisor and with the Commodity Futures Trading Commission (CFTC) as conditions warrant.

The Prime Broker

Prime brokerage is a service developed by major brokerage houses to facilitate the clearance, settlement, and custody of securities trades for hedge funds, institutions and high net worth individuals. Prime brokerage involves three distinct parties: the prime broker, the executing broker, and the hedge fund. To enter into a prime brokerage arrangement, the investment partnership executes an agreement with the prime broker. The prime broker, in turn, enters into agreements with each of the executing brokers whereby the prime broker agrees to clear each trade placed by the hedge fund.

The investor should inquire as to the identity of the prime broker since that broker's financial stability and strength are critical to the safety of the individual investment.

Accounting

There are numerous accounting issues facing a hedge fund. How are esoteric derivative securities valued and accounted for? What effect do illiquid positions have on new partners' valuations? Generally, the parameters governing the valuation of the securities in the portfolio are specifically included in the partnership document. If they are not, the investor should *beware*. The size of a hedge fund obviously affects the demands on the fund's accounting department; however, a four-million-dollar fund or a four-billion-dollar fund may need to deal with many of the same issues. Trading strategies as well as the frequency of changes in the partner roster determines complexity; size does not.

As a general rule, the hedge fund's investments are recorded at their original cost on the trade date. Realized gains and losses on securities sold as well as unrealized gains and losses on securities in the portfolio are recorded on the hedge fund's income statement for economic reporting.

An individual partner capital account is maintained for each partner in the fund. This account is increased by capital contributions as well as allocations of profits, and decreased by withdrawals as well as allocations of losses. Upon the effective date of any partner's contribution or withdrawal of capital, the partnership essentially closes its books, marks all of its investments to market or fair value and allocates appreciation or depreciation to the individual partners' capital accounts based upon their pro-rata share of capital. The period in time between each of these valuation dates is known as a "break period." The partnership's policy for allowing contributions and withdrawals during the year is specified in the partnership agreement and confidential offering document.

The difficulty in valuing the partnership at the end of each break period is determined by both the size and the complexity of the fund's portfolio. Most securities have readily available market prices while some do not. Investments in private or nonexchange traded securities, illiquid securities, or complex derivative instruments, such as swaps, may only be valued using computer models. In some partnership agreements there are few or no restrictions on the types of investments that a hedge fund can make. A hedge fund can be involved in cutting edge trading strategies using constantly evolving instruments. While this situation attracts the brightest fund managers and may yield substantial returns on investors' capital, it is a cause of much concern to all of the parties and professionals involved with the partnership. The past year has seen deliberations in Congress, a report by the General Accounting Office, investigations by the SEC, and new disclosure requirements promulgated by the Financial Accounting Standards Board (FASB) on the use of derivative securities. The disclosures necessary for the partnership agreement and offering document dictate the manner and powers a general partner has for the valuation of all instruments.

A fund with large investments in private placement or restricted securities can create issues of equitable allocations of gains and losses to its partners. Frequently, investments in nonpublic or illiquid investments are valued by the investment manager at cost or by a method designed to approximate a market price. These methods are at best only estimates based on individual judgment and the facts available at that time, and the real value of the investment will only be known upon its liquidation. If a partner withdraws from the fund between the time such an investment is made and the liquidation date of the investment, a procedure must be in place to allocate that partner's actual return on his or her investment. The typical method for dealing with this situation is through the use of "side pocket" accounts. Upon the date of acquisition of an illiquid investment, the fund creates a separate set of partner capital accounts. Each partner is allocated the pro-rata share of this investment from his regular partner capital account. New partners entering the fund after the acquisition of the illiquid investment do not share in any of the resultant gains and losses of the side pocket investment; instead, new partners only share in investments made after they were admitted. Upon the withdrawal of a partner, the balance in his or her regular partner capital account is distributed following the normal withdrawal procedures as specified in the partnership agreement, however the partner's capital balance in the side pocket account is retained in the fund. Upon the liquidation of the side pocket investment, the gain or loss is posted to the side pocket capital accounts, and the side pocket capital account balances are subsequently distributed to the original partners. In theory, a side pocket account can be established for each illiquid investment made by the fund, however for practical purposes side pockets can be established for groups of illiquid securities. The intended use of side pocket accounts should be discussed in the partnership agreement and the confidential offering document as the partner's ability to withdraw from the fund is impacted. The general partner usually receives an incentive allocation only upon the sale of the illiquid investment.

Investments in distressed debt securities and mortgage-backed securities can be problematic in that there may not be one central source for price quotes, and that multiple price quotes can differ significantly. In addition, due to the illiquidity of many of these securities, a price quote may not necessarily be the same price a dealer would be willing to pay to acquire those securities.

The National Association of Securities Dealers (NASD) has stringent rules regulating investing in newly issued securities that trade above their initial public offering price ("hot issues"). The gains and losses from trading in hot issues are to be allocated only to partners not deemed to be restricted persons. The topic of hot issues should be addressed in the partnership agreement and the subscription agreements should contain the necessary information concerning the investor's affiliation with members of the NASD.

Systems

The investment vehicle must have systems in place to not only account and give accurate information as to its cash balances, but be able to control security positions, partners' capital accounts, the appreciation/depreciation by accounting period, etc. The complexity of the system is a direct function of the size and complexity of the underlying portfolio. In any event, a prospective investor might be well advised to make inquiry of the general partner as to its accounting systems prior to finally committing to an investment.

Reports to Partners

In general, an investment partnership should provide, at a minimum, an annual audited financial statement to its partners (by the terms of its partnership agreement). This financial statement is prepared under generally accepted accounting principles (GAAP) as promulgated by the various accounting rule-making bodies and is reflective of common industry accounting practices. The annual financial statements include a statement of financial condition (at market value), a statement of income or operations (based on economics), a statement of changes in partners' capital, a statement of cash flows, and the related footnotes. There is currently a proposal outstanding to require investment partnerships to include a condensed statement of investments in their annual report. While many in the industry have been actively contesting this proposal, it now appears that this statement may be required as early as 1995. The partnership agreement describes the financial statements to be issued as well as the timing of their release. However, any funds that are registered with the CFTC are required to provide their annual report within 90 days after the year-end (unless an extension is granted, which can be difficult to obtain).

In recent years, there has been an increase in the disclosures required to be made as part of a financial statement prepared in accordance with GAAP. One of the primary areas of increased disclosure has been the use of financial instruments. Market risks and credit risks must be clearly described for each material instrument traded. In addition, the recently issued disclosure requirements for derivative financial instruments calls for a description of uses of such securities.

In addition to the annual financial statements of the investment partnership, the fund typically provides each investor with an audited capital letter showing their capital account at market value. This statement is designed to supplement the annual report and should be clearly marked so that it is not used for income tax purposes. The partnership may, at its option, also provide its partners with an audited statement of performance statistics.

Association of Investment Management and Research Performance Statistics

In late 1987, the Association of Investment Management and Research (AIMR) issued performance presentation standards, which were adopted in their final form in 1990. The objective of these standards was to increase the comparability and fairness of performance statistics. This is to be achieved through a combination of strictly defined performance calculations as well as full disclosure. The performance presentation standards are broken down into two categories: mandatory requirements and disclosures, and recommended requirements and disclosures.

The mandatory requirements and disclosures include the use of total return to calculate performance, the accrual basis of accounting, time-weighted rates of return and the comparison to representative composites, as well as many other specific calculations. The standards also call for mandatory disclosure of the number of portfolios and amount of assets comparable to a composite, as well as the percentage of total assets the composite represents. Additional mandatory disclosure requirements include the effect of investment manager fees on performance, the use of leverage in the portfolio as well as the tax rate assumptions if the performance is presented net of taxes.

AIMR's recommended guidelines and disclosures include the use of trade date accounting, presentation of statistics before taxes, and the revaluation of a portfolio whenever cash has flowed either in or out of the portfolio. For international portfolios, recommended disclosures include the disclosure of inconsistencies among portfolios in the treatment of foreign exchange rates and the presentation of portfolios exclusive of the effects of foreign exchange rates.

The selection of a comparable composite is an integral element of the performance presentation. A careful review of the standard composite indices available is necessary to determine which index or indices are the most comparable to the portfolio. In some cases a blended composite may be appropriate (such as 50 percent S&P 500 and 50 percent Salomon BIG bond index.)

An audited statement of performance statistics can be a useful marketing tool to the investment manager as well as an invaluable tool for the prospective investor.

Tax Considerations

Basic Principles of Partnership Taxation

Conduit Principle of Taxation

One of the main benefits of the partnership structure as a form of organization is the conduit principle of taxation. Under the conduit principle of taxation, a partnership's items of income, expense, gain, and loss flow through to its partners and are taxed at the partner level, rather than at the partnership level. This flow-through approach eliminates the double taxation inherent in the corporate form of organization. As items of income, expense, gain, and loss flow through from the partnership, they retain their tax character, timing, and source.

Character, Timing, and Source

Character, timing, and source are three basic tenets that govern federal income taxation.

Character refers to the type of income or expense, some examples being ordinary income and expense, capital gains or losses, and tax-exempt income. The character of the item will determine how it is treated at the partner level for income tax purposes. In the case of an individual, a long-term capital gain could be taxed at a lower rate than an ordinary gain, and a tax-exempt gain may not be taxed at all.

The concept of timing determines when an item of gain, loss, income, or expense should be recognized for tax purposes. Under general tax principles, gain or loss is not recognized until it is realized. For example, while unrealized appreciation or depreciation is accounted for on an economic basis, it generally would not be recognized for tax purposes until the position is actually disposed of at which point the gain becomes realized. Many trading partnerships however, trade certain securities that are taxed under special rules which may accelerate the timing of income or defer the timing of losses. If a partnership trades regulated futures contracts, subject to the provisions of I.R.C. Section 1256, the unrealized gains or losses on such contracts outstanding at the end of the tax year will be marked to market, and the partner will recognize gain or loss on the unrealized appreciation or depreciation. Certain hedge fund strategies may also inadvertently result in a deferral of trading losses.

The concept of source is used to determine the origin of partnership income (i.e., foreign source, domestic source, unrelated business taxable income, expenses with respect to short sales). For U.S. partnerships, the source of income, expenses, and withholding are used primarily for the calculation of the foreign tax credit at the partner level. Source may also be used to determine withholding requirements for any foreign partners.

Partner Capital Accounts and Allocations

Tax capital accounts are calculated under specific tax rules and will in many instances be different from book capital accounts calculated under GAAP. Since book income under GAAP includes both realized and unrealized gains and losses, partner's book capital accounts will reflect both realized and unrealized amounts. This distinction becomes especially important when allocating realized gains and losses for tax purposes.

A brief example may illustrate the importance of allocating realized gains and losses in a manner that follows the economic allocation reflected in the partners' book capital account. Assume A & B are equal partners in a partnership. At inception of the partnership, each partner contributed $50. At December 31, 1993, the sole asset in the partnership is a stock with a cost basis of $100 and a fair market value of $120. Further assume that C enters the partnership effective January 1, 1994 with a capital contribution of $60 (a

TABLE 12-1.   Example of Individual Partner's Allocation of Taxable Gains

	Prior Period Unrealized Realized	Current Period Unrealized Realized	Total Realized
Partner A	$10	$ 5	$15
Partner B	10	5	15
Partner C	0	5	5
	$20	$15	$35

1/3 interest). The partnership then sells the stock on December 31, 1994 for $135, generating a realized gain of $35. If the realized gain were to be allocated according to the partners respective book capital interests, it would be allocated $11.67 to each A, B, and C. That means that C would be taxed on a portion of the $20 of gain that economically accrued to A and B before C's entry into the partnership. However, by bifurcating the gain into prior period unrealized gains now realized and current period realized gains, the correct economic allocation would be achieved.

After bifurcating the gain, C is taxed only on his share, $5, of the appreciation in the security since his entry into the partnership. A and B are taxed on their respective shares of the appreciation before and after C's entry into the partnership.

Although there are several methods for allocating realized gains and losses, security by security layering (as demonstrated above) always provides the most accurate and equitable allocations for tax purposes.

Partnership Tax Returns and Partner Schedule K-1

Form 1065, U.S. Partnership Return of Income is used to report partnership income, deductions, gains, and losses. For domestic partnerships on a calendar year-end, the due date for the return is April 15th, although most investors will prefer to receive K-1s as soon after year-end as possible. Partner K-1s are used to report each partner's share of the partnership income, deductions, gains, and losses. The K-1s should also provide sufficient information to allow the partner to calculate its taxable income for both federal and state purposes. Information such as foreign income, deductions, and withholding; tax-exempt income and deductions related to tax-exempt income; income from U.S. government obligations; interest expense; and unrelated business taxable income (UBTI) should be listed on the face of the K-1, or provided in supplemental disclosures. Fund of funds may have additional considerations, with respect to K-1s received from investee partnerships. Items of profit or loss may be treated differently on different K-1s based upon whether the investee partnership is treated as a trader or an investor for tax purposes.

U.S. Federal Taxation of Partners—Traders versus Investors

A determination of whether or not a partnership engaged solely in investing and/or trading securities and other financial instruments for its own account is deemed to be carrying on a trade or business is of critical importance for tax purposes. Unfortunately, there is no statutory definition of trade or business. Ultimately, this determination is a question of fact, although case law does provide some guidance.

Based upon the relevant case law the indicia of a "trader" are: (1) predominant intent to earn a profit from the short-term market swings of securities by buying and selling securities frequently, (2) trading activities are continuous, regular and extensive, (3) vast majority of income is derived from short-term trading (as distinguished from dividends, interest, and long-term capital gain), (4) significant use of short term buying and selling of securities, margin purchases, borrowing to finance purchases, hedging transactions, short sales, put or call options, commodity transactions, stock lending, conversions and reverse conversions in order to manipulate security holdings in an attempt to produce the best possible return. While these criteria provide guidelines for determining trader versus investor status, the test is based solely on the facts and circumstances of the partnership.

The determination of trader versus investor will directly impact how the partners will be taxed on their respective distributive share of partnership income, deduction, gain, and loss. For example if under federal and state and local tax law, the partnership's activities do not constitute a trade or business, the partnership's operating expenses will be characterized as investment expenses. For an individual, for federal tax purposes, this means that the partnerships expenses will only be deductible as miscellaneous itemized deductions to the extent that they exceed 2 percent of such partner's adjusted gross income, (as opposed to being fully deductible if the partnership were deemed to be engaged in a trade or business). For federal purposes, interest expenses may be limited even further under the alternative minimum tax.

In contrast to domestic partners, foreign investors have several complex issues to deal with and are generally better advised to invest in either an offshore vehicle or be managed as an individual managed account.

Conclusion

Creating and managing an investment partnership is not an easy task. Selecting an investment vehicle is even more complex. As we have described, there are numerous accounting, tax, and business issues that need to be addressed. Although the tasks may seem monumental, they are not overwhelming to the person that seeks out sound professional advice.

CHAPTER 13

Unrelated Business Taxable Income Considerations for Tax Exempt Investors in Securities Partnerships

Daniel S. Shapiro, Senior Partner
Schulte Roth & Zabel

Tax-exempt entities, such as charitable organizations and pension plans, are increasingly becoming investors (i.e., limited partners) in securities investment and trading partnerships (securities partnerships). Although most forms of passive income of a tax-exempt organization are exempt from federal tax, income derived by a tax-exempt limited partner from certain investments and activities of a securities partnership may be classified as unrelated business taxable income (UBTI) to the tax-exempt limited partner, which would be subject to federal income tax. This chapter focuses on the UBTI consequences to tax-exempt limited partners of securities partnerships of various types of investments made by securities partnerships, including investments generating "unrelated debt-financed income." The method of calculating the amount of UBTI that a tax-exempt limited partner derives from UBTI-generating investments or activities of a securities partnership is also discussed.

The chapter concludes by addressing alternative ways in which a tax-exempt entity can participate in securities investments without incurring UBTI. These include investing in an offshore investment corporation, and investing in a domestic securities partnership as a lender rather than as a limited partner, typically through a debt instrument with a contingent or variable rate of interest tied to the profitability of the securities partnership.

Unrelated Business Taxable Income

UBTI Defined

Tax-exempt organizations are subject to tax on gross income derived (either directly or through a partnership) from any trade or business regularly carried on, which business is substantially unrelated to the exercise or performance of the organization's exempt purpose or function. IRC §512(a). If, for instance, a securities partnership receives fees for services performed, an exempt organization partner would be taxable on its share of the net fee income. An exempt organization will also be taxable on its share of a securities partnership's net income from investment in another partnership which itself operates a business.[1] Income from "dealer" activity will also be treated as UBTI. IRC §512(b)(5)(A),(B).

Statutory Exemptions from UBTI—Passive Income

Passive income earned by an exempt organization generally is exempt from UBTI. Thus, dividends and interest realized through a trading or investment partnership are exempt from UBTI. IRC §512(b)(1). Similarly, capital gains of such a partnership are exempt. IRC §512(b)(5). Statutory exemptions also apply to exempt from UBTI income from option writing (IRC §512(b)(5)), and payments with respect to fully collateralized securities loans (i.e., securities transferred under an agreement to repurchase to which IRC §1058 applies). IRC §§512(b)(1), 512(a)(5).

The Internal Revenue Service (the "Service") has ruled that, even when income is earned in an active business, if the character of the income fits within one of the statutory modifications, it will be exempt. For instance, in Rev. Rul. 79-349, 1979-2 C.B. 233, an exempt organization engaged in an active mortgage loan business. The Service ruled the exempt organization would not be taxable on its share of the interest income earned by the mortgage loan business because interest income is exempt from tax. The Service pointed out, however, that the exempt organization would be subject to tax on fees received by it for services performed in connection with a loan. In this connection, it should be noted that the 1993 Act added an additional exclusion to make clear that "loan commitment fees" received by exempt organizations are exempt from UBTI. For this purpose "loan commitment fees" means "nonrefundable charges made by a lender to reserve a sum of

---

[1] The 1993 Revenue Reconciliation Act (the "1993 Act") repealed a provision which automatically treated as UBTI any income received by an exempt organization from investment in a "publicly traded partnership."

money with fixed terms for a specified period of time." H.R. Rept. No. 103-11, H.R. 2141,p 182 (1993).

Other "Ordinary and Routine" Investment Transactions

Recently, the Service responded favorably to requests from the securities industry that it clarify that UBTI would not be applicable to income earned from interest rate and currency swap transactions, on the grounds that such transactions are ordinary and routine investments in connection with a securities portfolio which should not be subject to UBTI. Thus, in final regulations issued in July 1992 (Reg. §512(b)-1(a)(1)), the Service extended the Section 512(b)(1) UBTI exemption to "income from notional principal contracts . . . [and] other substantially similar income from ordinary and routine investments to the extent determined by the Commissioner."[2]

Investments in Controlled Corporations

Generally, an exempt organization investing (directly or indirectly) in the shares of a corporation will not be subject to UBTI on the receipt of dividends from, or gain on the sale of the shares of, the corporation, even if the corporation itself is actively engaged in a trade or business or incurs debt. See e.g., PLR 9414002, in which the Service did not subject an exempt organization to UBTI on the sale of shares of a wholly-owned subsidiary which itself incurred leverage.

If an exempt organization owns 80 percent or more of the shares of a corporation, however, any interest (or annuities, royalties or rents) derived from the corporation will be subject to UBTI to the extent that the income of the corporation, if earned directly by the exempt organization, would be subject to UBTI. See IRC §512(b)(13). See also discussion below on the possible "look through" taxation of a more than 10 percent exempt organization shareholder of a foreign corporation under present and proposed law.

Acquisition of Real Estate Mortgages

The primary tax concern arising out of the recent trend of purchases by investment partnerships of real estate mortgages or mortgage pools is how to characterize the gains upon the sale of the mortgages. Frequently, the strat-

---

[2] The Regulation refers to the definition of a "notional principal contract" in Reg. § 1.863-7, which defines such a contract as "a financial instrument that provides for the payment of amounts by one party to another at specified intervals calculated by reference to a specified index upon a notional principal amount in exchange for specified consideration or a promise to pay similar amounts."

egy in purchasing the mortgages is to restructure or rework them and sell them as quickly as possible to one or more purchasers. This raises the question whether the purchasing entity is holding the mortgages not in an investment or trading activity, but as a dealer, i.e., primary for the sale to customers in the ordinary course of business. If the purchasing partnership is a "dealer" with respect to the mortgages, a tax-exempt partner will be subject to UBTI on its share of the gain taxed as ordinary income. IRC §512(b)(5)(A),(B).

A critical issue, therefore, is whether the mortgage pools are held as "dealer" property. There appears to be no clear precedent on this issue. In the securities area, a taxpayer can be a very active trader, but will not be a "dealer" unless it makes a market in the securities, i.e., regularly engages in the purchase of securities and their resale to customers. See Treas Reg. §1.471-5. On the other hand, a taxpayer holding one or a few pieces of real property primarily for sale to customers can be a dealer. See, e.g., *S&H, Inc. v. Commissioner,* 78 T.C. 234 (1982). Since there appears to be no clear authority on how to treat a purchase and sale of real estate mortgages, the proper characterization will depend on each fact situation.

In the 1993 Act, Congress implicitly recognized the UBTI problem faced by pension funds acquiring distressed mortgages. It enacted a provision—Section 512(b)(16)—to encourage investment by pension plans and other exempt organization in mortgages and real estate acquired from certain financial institutions in conservatorship or receivership. Section 512(b)(16) provides an exception to the dealer UBTI rule by excluding from UBTI gains and losses from the sale of such mortgages and real property. However, the provision has so many requirements that it seems very unlikely that investment partnerships having tax-exempt partners will get much relief from it. These requirements include:

1. The property (real property or a mortgage) must be acquired from a "financial institution" which is in conservatorship or receivership or from the conservator or receiver of such institution (or any governmental agency succeeding to the rights or interest of the conservator or receiver).
2. The property must be designated as "disposal property" within 9 months of the acquisition, and disposed of within 2 1/2 years of acquisition (which date may be extended by the Treasury to assure an orderly liquidation).
3. No more than one-half by value of the properties acquired in a single transaction may be designated as disposal property!
4. The aggregate expenditures on development and improvement activities for the property cannot exceed 20 percent of its net selling price.

Unrelated Debt-Financed Income

UBTI also includes unrelated debt-financed income, which generally consists of

1. Income such as dividends or interest derived by an exempt organization (directly or through a partnership) from income producing property with respect to which there is "acquisition indebtedness" at any time during the taxable year.
2. Gains derived by an exempt organization (directly or through a partnership) from the disposition of property with respect to which there is "acquisition indebtedness" at any time during the 12-month period ending with the date of such disposition.

"Acquisition indebtedness" generally is the unpaid principal amount of indebtedness incurred in connection with the acquisition of property.

Consequences of a Tax-Exempt Partner Recognizing UBTI through a Partnership

General

In general, if UBTI is allocated from a partnership to an exempt organization partner, the portion of a partnership's income and gains which is not treated as UBTI will continue to be exempt from tax, as will the organization's income and gains from other investments which are not treated as UBTI. Therefore, except as indicated below, the possibility of realizing UBTI from its investment in a partnership generally should not affect the tax-exempt status of such an exempt organization.

Applicable Tax Rate for UBTI

To the extent that a partnership generates UBTI, the applicable federal tax rate for a tax-exempt partner would be either the corporate or trust tax rate, depending on the nature of the particular exempt partner.[3]

---

[3] With certain exceptions, tax-exempt organizations which are private foundations are subject to a 2 percent Federal excise tax on their "net investment income," without regard to the portion which is UBTI. The rate of the excise tax for any taxable year may be reduced to 1 percent if the private foundation meets certain distribution requirements for the taxable year. A private foundation will be required to make payments of estimated tax with respect to this excise tax.

Charitable Remainder Trusts

A charitable remainder trust will not be exempt from federal income tax under IRC §664(c) for any year in which it has *any* UBTI.

Trust Charitable Deduction

The charitable contribution deduction for a trust under Section 642(c) of the Code may be limited for any year in which the trust has UBTI.

Qualified Organizations

Certain exempt entities which realize UBTI in a taxable year will not constitute "qualified organizations" for purposes of Section 514(c)(9)(B)(vi)(I) of the Code, pursuant to which, in limited circumstances, income from certain real estate partnerships in which such exempt entities invest might be treated as exempt from UBTI.

Classification and Treatment of Unrelated Debt-Financed Income

"Unrelated debt-financed income" includes an exempt organization's share of a partnership's income and gains from its leveraged investments, including dividends and capital gains from securities purchased on margin.

Commodities Futures Contracts

The Service has held in a number of private rulings that investments in commodities futures contracts are not debt-financed and generally do not result in UBTI, even though the exempt organization is required to post margin. The Service's rationale has been that when a commodities contract is acquired, it involves only an executory contract which is not "acquisition indebtedness." See e.g., GCM 39620 (4/3/87). The Service has similarly ruled that a short commodity futures contract is an executory contract that does not give rise to acquisition indebtedness. See GCM 39620 supra (Service expressed no opinion as to treatment of short sales of stock).

Short Sales

The Transaction

In order to effect a short sale, a partnership will have its broker arrange on its behalf to borrow stock from a third party (the "Stock Lender"), which stock will then be delivered to the purchaser of the shares. The proceeds from the sale of the stock will be held as collateral for the obligation to redeliver the borrowed stock. In addition, the partnership will be required to post margin (equal at the outset to 50 percent of the short sale proceeds) pursuant to the Regulation T (Reg T) requirements for short sales promulgated by the Federal Reserve.[4] At such time as the partnership acquires stock which will be delivered to "cover" the short sale, the partnership will be entitled to the proceeds from the short sale. The partnership's profit or loss on the transaction will be measured generally by the difference between the cost of the stock acquired to cover the short sale and the proceeds of the short sale.[5]

PLR 8832052

Only one private ruling has been issued and, until recently, no public ruling had been issued on the question of whether a short sale transaction is subject to UBTI. The principal concern has been that the obligation of the short seller to return the stock to the Stock Lender can be characterized as "acquisition indebtedness," thereby subjecting to UBTI any gain on the transaction. PLR 8832052 involved a tax-exempt entity which conducted stock index arbitrage transactions, i.e., the sale (or purchase) of stock representative of a particular market index, and the purchase (or sale) of a futures contract on that index. When a short sale of stock was required, the exempt entity would obtain the stock through a "collateralized loan" of the shares. The ruling stated that "[a]ny such loans of stock would involve no net borrowing by [the exempt entity] because such loans would conform to the regulations of the Securities and Exchange Commission and would be secured by cash or Treasury securities owned by [the exempt entity] in an amount that is kept marked to a level that is not less than the current market price of the borrowed stocks." The ruling also stated that all cash or Treasury securities would be provided from cash or securities owned by the exempt entity, and no "net borrowing" would at any time be made. The Service ruled that, under these circumstances, the short sale portion of the arbitrage transactions would not involve acquisition indebtedness, and therefore the exempt entity would not have UBTI.

---

[4] While the short sale transaction is outstanding, the partnership will be required to pay the Stock Lender an amount equal to the dividends paid with respect to the stock.

[5] Of course, any in lieu of dividends paid to the Stock Lender (treated as "interest" pursuant to Section 163(d)(3)(C)) will reduce any profit on the transaction.

The Service's Position—Revenue Ruling 95-8[6]

A number of other private ruling requests have been filed with the Service, including one filed by this writer in October, 1987, in an attempt to obtain clarification of its position on short sales. Although the Service has not specifically responded to these private letter ruling requests, the Service issued Rev. Rul. 95-8 on December 30, 1994. In the ruling O, an exempt organization, sold short 100 shares of A stock for $500x. To sell the A stock short O, through its broker, borrowed A stock from a Stock Lender. O's broker retained the $500x sale proceeds (and income earned thereon) as collateral for O's obligation to return the A stock to the Stock Lender. In addition, O put up additional collateral of $250x cash "from its own (not borrowed) funds." The broker credited O's account with a "rebate fee" equal to a portion of the income earned on investment of the collateral.

The Service concluded in the ruling that the income derived by O upon closing the short sale of A stock for a profit would be subject to UBTI only if O incurs "acquisition indebtedness" with respect to the A stock. Citing *Deputy v. duPont*, 308 U.S. 488 (1940), in which the Supreme Court held that although a short sale created an obligation, it did not create indebtedness for purposes of the predecessor to Section 163 of the Code, the Service concluded that O had not incurred "acquisition indebtedness." Therefore, neither O's gain on closing the short sale nor income derived from the proceeds of the short sale, such as the rebate fee earned by O, is subject to UBTI. In summary, the Service held:

> *"[i]f an exempt organization sells publicly traded stock short through a broker, then neither the gain or loss attributable to the change in value of the underlying stock nor the rebate fee [received from the broker from investment of the short sale proceeds] is income or loss derived from debt-financed property. . . . No inference is intended with respect to a borrowing of property other than publicly traded stock sold short through a broker."*

Of significance, Rev. Rul. 95-8 clarifies that a tax-exempt organization will not be subject to UBTI on its short sale gains even though it obtains a form of leverage by effecting a short sale involving, at the outset, proceeds equal to twice the amount of its cash margin deposit. By contrast, the Service had implied in PLR 8832052, its only private ruling on the subject, that an exempt organization might have to maintain collateral equal in value to the market price of the borrowed stock. Moreover, in Rev. Rul. 95-8 the Service

---

[6] 1995-4 I.R.B. 1.

clarified for the first time that it would not take the position that the "rebate fee" received by a short seller is subject to UBTI.

The Service did not, in Rev. Rul. 95-8, deal with the situation of a short seller who collateralizes a short sale with Treasury securities or stock. Since it is not uncommon to use Treasuries or stock rather than cash as collateral for a short sale, the private ruling requests which have been pending have sought clarification that short sales involving the use of Treasuries or stock also will not be viewed as giving rise to UBTI. Assuming that the Treasuries or stock are owned outright and not financed by the short seller, it would seem that the reasoning of Rev. Rul. 95-8 should apply to short sales where Treasuries or stock are used as collateral. Under applicable margin rules, if the broker is required to cause more collateral to be given to the Stock Lender (i.e., when the borrowed stock goes up in value), the broker must put up cash collateral and will charge the short seller "interest" even though the short seller puts up additional stock or Treasuries. Thus, at least until private rulings interpreting Rev. Rul. 95-8 are issued, it may be prudent for a short seller who must put up additional collateral to put up cash, rather than stock or Treasuries, to avoid a possible argument by the Service that the broker is "lending" the short seller cash against the additional stock or Treasuries furnished as additional collateral by the short seller.

Hedged Investments

According to a private letter ruling issued by the Service, a position for which there is no acquisition indebtedness may be treated as debt-financed property if such position is fully hedged by another position which is debt-financed. In PLR 8717066, the Service held that if an exempt entity purchases on margin a portfolio of stocks representative of a market index, and hedges the portfolio with a short futures contract position on the index, gain from a disposition of the futures contract would constitute UBTI to the extent of the loss from a simultaneous sale of the leveraged stock. Although a futures contract position, standing alone, is not treated as debt-financed property, the Service ruled that the futures contract's hedge relationship with the leveraged stock position caused gain from the futures contract to be treated as gain attributable to debt-financed property. Thus, losses from the sale of the margined stock must be reduced by gain from the futures position, and could not offset other UBTI of the exempt entity. Conversely, the Service held that, in computing its UBTI, the exempt entity could reduce its gains from the leveraged stock position by its loss from the futures contract, since such losses are treated as attributable to debt-financed property.

The scope of this ruling is presently unclear. The holding of the ruling could possibly be extended to apply to all offsetting securities positions held by a partnership, thus requiring gain and loss from any "hedge" position relating to debt-financed property to be taken into account in computing a tax-exempt partner's UBTI. Alternatively, the ruling may be applicable only to situations such as the index arbitrage transactions, in which the hedged positions are simultaneously purchased and sold as a unit, and thus would not affect occasional positions acquired by a partnership which may "hedge" other investments in its portfolio.

Computation of Unrelated Debt-Financed Income

UBTI Reporting Requirement

In the case of a partnership having UBTI, the partnership is required to furnish each exempt organization partner with such information as is necessary to enable it to compute its distributive share of UBTI. IRC §6031(d).

Computation Rules

The computation of "unrelated debt-financed income" is complex:

a. Generally, to the extent a partnership recognizes ordinary income (i.e., dividends and interest) from securities with respect to which there is "acquisition indebtedness" during the taxable year, the percentage of such income which will be treated as UBTI will be based on the percentage calculated by dividing

(i) The "average acquisition indebtedness" incurred with respect to such securities by

(ii) The "average amount of the adjusted basis" of such securities during the taxable year.

b. To the extent a partnership recognizes gain or loss from securities with respect to which there is "acquisition indebtedness" at any time during the 12-month period ending with the date of their disposition, the percentage of such gain or loss which will be taken into account in computing UBTI will be based on the percentage calculated by dividing

(i) The highest amount of acquisition indebtedness during such period by

(ii) The "average amount of the adjusted basis" of such securities during the taxable year.

c. In determining the unrelated debt-financed income of a partnership, an allocable portion of deductions directly connected with the partnership's debt-financed property is taken into account. Thus, for instance, a percentage of capital losses from debt-financed securities (based on the debt/basis calculation described above) would be offset against gains treated as UBTI.

    d. An exempt organization's share of the income of a partnership which is treated as UBTI may not be affected by losses of the exempt organization either from the partnership or otherwise, unless such losses are treated as attributable to an unrelated trade or business (e.g., losses from securities for which there is acquisition indebtedness).

    e. Definitions.

  (i) "Average acquisition indebtedness" is the average of the outstanding acquisition indebtedness as of the first day of each calendar month in which the debt-financed property is held during the taxable year.

  (ii) "Average amount of the adjusted basis" is the average of the adjusted basis of the debt-financed property as of the first day and the last day on which the property is held during the taxable year.

    f. Accounting Conventions for UBTI Computations. As indicated above, the regulations require a very specific property-by-property calculation to determine the "average acquisition indebtedness" with respect to a security, the "average amount of the adjusted basis" of the security, and the highest amount of acquisition indebtedness relating to the security in the twelve month period ending with its sale. Although computer models conceivably can be constructed to make these calculations for investment partnerships not having a large number of transactions, it is extremely difficult—and perhaps impossible—to calculate UBTI on a security by security basis for trading partnerships. An informal survey of accounting firms active in this area indicates that they have adopted conventions to make the UBTI computations on an aggregate basis, rather than on a security by security basis. The objective in using the convention is to make a UBTI computation which reasonably approximates what would be achieved if a security by security method were possible to use.

    In summary, it is understood that the following type of convention has been used to calculate UBTI on the partnership's investment income such as dividends and interest (not including gain on sale of securities). Instead of calculating a debt/basis percentage for each security, an average debt/average adjusted basis percentage is computed. The "average debt" is computed by totaling the partnership debt balances outstanding on the first day of each month in the year (assuming a full year of operations) and dividing that amount by 12. The "average adjusted basis" is calculated by adding the total adjusted tax basis of all of the partnership's long securities positions on the first day of each month of the year, and dividing that amount by 12.

Under this method, the total gross income from the partnership's long securities positions for the year is determined. These amounts (e.g., dividends, interest) are then multiplied by the average debt/average adjusted basis percentage. (Generally, accounting firms do not treat interest or rebate income from short sales as being subject to UBTI—see discussion above). Deductions directly attributable to debt-financed property are calculated by determining all interest expenses, management fees, and other expenses during the year (expenses attributable to short sales (e.g., in lieu of dividends) are not taken into account). These deductions, multiplied by the average debt/average adjusted basis percentage, offset the investment income which is determined to be UBTI.

The amount of a partnership's capital gain or loss attributable to debt-financed property is calculated by reference to the *highest* average debt/average adjusted basis percentage for the month in which gains or losses are realized and the previous 11 months. The highest percentage is then used to compute the gain attributable to debt-financed property. Some accounting firms apparently attempt to determine the average monthly holding period of securities, and use that period rather than 12 months as the reference point in calculating the highest average debt percentage.

Methods to Avoid UBTI

U.S. Federal Tax Issues Raised by U.S. Tax-Exempt Entities Investing in Offshore Funds

U.S. Income Tax Concerns of U.S. Tax-Exempt Shareholders of a Fund

a. **Controlled Foreign Corporations (CFCs)**

   (i) *General.* The CFC rules generally apply only if more than 50 percent of the stock of a foreign corporation (in vote or value) is owned or is deemed owned by "U.S. shareholders." A "U.S. shareholder" is a U.S. person who owns or is deemed to own at least 10 percent of the combined voting power of such corporation. A U.S. shareholder in a CFC is generally required to include in its income a pro-rata share of the CFC's income.

(ii) *Tax-Exempt Investors.* Although the Service's ruling position is inconsistent on the subject, the Service has issued a private letter ruling which suggests that the Service would look through, under the CFC rules, to the ultimate earnings of a fund that is a CFC and would tax the income to a tax-exempt U.S. shareholder as if earned by such U.S. shareholder itself.[7] Under this rationale, if a fund's portfolio is leveraged, presumably the borrowing would be treated as if it had been made directly by its tax-exempt U.S. shareholders with the consequence that the leverage would result in UBTI. This risk can be avoided if a fund's U.S. shareholders own, in the aggregate, less than 50 percent of its shares. Moreover, a single U.S. tax-exempt investor owning less than 10 percent of the voting shares of the fund will not be subject to this "look-through" risk.

b. Passive Foreign Investment Corporations (PFICs)

(i) *General.* A PFIC is defined as a foreign corporation in which either (1) 75 percent or more of its gross income for any taxable year is "passive income" or (2) 50 percent or more of its assets (by value) either produce passive income or are held for the production of passive income.

U.S. persons are generally subject to U.S. federal income taxation with respect to their investment in a PFIC under one of two methods. Under the "interest charge" method, a U.S. person is generally liable for tax (at ordinary income rates) plus an interest charge reflecting the deferral of tax liability when it sells its stock in the PFIC at a gain or receives a distribution from the PFIC.

Alternatively, a U.S. person can make an election to have the PFIC treated as a qualified electing fund (QEF) with respect to its PFIC shares. A shareholder that had made the QEF election is generally taxed currently on its proportionate share of the ordinary earnings and net long-term capital gains of the fund whether or not the earnings or gains are distributed. In order for a shareholder to be eligible to make a QEF

---

[7] PLR 9043039. But see PLR's 8922047 and 9024026, which conclude that CFC income passes through to tax-exempt U.S. shareholders as dividend income (without regard to the nature of such income to the CFC), which is not UBTI. These rulings do not discuss the effect of leverage incurred by a CFC on a tax-exempt U.S. shareholder of such CFC.

election, the PFIC would have to agree to provide certain tax information to such shareholder on an annual basis.

(ii) *Tax-Exempt Shareholders.* Although it is not entirely clear under current law, a tax-exempt U.S. person investing in a PFIC generally should be exempt from tax with respect to its shares in a PFIC, assuming that such tax-exempt U.S. person does not make a QEF election. Proposed legislation[8], if enacted (subject to the discussion below) and proposed regulations, if adopted, would clarify the exemption for such tax-exempt U.S. persons if the tax-exempt U.S. person does not make a QEF election. (This assumes the tax-exempt investor would not otherwise be subject to tax under the UBTI provisions (because, for example, its investment in the fund is debt-financed).

c. **Proposed Legislation.** Legislation has been proposed[9] which would cause tax-exempt entities owning 10 percent or more of the voting stock of a fund to recognize UBTI in the following circumstances:

(i) Dividend distributions from a fund to a 10 percent tax-exempt shareholder would be treated as UBTI in the same proportion that earnings and profits of the fund would be treated as UBTI if received directly by such 10 percent tax-exempt shareholder, whether or not the fund is a CFC; and

(ii) Income inclusions under the CFC rules to a 10 percent tax-exempt investor in a fund that is a CFC would be treated as UBTI to such 10 percent tax-exempt shareholder to the extent that such income of the CFC would be treated as UBTI if received directly by the 10 percent tax-exempt shareholder.

At this time it is unclear whether this legislation, which had been passed by the House of Representatives in 1994, will be reintroduced for consideration by the current Congress. Moreover, the legislation appears not to apply to *gains* realized by an exempt organization upon redemption or sale of its shares in a fund, at least if the fund is not a CFC. Since in a typical offshore fund structure a shareholder does not receive dividends, the legislation may not have an adverse impact on U.S. exempt organizations seeking to invest in a fund. Moreover, it appears that if U.S. exempt organizations own only nonvoting shares, they should be exempt from tax under the proposed legislation even if they own more than 10 percent of the fund's equity.

---

[8] Section 402 of H.R 3419, The Tax Simplification and Technical Corrections Act of 1993 (the "Act").

[9] Section 901 of the Act.

U.S. Federal Income Tax Concerns of the Offshore Fund Having U.S. Tax-Exempt Shareholders

a. Is Fund Engaged in a U.S. Trade or Business?—The 10 Commandments

(i) *General.* A fund whose principal business is trading stock and securities for its own account that is deemed to be engaged in a trade or business in the United States will be subject to the regular corporate income tax (35 percent top tax rate) and branch profits tax (30 percent rate) on its income and gains which are effectively connected with its U.S. trade or business. However, if such a fund avoids engaging in a trade or business within the United States, generally it will not be subject to such U.S. income taxes with respect to its capital gains, even if its trading activities are conducted by U.S. investment advisors who are given discretionary authority to effect transactions for the fund.

(ii) *Location of Principal Office.* A fund engaged in trading in stocks and securities for its own account will not be treated as engaged in a U.S. trade or business if its principal office is located outside the United States. For federal income tax purposes, a foreign corporation is considered to have only one principal office. The Treasury regulations provide that the principal office of a fund which conducts most or all of its investment activities in the United States is deemed to be maintained outside the United States if the fund's management is located in a general business office outside the United States and "all or a substantial portion" of the following 10 functions are conducted from an office or offices outside the United States:

(1) communicating with its stockholders (including the furnishing of financial reports);

(2) communicating with the general public;

(3) soliciting sales of its own stock;

(4) accepting the subscriptions of new stockholders;

(5) maintaining its principal corporate records and books of account;

(6) auditing its books of account;

(7) disbursing payments of dividends, legal fees, accounting fees, and officers' and directors' salaries;

(8) publishing or furnishing the offering and redemption price of the shares of stock issued by it;

(9) conducting meetings of its stockholders and board of directors; and

(10) making redemptions of its own stock.

(iii) *Compliance with the 10 Commandments.* With the exception of function (3) (discussed below), the 10 functions enumerated above generally can be satisfied by technical compliance. Because there is no clear guidance as to what constitutes a "substantial portion" of the 10 functions[10], it is desirable for a fund to attempt to locate all 10 functions at offshore offices in order to avoid being engaged in a U.S. trade or business.

(iv) *Solicitations.* If a fund has substantial U.S. investors, its strict compliance with function (3) is very difficult. To the maximum extent possible, efforts should be made to have solicitations of U.S. investors performed from outside of the United States by the fund's agents or employees.

b. Minimum Foreign Ownership of the Fund. The exemption from U.S. taxation for foreign corporations trading in stocks and securities for their own account was added to the federal tax law in the Foreign Investors Tax Act of 1966 (the "Act"). It is clear from the legislative history of the Act that Congress intended the exemption to be available to facilitate investment by foreign investors in the United States. Nevertheless, neither the statute nor the applicable regulations stipulates that the exemption from tax for a foreign corporation such as a fund is based on the shareholders of the corporation being comprised of any particular percentage of foreign—as opposed to U.S.—investors. In fact, the regulations imply strongly that a fund having U.S. investors can qualify for the 10 commandments safe harbor.[11] The critical test under the regulations is whether a fund is engaged in a trade a business in the United States and, as discussed above, a fund can ensure that it will not be treated as engaged in a U.S. trade or business if its "principal office" is located outside of the United States. Under the regulations, a determination as to where the fund's "principal office" is located is made without regard to the percentage of its U.S. stock ownership. Nevertheless, where the U.S. ownership of a fund is significant, arguably the factual circumstances are not those contemplated by Congress when the Act was passed. Thus, it seems prudent for a substantial percentage (e.g., 50 percent) of the shares of a fund to be held by non-U.S. persons. Maintaining a 50 percent foreign investor threshold would also ensure that the fund does not become a CFC.

---

[10] It is unclear whether this means a "substantial portion" of each of the ten functions must be carried on from outside the U.S., or a substantial number (8–9?) of the functions must be so performed.

[11] See Treas. Reg. §1.864-2(c)(2)(ii) (Example 1) (10 commandments test applies for purposes of determining whether a widely held trading partnership is engaged in U.S. trade or business; example discusses partnership consisting of U.S. citizens, nonresident aliens, and foreign corporations).

Use of Variable Rate Debt for Tax-Exempt Investors

Some sponsors of U.S. securities partnerships utilizing leverage have offered exempt organizations the ability to invest in the partnership as a lender rather than as a partner, so that the exempt organization is not subject to UBTI. The type of debt instrument typically will provide for a low fixed interest rate and an additional contingent or variable rate of interest tied to the profitability of the partnership. It is, of course, crucial that the debt be structured carefully so that the Service cannot successfully contend that the debt is in fact equity of the partnership.

The factors governing the debt vs. equity issue in the corporate context generally will be applicable in determining whether a partnership's debt instruments should be treated as debt.[12] Some of the factors which typically support debt treatment for a variable rate note include:

- A fixed amount of interest must be paid annually.
- The debt has a fixed maturity.
- The holders of the debt are not sharing in losses of the partnership.

The fact that the variable rate interest is based on a sharing of the partnership's profits does not, of itself, make the exempt organization a partner.[13] However, most practitioners have concluded that, in order for a variable rate debt to qualify as debt, the exempt organization's share of profits must be subject to a maximum return or "cap," rather than being an unlimited share of profit. If the exempt organization's return on the variable rate notes is subject to the "cap" which could realistically be reached, its profit share will then look more like a return of a lender rather than equity return.[14]

---

[12] See *Joseph W. Hambuechen*, 43 T.C. 90 (1964).

[13] See, e.g., *Kena, Inc. v. Commissioner*, 44 B.T.A. 217 (1941); *Dorzback v. Collison*, 195 F.2d 69 (3rd Cir 1952); Rev. Rul. 85-51, 1983-1 C.B. 48; Compare *Farley Realty Corp. v. Commissioner*, 279 F.2d 701 (2nd Cir. 1960), and *Portage Plastics Co. v. United States*, 486 F.2d 632 (7th Cir. 1973).

[14] There are other indications that Congress has not taken steps to treat all contingent interest received by an exempt organization as UBTI. Compare IRC §512(b)(3)(B)(ii), which treats rent as UBTI if it is determined in whole or in part by "income or profits." No analogous provision applies to contingent interest. Moreover, in the 1993 Act Congress enacted IRC §871(b)(4), a provision which makes "contingent interest" paid to a foreign lender subject to 30 percent withholding tax. Compare also IRC §512(b)(13), discussed above, which treats as UBTI interest received from a controlled corporation.

CHAPTER 14

Prime Brokerage

Glen C. Dailey, Executive Vice President
Montgomery Prime Brokerage Services

Background

Banks have offered custody services to pension funds, mutual funds, and investment management firms for many years. The arrival of hedge funds caused a need for a firm that could provide consolidated clearing and custody for short sellers and option traders as well as for traditional investment manager. Several brokerage firms saw this as an opportunity to offer a service to a limited number of large customers. This clearing service that eventually became known as prime brokerage allowed an investment manager to execute trades in multiple financial instruments at various broker dealers while safekeeping all cash and securities at one firm.

History of Prime Brokerage

A. W. Jones and Associates were the pioneers of the hedge fund business. The fund began quietly operating in the 1950s with the idea of being long and short securities that would provide a reasonable return in bull and bear markets. Wall Street began to take notice of hedge funds when the surge of start up funds that occurred in the early 1970s started to become a significant trading factor in the investment business. Hedge funds were the original prime brokerage customers and continue to be the major force in the business today. Given the ability to trade with various brokers while financing both the long and short sides of their portfolio at one firm gave hedge fund managers the flexibility they needed to execute their strategies.

By processing trades on a same-day substitution basis, clearing brokers were able to provide automatic settlement to hedge fund customers by assuming the delivery or receive responsibility for each trade. The executing broker for each of these trades had to request a "letter of free funds" from the clearing firm for every trade that stated the account was in compliance with Federal Reserve margin requirements. The volume of letters became a problem as activity continued to increase over time. To alleviate the paperwork blizzard, clearing brokers agreed to sign a letter with each broker executing trades on behalf of a customer that stated the clearing firm would take compliance responsibility for Federal Reserve margin rules. This letter became known as a "prime broker letter" and was the origin of the term "prime broker."

The firm of Neuberger and Berman was the original prime broker since they were the firm that provided clearing services to A. W. Jones and Associates. A limited number of firms offered a prime brokerage service to clients in the early years of the hedge fund business. The hedge fund boom of the late 1980s presented an opportunity for brokerage firms with excess clearing capacity to set up prime brokerage operations. The prospect of having a steady flow of revenues from the commissions, ticket charges, and financing generated by hedge funds seemed enticing for many brokerage firms.

The prime brokerage business prospered in unison with hedge funds in the late 1980s as demand for alternative investment styles increased and the entrepreneurial spirit of investment managers grew. Investors have embraced the idea of having their assets managed by a money manager that has a major portion of his or her own net worth at risk in the same fund. Many times the general partner is the largest investor in a fund and stands to lose the most should investment decisions turn sour.

Getting Started

Starting a fund takes six to 12 weeks and requires three fundamental relationships. The relationships are with legal, accounting, and brokerage organizations.

Attorneys will write a partnership agreement and offering memorandum that will outline strategies and risks. These documents will always decide any issue of controversy or contention that may arise during the life of the fund. An experienced attorney will incorporate disclosures and investment powers into the partnership agreement that are broad enough to avoid unnecessary and expensive amendments. The number of states a fund is offered in and the amount of time it takes those states to process the appropriate partnership filing applications will dictate how long it takes for a fund to become operational relates directly to the number of states in which the partnership is being offered and the application process of each state.

An accountant will review a final draft of the partnership agreement to ensure accounting methods are acceptable and relevant tax issues addressed. The accountant will have an ongoing relationship with the partnership that will include responding to any tax issues that arise during the year and performing the annual audit.

The prime broker is the third essential component for a hedge fund and is the relationship that will interact with the operation of a hedge fund everyday. The prime broker's statements are the first report a fund manager sees in the morning and reporting the day's trading activity is the last task performed at night. Choosing a prime broker that will work well with an organization is crucial.

The Role of the Prime Broker

The basic service of a prime broker is to clear and finance trades. Services have expanded over the years to include research, institutional trading, portfolio accounting, soft dollar services, and consulting. Services continue to evolve as prime brokers become more resourceful and hedge funds continue to form and grow. For a hedge fund to maximize the value that a prime broker adds to their operation, they must look at the various services offered by firms and decide upon the issues important to their operation.

Wall Street research is a resource many fund managers use for generating investment ideas or for verifying their own feelings on a stock. Access to a prime broker's research reports and analysts should be part of the criteria an investment manager requires when choosing a prime broker. Direct access to the main trading desk of a firm that will provide a cost effective yet competitive execution is of equal importance. Participation in syndicate offerings can also be a major plus.

Operational services range from real-time profit and loss systems to individualized operational support. Prime brokerage portfolio systems will save time on the year-end audit by reducing the hours of manual work that accountants must perform.

The daily portfolio system reports supplied by prime brokers can vary but may include:

Performance statistics

Balance sheets

Profit and loss by security

Transaction ledger

Positions by taxlot

Positions by industry

Realized gains/losses

Monthly reports may include:

Transaction history

Capital gains listings

Income summary statements

Wash sale identification

Reporting systems can be very sophisticated and vary greatly between prime brokers. A review of operational systems and reporting capability is as important as reviewing the investment support services of a prime broker.

Marketing has become an important issue as the number of funds has increased in recent years. Competition among funds for the limited pool of investment capital available has grown. To compete for assets, a general partner needs a clear marketing plan as well as good performance numbers. A prime broker's assistance in this area can range from providing guidance in establishing a marketing plan to making introductions to potential investors.

Prime brokerage services have expanded from clearing trades to include much more. Potential users of prime brokerage services should understand their own internal capabilities and needs in order to ensure that they make the right choice when starting or expanding in the hedge fund business.

Operations

Every trade executed in the stock market requires an exchange of cash and securities between a buyer and seller. There are several internal departments of a brokerage firm involved in trade settlement as well as several outside organizations. These organizations, services, and operations may not be visible to the investor but are essential to the daily operations of Wall Street. Outlined below are some of the vital organizations, departments, and systems.

DTC—Depository Trust Company

The Depository Trust Company (DTC) is a member-owned organization that is the center point of all Wall Street settlement activity. DTC is the bank, post office, and telephone company for Wall Street. By acting as a centralized clearing facility, DTC empowers banks and brokers to clear and settle the high volume of transactions that occur in today's financial markets.

Every major bank and broker is a participant in DTC or clears through a company that is. Virtually all securities that investment firms and banks have on their books are in the vault of DTC. The DTC computer system records all of these security positions and allows its participants to transfer securities and money between each other each business day by computer terminal entries. The computer system of DTC tracks and updates thousands of transactions that occur between participants every business day. Security positions and balances update with every delivery or receive that occurs. DTC summarizes delivery and receive information of each participant and requires each to pay or receive one check for the net of all the participants' activity at the end of each business day.

The DTC Institutional ID System is the common link between brokers, banks and institutional clients that allows for notification and verification of trade executions. The ID system takes in computer feeds from every broker of all trades executed on behalf of institutional clients. This system has eliminated the need for mailed confirms and has expedited the information process between brokers, their largest customers, and banks that act as custodian for these customers. With timely trade information, institutions are able to instruct their agent banks with accurate trade settlement information more quickly. The ID system has helped to minimize trade settlement problems and has saved millions of dollars in carrying costs associated with failed deliveries.

Acting as the depository for most U.S. securities also allows DTC to collect dividends and facilitate exchanges and tender offers in a consistent manner for all its participants. Through the DTC computer system, brokers can pledge collateral to banks for loans and change the collateral daily. These computer communications facilitated by DTC give brokers great financing flexibility while maintaining compliance with regulatory requirements.

DTC has automated many functions and provided innovative steps to solving operational issues within the brokerage business. The efficient and cost effective services offered by DTC has made the U.S. settlement system the best in the world.

CNS—Continuous Net Settlement System

The Securities Industry Automation Corporation (SIAC), the computer processing company for the New York Stock Exchange, developed the CNS system to net buyers and sellers of the same security. There are times that a broker acts a buy and seller of the same stock several times in one trading day. To avoid receiving and delivering stock for every trade, the CNS system nets a single firm's trades for a day and requires only one net delivery or receive. The CNS system saves firms from having to make thousands of deliveries each day. Wall Street veterans believe the CNS system saved many brokerage firms from being crushed in the paper blizzard that occurred when 20 million shares was an average day's volume. Today the street could not operate without it.

OCC—Option Clearing Corporation

An option trade involves two parties that have taken opposing views of an investment. A buyer of an option contract needs a seller willing to accept the risk of being forced to buy or sell an underlying security, depending if the option is a put or call. To facilitate option trading and eliminate counter-party risk, the OCC standardized option contracts and became the counter-party to every option trade. The OCC computer system is the bookkeeping system for all option contracts. The OCC computer system will track every option contract from inception to expiration. OCC is the option market equivalent of DTC.

Same-Day Substitution Trades

A prime broker processes trades for hedge fund clients through its computer system as same day substitution trades. A same day substitution trade requires a two-sided bookkeeping entry on the brokerage system for balancing and clearance purposes.

For a customer who is buying a stock, the prime broker processes a buy trade in the customer account by making the account long the stock and debiting the value of the trade. In a clearance account the prime broker processes an offsetting sell trade that makes the clearance account short stock and credits the value of the trade. On settlement date the clearance account receives the stock against the short position at the same time the credit balance is being paid to the executing broker to complete the transaction.

The result is the trade settles, the clearance account is flat and the customer account is long the purchase of the stock. The customer account receives automatic settlement as if the account did all of its trading with the prime broker's trading desk. This method of trade processing makes the record keeping of an active account much easier.

Cashiers

The cashier's department is a secured area that is responsible for the physical processing of stock and bond certificates. Also known as "the cage" because of its enclosed nature and limited accessibility, the cashier's department processes delivery and receive transactions as well as stock transfers, reorganizations, buy-ins, and dividend payments.

Purchase and Sales

The purchase and sales department processes all trades executed by a firm's trading room. The department matches trades executed on an exchange to a customer or firm trading account. This department is responsible for ensuring that a counterparty knows and will settle each trade on the firm's books on settlement date.

Margin

The margin department is responsible for monitoring credit exposure in customer accounts and enforcing compliance of Federal Reserve margin regulations. The margin department will normally act as the liaison between customers and the operations department. Margin clerks control delivery, receive, and payment instructions related to customer accounts.

Stock Loan

The stock loan department of a brokerage firm serves several purposes. Their first mission is to maximize the number of deliveries made on settlement date. The stock loan department will borrow securities from various sources in an attempt to meet the settlement date trade commitments of their brokerage firm. Second, the stock loan department will borrow stock for customers that are short sellers.

For whatever purpose borrows are being made, there are several sources brokers use to satisfy their borrowing needs. Their own box (vault) is always the primary source. A brokerage firm can use securities in a customer margin account up to 140 percent of that customer's debit balance. Alternate sources for borrowing securities include other broker dealers that have customers on margin, pension funds, and mutual funds that participate in a bank's stock lending program. Pension funds and mutual funds are among the largest and most active players in the stock loan business.

The organizations, systems, and departments mentioned above are integral parts of daily operations in the prime brokerage business. The role each plays in the daily trade activity of a hedge fund is critical to understanding the settlement process of a prime broker.

Trading

An active hedge fund may interact with the trading desks of many different brokerage firms in order to obtain research, trade execution, soft dollars, or other services. The markets are global and methods of execution can vary. Executing trades through the right broker may be the difference between a winning or losing trade.

Equities

Equity securities can trade in many locations: where floor brokers walk out to a specialist post, electronically through a DOT machine, by an NASDAQ terminal, through a third market firm (i.e., Instinet), or even in London. Most equity trades clear through DTC from standard delivery instructions that brokers keep on their computer systems. This is the easiest and most efficient settlement process in the investment business.

Options

Multiple brokers can execute option trades for a customer. The settlement process for options begins at the time of execution. The floor broker must state that the option order will clear as a Clearing Member Transfer Authorization (CMTA) when entered. By stating the option trade is a CMTA, the floor broker is informing the exchange and the OCC that a prime broker will clear the trade. The customer must report the trade to the prime broker on trade date so the prime broker records the trade on its computer and reports to OCC that it is expecting the option trade. Option trades settle in one day. An accurate and timely exchange of information between the customer and prime broker is critical.

Fixed Income

Fixed-income securities generally settle in the same manner as equities since most fixed-income securities are eligible for DTC. Government securities settle by the Federal Reserve's book entry system.

Fixed-income investors who use a high degree of leverage must hold collateral at the firm that is providing repo financing for their bonds. Most firms do not want the exposure of high leverage concentrated in one account, therefore the firm that will provide the repo financing is the firm that will execute and clear the fixed-income trade for the customer. Since the comfort level on different issues varies from firm to firm, a leveraged fixed income trader may have a portfolio spread over several firms.

Global Investments

As the investment horizons of many money managers have expanded, so has the operational abilities of many prime brokers. To be an effective prime broker, a firm must have a network of agent banks that can facilitate the clearance of trades in markets around the world. The benefits of having a prime broker to consolidate your trading activity is even more important when dealing outside the United States.

Among the areas to be concerned with when dealing in foreign markets are the trading, delivery, and buy-in policies of each country. Most countries do not permit short selling by investors and failure to make settlement of a trade, in as little as two days in some countries, can result in the close out of the trade by the executing broker. Investors selling securities should be aware of registration policies. Failure to properly follow registration rules may result in the loss of dividends or the inability to sell a security in registration.

Regulations

As the prime brokerage business has grown, so has the level of scrutiny from regulatory authorities. On October 6, 1994, a no-action letter issued by the Securities and Exchange Commission became effective, outlining the procedures for parties participating in a prime brokerage transaction. The regulations require

1. Agreements detailing obligations and responsibilities among the prime broker, executing broker, and customer.
2. Minimum equity requirements of $100,000 for an account managed by a registered investment advisor and $500,000 for an account managed by a nonregistered investment advisor.
3. Executing brokers to be responsible for borrowing securities before executing a short sale.
4. Executing brokers to be responsible for the "know your customer" rule.

Compliance

There are basic issues of compliance that brokerage firms look for from a partnership. In the partnership agreement there should be disclosures or powers granted to the general partner that discuss:

> Opening margin accounts
>
> Investment strategy
>
> Trading options (covered and uncovered)
>
> Short selling
>
> Soft dollars

Short Sales

A customer executing a short sale of stock must know that the prime broker has stock available to borrow before entering an order. Short sales executed on a regional exchange require an uptick or a plus bid if sold in the OTC market. The settlement process is the same for short sales and long sales.

New Issues

When the syndicate market is hot, hedge funds are active participants. Partnerships must comply with the free-riding and withholding rule that pertains to the fair public offering of securities. Partnerships that have investors that include individuals employed by brokers, banks, or insurance companies cannot participate in a syndicate offering if prohibited individuals participate in the gains. To comply with this rule, a partnership must disclose its investors or provide a letter from the partnership's accountant or lawyer that states that they are aware of the free-riding and withholding rule and the fund is in compliance with the rule.

Margin

The purchase or short sale of a security is subject to Federal Reserve margin rules. The current Reg T margin rules require a minimum deposit of 50 percent of the purchase cost or short sale proceeds of a trade. The Federal Reserve Board may change margin requirements as a method for controlling monetary policy. The current lending rate of 50 percent has not changed in more than 20 years. After initial margin requirements, clients must maintain an equity level acceptable to support their debit balance.

The New York Stock Exchange is the regulatory agency that sets maintenance margin requirements. A brokerage firm expects customers to maintain enough equity in their account to support their margin debit balance. If the value of the securities falls below 125 percent of the margin debit balance in the account, a brokerage firm will ask the customer to add cash or sell securities to reduce the customer's debit balance. A customer must respond to a maintenance call promptly or face an automatic liquidation of securities to cover the maintenance shortfall.

For a security to be marginable it must trade on a listed stock exchange within the United States or be on the Federal Reserve's list of marginable OTC securities. All brokers are subject to the same Federal Reserve margin rules.

Financing and Fees

The main sources of revenue to a prime broker are financing and service fees. A customer pays a service fee for each transaction that a prime broker clears. Financing debit, credit, and short balances are an equally important revenue source. The larger the balances a fund carries, the more appealing that fund is to a prime broker. Consolidating balances with a prime broker to receive competitive rates on balances is one of the attractive reasons for using a prime broker. The financing component of the prime brokerage relationship will also affect the rates charged for clearance of trades.

Conclusion

The prime brokerage business has grown tremendously over the past 20 years and is likely to continue as the hedge fund format becomes more common. A prime broker can simply clear trades or can supply the infrastructure for operating in a hedge fund business. From getting started to daily trading, from portfolio reporting to K-1s, a prime broker can make a significant difference in the setup and smooth operations of a hedge fund business. A prime broker can make operations seem very easy or very painful. Choosing the right prime broker that has the operational and systems ability to support your operational, financial, and investment needs is critical.

Profiling Hedge Fund Styles

Lois Peltz, Managing Editor
Managed Account Reports, Inc.

One of the greatest myths is that all hedge funds are alike. This is untrue—some use diverse strategies while others specialize. Some are global while others are country specific. As would be expected, performance differs by styles. While there are many ways to categorize hedge funds and sometimes, it is difficult to pigeonhole a fund, *MAR/Hedge* uses the following categorizations.

Event-driven

- Distressed securities—Manager focuses on securities of companies in reorganization and/or bankruptcy, ranging from senior-security debt (low risk) to common stock (high risk).
- Risk arbitrage—Manager simultaneously buys stock in a company being acquired and sells stock in its acquiree. If the takeover falls through, traders can be left with large losses.

Global

- International—Manager pays attention to economic change around the world (except the United States). More bottom-up oriented in that they tend to be stock-pickers in markets they like, and use index derivatives to a much lesser extent than macro managers.
- Emerging—Manager invests in less mature financial markets of the world, e.g., Hong Kong, Singapore, Pakistan, India. Because shorting is not permitted in many emerging markets, managers must go to cash or other markets when valuations make being long unattractive.
- Regionals—Manager focuses on specific regions of the world, e.g., Latin America, Asia.

Global macro

Opportunistic manager profits from changes in global economy typically based on major interest-rate shifts, and uses leverage and derivatives.

Market neutral

Half long/half short. Manager attempts to lock-out or neutralize market risk. In theory, market risk is greatly reduced, but it is very difficult to make a profit on a large diversified portfolio, so stock-picking is critical.

- Convertible arbitrage—One of the most conservative styles. Manager goes long convertible securities and short underlying equities. Profits from mispricing in the relationship of the two.
- Stock index arbitrage—Manager buys a basket of stocks and sells short stock index futures contracts, or reverse.
- Fixed-income arbitrage—Manager buys T-bonds and sells short other T-bonds that replicate the bond purchased in terms of rate and maturity.

Short seller

Manager takes a position that stock prices will go down. A hedge fund borrows stocks and sells them, hoping to buy them back at a lower price. Managers short only overvalued securities. A hedge for long-only portfolios and those who feel market is approaching a bearish trend.

U.S. opportunity

- Value—Manager focuses on assets, cash flow, book value, or out-of-favor stocks.
- Growth/small-cap—Manager invests in growth stocks. Revenues and earnings and potential for growth are key.
- Short-term—Manager holds positions for a short term only.

Funds of funds

Capital is allocated among funds, providing investors with access to managers with higher minimums than they might otherwise be able to afford.

Performance Characteristics

Each investment style has different risk and return parameters. Table A-1 shows returns, standard deviations, and Sharpe ratios for each style for 1994, 1992–94, and 1990–94.

TABLE A-1. Median Comparisons by Style

	Event-Driven	Global	Global Macro	Market Neutral	Short Sellers	U.S. Oppty.	Fund of Funds	Futures	S&P
Returns									
1994	1.98	-2.59	-1.20	1.06	3.29	1.18	-6.97	-2.18	1.32
3 year	11.83	10.58	13.83	8.02	1.39	12.19	8.90	4.40	6.28
5 year	9.62	11.39	14.19	11.25	0.84	10.77	8.62	8.53	8.70
Standard Deviation									
1994	9.68	10.87	10.35	5.36	17.79	11.99	7.26	6.51	10.55
3 year	9.82	19.48	16.47	6.76	15.62	13.58	10.31	8.99	8.06
5 year	13.34	19.21	16.69	8.74	19.37	12.74	8.74	11.09	12.52
Sharpe Ratio									
1994	-0.18	-0.61	-0.47	-0.37	-0.01	-0.13	-1.27	-0.99	-0.23
3 year	1.16	0.57	0.69	0.86	-0.18	0.80	0.71	0.14	0.36
5 year	0.90	0.48	0.81	0.76	-0.04	0.53	0.55	0.36	0.34

1994		T-bill rate = 4.4%
3 year	1992–1994	T-bill rate = 3.6%
5 year	1990–1994	T-bill rate = 4.8%

Analysis by Time Frame

In 1994, short sellers and event-driven managers did the best, as illustrated by their median performer. Fund of funds managers did the worst and are one of three categories to have negative returns.

Over the three-year period, global macro managers reflect the highest returns while global managers have the highest volatility. Most categories generated returns in the 8–14 percent range which generally beats the S&P 500 at 6.3 percent.

In the long term, most hedge fund styles returned 8–14 percent except for short sellers.

Analysis by Style

Global Macro

Global macro managers tend to hold their positions for the medium term. Median returns for 1994 were down 1.2 percent but consistently they have been high performers for the long and medium term with annualized returns at about 14 percent. Volatility is about moderate. The Sharpe ratio has been excellent over the long term as well.

MAR/Hedge data indicate that global macro managers, who represent the largest category and have the longest history as a style, tend to follow a seasonal pattern—April is the low month and December is the strongest. The analysis of variance showed quarter-ends are strong, but not as strong as December.[1] While a significant December effect was shown, one caveat is that factors other than seasonality may be the reason.

Global

Managers who focus on specific regions include Peter Gruber of LatinVest and Martin Shefield of Ki Asset Management. This style category tends to hold positions for the medium term. Median returns for 1994 were down 2.6 percent. Over the medium to long term, returns have been good.

Emerging managers say their performance generally lacks patterns. But every October, says Mark Yale of Bankers Trust, the Mexican government, businesses, and unions agree not to increase wage or prices that could boost inflation. "As the Mexican economy and financial system strengthen, investors pay close attention at this time of year to the central bank's implicit vision of the coming 12 months and the extent capital markets are allowed to dictate foreign exchange prices," said Yale.

---

[1] *MAR/Hedge*, "Coming out of the summer doldrums," Sept. 1994, p. 10.

U.S. Opportunity

Value managers tend to hold investments for the long haul and have moderate volatility while growth managers hold trades for the medium term with generally moderate volatility.

Returns for 1994, as illustrated by the median performer, were positive, up 1.2 percent. Over the three- to five-year time frame, returns have been one of the highest. Volatility tends to be moderate to high.

Small caps do exhibit some seasonality. Edwin Vroom of Roanoke Asset Management says that most small-cap managers own technology stocks which peter out in March/April in anticipation of a slow summer. Few capital spending decisions are made in the summer and many European customers are on vacation. But the technology stocks tend to be revisited in late July/August.

Market Neutral

Chancellor's QLS, Fenchurch III, and Coast Arbitrage are examples of market-neutral managers. Convertible arbitrageurs are among the most conservative styles and had good performance in 1994 with a median gain of 1.1 percent. Over the last three and five years, performance has been good as well. They tend to have very low volatility. As a result, the Sharpe ratio has been excellent over all time frames.

Short Sellers

Short sellers were the best performing style in 1994, up 3.3 percent. Over the last three to five years, they have been poor performers and have been characterized by high volatility.

Event-Driven

M.D. Sass and Dickstein are examples of event-driven managers. This style had the second best performance for 1994, up 2.0 percent. They've had good performance over the medium and long term with moderate to high volatility.

Distressed managers note that their "hunting season" is year-end as they snap up great bargains that occur when banks, insurance companies, mutual funds, etc., sell out poor performers at distressed levels for year-end window dressing.

Funds of Funds

Optima Fund Management, Olympia Capital, Glenwood, Momentum, and Grosvenor are all funds of funds. They allocate assets to multiple managers with multiple strategies. As a result, volatility is usually on the lower end, as are returns. One of their main benefits is that for a lower minimum invest-ment than most hedge funds, investors can gain access to hedge fund man-agers with high minimums. In 1994, the median performance for funds of funds was down 7.0 percent, the largest decline of any category style.

Universe Graphs and Medians[2]

The universe graphs and statistical tables for each style (Figures A-1 through A-7) illustrate the annual rates of return, and medians and quartiles for the different styles over the last five years. These medians and quartile graphs serve as references to compare against each of the individual hedge funds.

Medians rather than means are used because outliers do not impact medians as they do means. For example, if we are averaging 10 funds' annual returns and one has a 1993 return of 230 percent (this may be due to the small assets under management, special focus, etc.), that fund might be categorized as atypical or an outlier. If this fund's return is included in a mean average, the result would be inflated or distort reality. Of course, an outlier may skew results to the downside as well.

However, by computing the median, we are able to find the hedge fund which in the middle of the universe (at the 50th percentile). The fund with a return of 230 percent does not directly impact the median. The outlier is considered as just another fund above the median.

Rankings[3]

Table A-2 shows the top performers over the last 60 and 36 months for the different styles. Rankings are done by return, standard deviation, Sharpe ratio, and assets.

HFQPR[4]

Tables A-3 and A-4 show recent performance for the hedge funds and funds of funds tracked by *MAR/Hedge*.

---

[2] *MAR/Hedge* Performance & Evaluation Directory, Q2 1994.

[3] Ibid.

[4] Ibid.

FIGURE A-1.   Performance Summary by Quartile: Global
Annual returns, 1990–1994

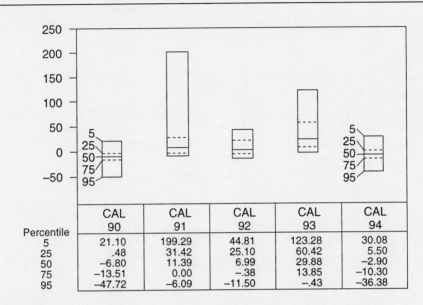

Percentile	CAL 90	CAL 91	CAL 92	CAL 93	CAL 94
5	21.10	199.29	44.81	123.28	30.08
25	.48	31.42	25.10	60.42	5.50
50	−6.80	11.39	6.99	29.88	−2.90
75	−13.51	0.00	−.38	13.85	−10.30
95	−47.72	−6.09	−11.50	−.43	−36.38

FIGURE A-2.   Performance Summary by Quartile: Global Macro
Annual returns, 1990–1994

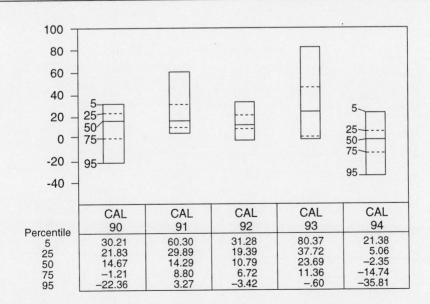

Percentile	CAL 90	CAL 91	CAL 92	CAL 93	CAL 94
5	30.21	60.30	31.28	80.37	21.38
25	21.83	29.89	19.39	37.72	5.06
50	14.67	14.29	10.79	23.69	−2.35
75	−1.21	8.80	6.72	11.36	−14.74
95	−22.36	3.27	−3.42	−.60	−35.81

FIGURE A-3.   Performance Summary by Quartile: Event-Driven
Annual returns, 1990–1994

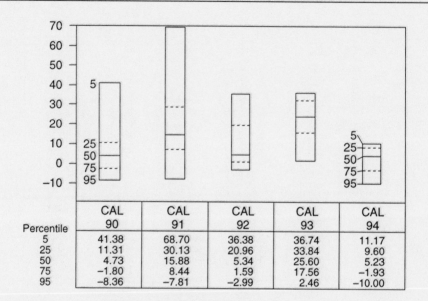

Percentile	CAL 90	CAL 91	CAL 92	CAL 93	CAL 94
5	41.38	68.70	36.38	36.74	11.17
25	11.31	30.13	20.96	33.84	9.60
50	4.73	15.88	5.34	25.60	5.23
75	−1.80	8.44	1.59	17.56	−1.93
95	−8.36	−7.81	−2.99	2.46	−10.00

FIGURE A-4.   Performance Summary by Quartile: U.S. Opportunity
Annual returns, 1990–1994

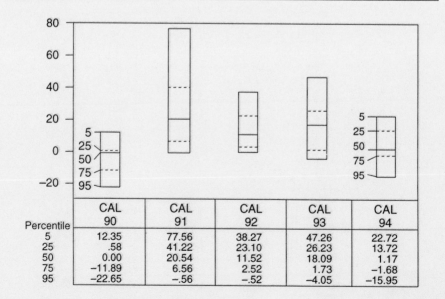

Percentile	CAL 90	CAL 91	CAL 92	CAL 93	CAL 94
5	12.35	77.56	38.27	47.26	22.72
25	.58	41.22	23.10	26.23	13.72
50	0.00	20.54	11.52	18.09	1.17
75	−11.89	6.56	2.52	1.73	−1.68
95	−22.65	−.56	−.52	−4.05	−15.95

FIGURE A-5. Performance Summary by Quartile: Short Sellers
Annual returns, 1990–1994

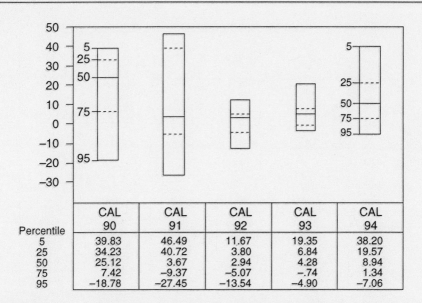

Percentile	CAL 90	CAL 91	CAL 92	CAL 93	CAL 94
5	39.83	46.49	11.67	19.35	38.20
25	34.23	40.72	3.80	6.84	19.57
50	25.12	3.67	2.94	4.28	8.94
75	7.42	–9.37	–5.07	–.74	1.34
95	–18.78	–27.45	–13.54	–4.90	–7.06

FIGURE A-6. Performance Summary by Quartile: Market Neutral
Annual returns, 1990–1994

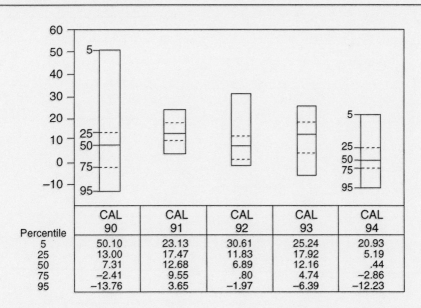

Percentile	CAL 90	CAL 91	CAL 92	CAL 93	CAL 94
5	50.10	23.13	30.61	25.24	20.93
25	13.00	17.47	11.83	17.92	5.19
50	7.31	12.68	6.89	12.16	.44
75	–2.41	9.55	.80	4.74	–2.86
95	–13.76	3.65	–1.97	–6.39	–12.23

FIGURE A-7. Performance Summary by Quartile: Fund of Funds
Annual returns, 1990–1994

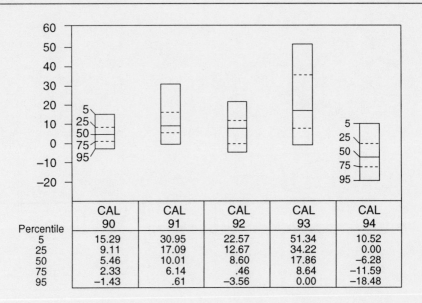

Percentile	CAL 90	CAL 91	CAL 92	CAL 93	CAL 94
5	15.29	30.95	22.57	51.34	10.52
25	9.11	17.09	12.67	34.22	0.00
50	5.46	10.01	8.60	17.86	−6.28
75	2.33	6.14	.46	8.64	−11.59
95	−1.43	.61	−3.56	0.00	−18.48

TABLE A-2a. Top 10 Rankings of Event-Driven Managers

Returns (%)		Standard Deviation (%)		Sharpe Ratio	
Ranking over the Last 60 Months					
1. Dickstein & Co. L.P.	317.25	1. Gabelli Associates Fund	2.78	1. Dickstein & Co. L.P.	1.65
2. M.D. Sass Re/Enterprise Partners	154.14	2. Gabelli Associates Ltd.	3.65	2. M.D. Sass Re/Enterprise Partners	1.40
3. GAM Arbitrage Inc.	77.15	3. WCM Partners L.P.	5.71	3. GAM Arbitrage Inc.	1.12
4. Hudson Valley Partners L.P.	74.95	4. GAM Arbitrage Inc.	7.27	4. Hudson Valley Partners L.P.	1.01
5. Aetos Corp. Class A Common Shares	58.34	5. Hudson Valley Partners L.P.	7.89	5. Gabelli Associates Ltd.	0.94
6. WCM Partners L.P.	58.19	6. Aetos Corp. Class A Common Shares	11.49	6. CM Partners L.P.	0.92
7. Calamos Convertible Hedge L.P.	50.54	7. M.D. Sass Re/Enterprise Partners	13.34	7. Gabelli Associates Fund	0.71
8. Gabelli Associates Ltd.	47.29	8. Sonz Partners L.P.	18.88	8. Aetos Corp. Class A Common Shares	0.46
9. Sonz Partners L.P.	39.22	9. Dickstein & Co. L.P.	22.53	9. Calamos Convertible Hedge L.P.	0.17
10. Gabelli Associates Fund	38.26	10. Calamos Convertible Hedge L.P.	23.94	10. Sonz Partners L.P.	0.12
Ranking over the Last 36 Months					
1. York Investment Ltd.	99.34	1. Gabelli Associates Fund	2.50	1. Otter Creek Partners I L.P.	3.39
2. Dickstein & Co. L.P.	97.90	2. WCM Partners L.P.	3.86	2. York Investment Ltd.	2.71
3. York Capital Mgt.	93.96	3. Gabelli Associates Ltd.	4.17	3. York Capital Mgt.	2.37
4. M.D. Sass Re/Enterprise Partners	70.62	4. Otter Creek Partners I L.P.	4.31	4. Hudson Valley Partners L.P.	2.33
5. Otter Creek Partners I L.P.	57.65	5. Hudson Valley Partners L.P.	5.04	5. Dickstein & Co. L.P.	2.13
6. Hudson Valley Partners L.P.	48.29	6. GAM Arbitrage Inc.	5.16	6. GAM Arbitrage Inc.	1.97
7. GAM Arbitrage Inc.	43.31	7. Aetos Corp. Class A Common Shares	9.82	7. WCM Partners L.P.	1.68
8. Aetos Corp. Class A Common Shares	39.72	8. York Investment Ltd.	10.16	8. M.D. Sass Re/Enterprise Partners	1.31
9. WCM Partners L.P.	31.54	9. York Capital Mgt.	10.97	9. Gabelli Associates Ltd.	1.31
10. Gabelli Associates Ltd.	28.46	10. Dickstein & Co. L.P.	12.69	10. Gabelli Associates Fund	1.09

1. Ranking through December 1994. Ranking based on data supplied by March 1, 1995.
2. To be included in the ranking, track record must include the full trading period for each time frame.
3. Ranking reflects lowest standard deviation.

TABLE A-2b. Top 10 Rankings of Global Managers

Ranking over the Last 60 Months

	Returns (%)		Standard Deviation (%)		Sharpe Ratio	
1.	Sintra Fund Ltd.	279.78	Chinook Global Opportunity Pro	9.45	GAM Selection Inc.	0.94
2.	GAM East Asia Inc.	249.73	Ermitage International Bond Fund	11.42	GAM Asean Inc.	0.76
3.	GAM Singapore/Malaysia Inc.	196.04	GAM Selection Inc.	12.66	Sintra Fund Ltd.	0.71
4.	GAM Asean Inc.	152.08	GAM France Inc.	14.11	GAM Singapore/Malaysia Inc.	0.70
5.	GAM Selection Inc.	102.55	GAM European Inc.	14.65	GAM East Asia Inc.	0.60
6.	GAM Japan Inc.	71.89	Ermitage Equities Fund	15.25	Chinook Global Opportunity Pro	0.53
7.	GAM Pacific Inc.	71.22	GAM Pacific Inc.	16.04	GAM Pacific Inc.	0.46
8.	Chinook Global Opportunity Pro	57.39	GAM U.S. Inc.	17.94	GAM Japan Inc.	0.34
9.	GAM Australia Inc.	46.45	GAM Australia Inc.	19.21	GAM Australia Inc.	0.17
10.	Ermitage Equities Fund	29.87	GAM Franc-Val Inc.	20.80	Ermitage Equities Fund	0.04

Ranking over the Last 36 Months

	Returns (%)		Standard Deviation (%)		Sharpe Ratio	
1.	GAM Singapore/Malaysia Inc.	209.13	Everest Capital Intl. Ltd.	7.83	GAM Singapore/Malaysia Inc.	1.61
2.	GAM East Asia Inc.	164.83	Chinook Global Opportunity Pro	8.63	Maverick Fund USA	1.49
3.	McGinnis Partners Focus Fund Ltd.	158.20	Chinook Global Opportunity Fund	8.78	Maverick Fund	1.45
4.	Maverick Fund USA	139.39	Ermitage Equities Fund	12.84	GAM Asean Inc.	1.22
5.	Maverick Fund	128.70	Ermitage International Bond Fund	13.38	GAM Pacific Inc.	1.04
6.	GAM Asean Inc.	121.07	GAM France Inc.	13.85	Sintra Fund Ltd.	0.94
7.	Sintra Fund Ltd.	100.29	GAM Selection Inc.	14.42	Ermitage Crosby Asia Fund	0.87
8.	Ermitage Crosby Asia Fund	82.30	GAM Pacific Inc.	15.63	McGinnis Partners Focus Fund Ltd.	0.75
9.	GAM Overseas Inc.	63.80	GAM European Inc.	16.26	GAM East Asia Inc.	0.74
10.	GAM Pacific Inc.	62.20	GAM U.S. Inc.	16.82	GAM Australia Inc.	0.67

1. Ranking through December 1994. Ranking based on data supplied by March 1, 1995.
2. To be included in the ranking, track record must include the full trading period for each time frame.
3. Ranking reflects lowest standard deviation.

TABLE A-2c. Top 10 Rankings of Global Macro Managers

Returns (%)		Standard Deviation (%)		Sharpe Ratio	
Ranking over the Last 60 Months					
1. Quantum Fund N.V.	354.43	1. Regal Trading Partners Ltd.	5.70	1. Regal Trading Partners Ltd.	1.84
2. Gamut Investments Inc.	179.61	2. Colobus International Ltd.	7.44	2. JRO Associates L.P.	1.59
3. Alpha Max L.P.	140.85	3. JRO Associates L.P.	7.60	3. Colobus International Ltd.	1.50
4. Ermitage Selz Fund	108.05	4. Iliad Partners L.P.	11.69	4. Gamut Investments Inc.	1.14
5. JRO Associates L.P.	100.31	5. Ermitage Selz Fund	11.99	5. Ermitage Selz Fund	1.10
6. Colobus International Ltd.	94.13	6. Alpha Max L.P.	16.82	6. Alpha Max L.P.	1.06
7. Iliad Partners L.P.	90.52	7. Gamut Investments Inc.	19.82	7. Quantum Fund N.V.	0.96
8. Regal Trading Partners Ltd.	90.05	8. Aquila Intl. Fund Ltd. A Shares	21.23	8. Iliad Partners L.P.	0.91
9. Aquila Intl. Fund Ltd. A Shares	89.70	9. Permal Euromir (ECU) Ltd.	25.47	9. Aquila Intl. Fund Ltd. A Shares	0.51
10. Permal Euromir (ECU) Ltd.	39.67	10. JGM Hedge Fund L.P.	30.55	10. Permal Euromir (ECU) Ltd.	0.10
Ranking over the Last 36 Months					
1. Oak Tree Partners L.P.	127.08	1. Regal Trading Partners Ltd.	3.91	1. JRO Associates L.P.	1.88
2. Aquila Intl. Fund Ltd. A Shares	84.49	2. Colobus International Ltd.	7.29	2. Colobus International Ltd.	1.61
3. Quantum Fund N.V.	72.89	3. JRO Associates L.P.	7.49	3. Oak Tree Partners L.P.	1.38
4. Moore Global Investment+	69.37	4. Select Strategic Partners L.P.	9.25	4. Regal Trading Partners Ltd.	1.28
5. JGM Hedge Fund L.P.	68.60	5. Iliad Partners L.P.	9.95	5. Select Strategic Partners L.P.	1.17
6. Gamut Investments Inc.	68.01	6. Alpha Max L.P.	11.63	6. Aquila Intl. Fund Ltd. A Shares	1.07
7. La Jolla Intl. Growth Fund Ltd.	55.88	7. Rosebury L.P.	12.12	7. Moore Global Investment+	1.06
8. JRO Associates L.P.	55.49	8. Ermitage Selz Fund	13.37	8. Iliad Partners L.P.	1.02
9. La Jolla Partners L.P.	48.75	9. Meteoric L.P.	16.29	9. Gamut Investments Inc.	0.97
10. Colobus International Ltd.	48.02	10. Momentum Guild Ltd.	16.65	10. Alpha Max L.P.	0.93

1. Ranking through December 1994. Ranking based on data supplied by March 1, 1995.
2. To be included in the ranking, track record must include the full trading period for each time frame.
3. Ranking reflects lowest standard deviation.

TABLE A-2d. Top 10 Rankings of Market Neutral Managers

Returns (%)		Standard Deviation (%)		Sharpe Ratio	
Ranking over the Last 60 Months					
1. Fenchurch Gamma Fund Ltd.	159.75	1. Lindahl Capital Mgt.	2.80	1. III L.P.	2.41
2. Fenchurch Beta Fund	143.74	2. III L.P.	3.40	2. Fenchurch Gamma Fund Ltd.	2.01
3. MCD Financial Arbitrage Fund Ltd.	105.45	3. Intermarket Fund S.A.	4.84	3. Lindahl Capital Mgt.	1.96
4. Millennium Partners L.P.	101.11	4. GAM Bond Fund Inc. (DM)	5.08	4. Millennium Partners L.P.	1.89
5. New World Partners (SPH) L.P.	89.70	5. Millennium Partners L.P.	6.14	5. Fenchurch Beta Fund	1.84
6. III L.P.	78.11	6. GAM Bond Fund Inc. (£)	8.52	6. MDC Financial Arbitrage Fund Ltd.	1.25
7. GAM Bond Fund Inc. (£)	63.27	7. GAM Bond Fund Inc. (SF)	8.87	7. New World Partners (SPH) L.P.	0.91
8. Lindahl Capital Mgt.	60.13	8. Fenchurch Beta Fund	9.40	8. GAM Bond Fund Inc. (£)	0.71
9. GAM Swiss Franc Special Bond Fund	31.63	9. Fenchurch Gamma Fund Ltd.	9.63	9. GAM Swiss Franc Special Bond Fund	0.08
10. Intermarket Fund S.A.	27.35	10. MCD Financial Arbitrage Fund Ltd.	9.78	10. Intermarket Fund SA	0.02
Ranking over the Last 36 Months					
1. Fenchurch Beta Fund	90.49	1. Lindahl Capital Mgt.	3.24	1. III L.P.	3.51
2. Fenchurch Gamma Fund Ltd.	90.28	2. III L.P.	3.26	2. Fenchurch Beta Fund	2.44
3. MCD Financial Arbitrage Fund Ltd.	77.63	3. Intermarket Fund S.A.	4.06	3. Fenchurch Gamma Fund Ltd.	2.41
4. Millennium Partners L.P.	49.17	4. GAM Bond Fund Inc. (SF)	4.31	4. Lindahl Capital Mgt.	2.10
5. III L.P.	47.72	5. GAM Bond Fund Inc. (DM)	4.63	5. Millennium Partners L.P.	1.83
6. GAM Bond Fund Inc. (£)	36.27	6. Convertible Opportunities L.P.	4.70	6. GAM Bond Fund (£)	0.98
7. Lindahl Capital Mgt.	32.71	7. GAM Swiss Franc Special Bond Fund	6.00	7. GAM Swiss Franc Special Bond Fund	0.89
8. GAM Swiss Franc Special Bond Fund	28.14	8. Millennium Partners L.P.	6.63	8. GAM Bond Fund Inc. (SF)	0.80
9. GAM Sterling Special Bond Fund Inc.	23.94	9. New World Partners (SPH) L.P.	7.08	9. Convertible Opportunities L.P.	0.80
10. Convertible Opportunities L.P.	23.16	10. GAM Bond Fund Inc. (£)	8.16	10. GAM Bond Fund Inc. (DM)	0.74

1. Ranking through December 1994. Ranking based on data supplied by March 1, 1995.
2. To be included in the ranking, track record must include the full trading period for each time frame.
3. Ranking reflects lowest standard deviation.

TABLE A-2e. Top Rankings of Short-Selling Managers

Returns (%)		Standard Deviation (%)		Sharpe Ratio	
Ranking over the Last 60 Months					
1. Emerging Growth Management	207.24	1. Permal Noscal Ltd.	6.21	1. Emerging Growth Management	0.92
2. Permal Noscal Ltd.	36.42	2. Permal Media & Communications	21.74	2. Permal Noscal Ltd.	0.27
3. Permal Media & Communications	-0.40	3. Emerging Growth Management	28.02	3. Permal Media & Communications	-0.23
Ranking over the Last 36 Months					
1. Emerging Growth Management	47.06	1. Permal Noscal Ltd.	6.23	1. Emerging Growth Management	0.60
2. Skye Short-Selling Fund L.P.	29.06	2. Permal Media & Communications	12.06	2. Skye Short-Selling Fund L.P.	0.27
3. Lynx Partners L.P.	11.41	3. Lynx Partners L.P.	18.82	3. Lynx Partners L.P.	0.00
4. Permal Noscal Ltd.	11.20	4. Emerging Growth Management	19.18	4. Permal Noscal Ltd.	-0.01
5. Permal Media & Communications	-5.22	5. Skye Short-Selling Fund L.P.	21.37	5. Permal Media & Communications	-0.45

1. Ranking through December 1994. Ranking based on data supplied by March 1, 1995.
2. To be included in the ranking, track record must include the full trading period for each time frame.
3. Ranking reflects lowest standard deviation.

TABLE A-2f. Top 10 Rankings of U.S. Opportunity Managers

Ranking over the Last 60 Months

Returns (%)		Standard Deviation (%)		Sharpe Ratio	
1. Adit Partners	187.12	1. GAM Money Mkts. Fund Inc.	2.83	1. Technology Yield Fund	1.38
2. Alphi Fund L.P.	182.34	2. GAM Money Mkts. Fund (SF)	4.11	2. Roanoke Partners L.P.	1.30
3. Technology Yield Fund	135.51	3. GAM Money Mkts. Fund (DM)	4.74	3. Adit Partners	0.94
4. Sharevest Partners L.P.	104.75	4. GAM Money Mkts. Fund (£)	6.56	4. Carl Marks Strategic Investments	0.77
5. Gabelli Intl. Ltd.	100.48	5. MCD Merger Arbitrage Fund Ltd.	9.20	5. Targat Associates L.P.	0.75
6. Carl Marks Strategic Investments	91.32	6. GAM High Yield Inc.	11.31	6. Alphi Fund L.P.	0.74
7. Targat Associates L.P.	79.32	7. Targat Associates L.P.	11.35	7. MCD Merger Arbitrage Fund Ltd.	0.67
8. Gamerica Inc.	78.14	8. First Eagle Fund N.V.	11.68	8. Gabelli Intl. Ltd.	0.65
9. GAM High Yield Inc.	70.01	9. Technology Yield Fund	11.89	9. GAM High Yield Inc.	0.62
10. MCD Merger Arbitrage Fund Ltd.	63.62	10. GAM Whitethorn Fund Inc.	12.08	10. Sharevest Partners L.P.	0.57

Ranking over the Last 36 Months

Returns (%)		Standard Deviation (%)		Sharpe Ratio	
1. Abraham & Sons L.P.	130.91	1. GAM Money Mkts. Fund Inc.	1.76	1. Peregrine Capital Partners	2.35
2. Avanti Partners L.P.	116.43	2. GAM Money Mkts. Fund (SF)	3.65	2. Abraham & Sons L.P.	1.88
3. Peregrine Capital Partners	95.72	3. GAM Money Mkts. Fund (£)	4.66	3. Technology Yield Fund	1.55
4. Alphi Fund L.P.	90.05	4. GAM Money Mkts. Fund (DM)	4.87	4. Eagle Capital Partners L.P.	1.53
5. Gabelli Intl. Ltd.	87.80	5. GAM High Yield Inc.	5.84	5. GAM High Yield Inc.	1.51
6. Alvarado Partners L.P.	85.84	6. MCD Merger Arbitrage Fund Ltd.	5.90	6. MCD Merger Arbitrage Fund Ltd.	1.44
7. Adit Partners	80.12	7. GAM Whitethorn Fund Inc.	7.06	7. Gabelli Intl. Ltd.	1.43
8. Roanoke Partners L.P.	76.43	8. Targat Associates L.P.	7.29	8. Adit Partners	1.31
9. Exponential Ptnrs. Max. Capital	73.62	9. Gabelli Performance Partnership L.P.	8.06	9. Alvarado Partners L.P.	1.23
10. Eagle Capital Partners L.P.	71.57	10. Technology Yield Fund	8.66	10. Avanti Partners L.P.	1.19

1. Ranking through December 1994. Ranking based on data supplied by March 1, 1995.
2. To be included in the ranking, track record must include the full trading period for each time frame.
3. Ranking reflects lowest standard deviation.

TABLE A-2g. Top 10 Rankings of Fund of Funds Managers

Returns (%)		Standard Deviation (%)		Sharpe Ratio	
Ranking over the Last 60 Months					
1. Haussmann Holdings N.V.	107.25	1. Ivy Asset Mgt. Corp.	3.15	1. Haussmann Holdings N.V.	1.25
2. Glenwood Partners L.P.	69.57	2. Rosewood Associates	3.96	2. Ivy Asset Mgt. Corp.	1.05
3. GAM Multi-Global US$ Fund Inc.	65.27	3. Oakwood Associates	4.34	3. Glenwood Partners L.P.	0.95
4. Anabasis Fund Inc.	61.38	4. Birchwood Associates	5.19	4. Anabasis Fund Inc.	0.59
5. GAM Allocated Multi-Fund Inc.	55.68	5. Rainier Partners	5.45	5. GAM Multi-Global US$ Fund Inc.	0.57
6. GSAM Composite Inc.	46.99	6. Optima Fund L.P.	6.22	6. GAM Allocated Multi-Fund Inc.	0.55
7. Ivy Asset Mgt. Corp.	46.08	7. Glenwood Partners L.P.	7.30	7. Optima Fund L.P.	0.47
8. Optima Fund L.P.	43.88	8. GAM Allocated Multi-Fund Inc.	8.74	8. Rosewood Associates	0.47
9. Birchwood Associates	37.40	9. Diversified Investments Assoc.	8.78	9. GSAM Composite Inc.	0.35
10. Rosewood Associates	37.26	10. GSAM Composite Inc.	9.61	10. Birchwood Associates	0.35
Ranking over the Last 36 Months					
1. Quasar Intl. Fund N.V.	127.65	1. Ivy Asset Mgt. Corp.	3.55	1. Summit Private Investments L.P.	1.83
2. Summit Private Investments L.P.	54.66	2. Birchwood Associates	4.18	2. Pan Domestic L.P.	1.78
3. Genesee Fund Ltd. (Portfolio A)	51.10	3. Rosewood Associates	4.77	3. Genesee Fund Ltd. (Portfolio A)	1.49
4. Hedge Ventures L.P.	46.05	4. Oakwood Associates	4.92	4. Equity Fund L.P.	1.38
5. Pan Domestic L.P.	43.98	5. Rainier Partners	5.20	5. Ivy Asset Mgt. Corp.	1.12
6. Haussmann Holdings N.V.	40.91	6. Equity Fund L.P.	5.41	6. Birchwood Associates	1.07
7. GAM Trading US$ Fund Inc.	40.38	7. Pan Domestic L.P.	5.85	7. Hedge Ventures L.P.	1.06
8. GAM Multi-Global US$ Fund Inc.	37.28	8. Glenwood Partners L.P.	5.98	8. Quasar Intl. Fund N.V.	1.02
9. Equity Fund L.P.	34.63	9. Optima Fund L.P.	6.95	9. Haussmann Holdings N.V.	0.98
10. GAM Allocated Multi-Fund Inc.	30.60	10. Diversified Investments Assoc.	7.48	10. GAM Trading US$ Fund Inc.	0.92

1. Ranking through December 1994. Ranking based on data supplied by March 1, 1995.
2. To be included in the ranking, track record must include the full trading period for each time frame.
3. Ranking reflects lowest standard deviation.

TABLE A-3. Performance of Hedge Funds

Fund Name	General Partner	Fund Manager (a)	Minimum Investment Required	Currency	Start Date	Start NAV/ Unit
ABRAHAM & SONS L.P.	98	306	250,000	$	1/92	1,000
* ABSOLUTE PERFORMANCE FUND LTD.	=	199,200	5,000,000	$	2/92	
ADIT PARTNERS	=	11	500,000	$	12/86	100
ADVANCED CASH MGT./SHORT DURATION	=	21	1,000,000	$	4/94	1,000
* AETOS CORP. CLASS A COMMON SHARES	28	91	5,000	$	2/86	2,500
AGGRESSIVE GROWTH PARTNERS L.P.	=	15	1,000,000	$	5/93	100
* AJR INTERNATIONAL	30	104	100,000	$	2/93	100
ALLIANCE ALPHA I PARTNEFS L.P.	108	319	1,000,000	$	4/94	1,000
ALPHA MAX L.P.	=	16	2,000,000	$	10/82	1,000
ALPHI CAPITAL L.P.	=	108	50,000	$	8/92	1,000
ALPHI FUND L.P.	=	108	250,000	$	11/88	1,000
ALVARADO PARTNERS L.P.	107	318	1,000,000	$	12/82	
AQUILA INTL. FUND LTD. A SHARES	24	60	100,000	$	1/85	104
THE ARBITRAGE GROUP L.P.	=	7	250,000	$	9/92	1,000
* ARDEN INTL. CAPITAL LTD.	106	315	100,000	$	10/93	100
* ASIA INTERSTRUCTURE DEVELOPMENT	=	38	Closed	$	5/94	99.16
AVANTI PARTNERS L.P.	=	264	100,000	$	9/90	1,000
BAY CAPITAL MGT.	112	320	1,000,000	$	9/87	1,000
BENCHMARK PARTNERS L.P.	23	59	500,000	$	12/89	1,000
BENNETT/LAWRENCE PARTNERS L.P.	89	158	500,000	$	2/94	1,019
* BLUE RIDGE OVERSEAS LTD	109	321	100,000	$	5/94	1,000
BV PARTNERS L.P.	77	265	1,000,000	$	9/94	1,000
CADUCEUS CAPITAL L.P.	=	133	1,000,000	$	1/93	1,000
CALAMOS CONVERTIBLE HEDGE L.P.	51	169	250,000	$	1/89	1.00
CALIBER FUND L.P.	43	999	250,000	$	8/92	1,000
* CASTALIA OFFSHORE PARTNERS LTD.	=	194	1,000,000	$	10/92	10,000
CAYWOOD CAPITAL FUND, L.P.	=	322	500,000	$	2/93	100
* CFP INTEREST RATE ARBITRAGE FUND	=	213	1,000,000	$	10/94	10.00
CHAMPLAIN PARTNERS LP	=	323	250,000	$	2/92	1,000
CHINOOK GLOBAL OPPORTUNITY FUND, L.P	35	#	100,000	$	4/91	1,000
CHINOOK GLOBAL OPPORTUNITY PROGRAM	35	#	5,000,000	$	4/88	1,000
* CNK CAPITAL GROWTH FUND	=	199,200	500,000	$	7/93	9.99
* THE COAST ARBITRAGE FUND LTD.	25	66	100,000	$	12/92	1,000
* COAST ENHANCED INCOME FUND II LTD.	25	66	500,000	$	12/92	1,000
COAST TREASURY BILL PLUS FUND II LTD	25	66	1,000,000	$	10/94	1,000
C&O INVESTMENT PARTNERSHIP L.P.	=	298	250,000	$	2/94	1,003
* COLOBUS INTERNATIONAL LTD.	=	61	250,000	$	12/86	100
COLUMBINE DYNAMIC STRATEGY LP	=	324	500,000	$	9/93	1,000
COMAC PARTNERS L.P.	87	154	500,000	$	4/93	1,000
COMPASS SERIES E LTD.	102	310	1,000,000	$	12/94	5,000
* COMPASS SERIES N LTD.	102	205	100,000	$	5/93	4,553
COMPUTIME INSTIT SERVS DOS PORTFOLIO	82	270	300,000	$	1/93	1,000
COMPUTIME INSTITUTIONAL SERVICES INC	82	270	300,000	$	5/92	1,000
CONVERTIBLE OPPORTUNITIES L.P.	=	18	1,000,000	$	6/91	1,000
* THE COVERED BRIDGE FUND INC.	=	10	3,000,000	$	10/93	10.00
* DELPHI OFFSHORE PARTNERS LTD.	=	194	500,000	$	12/93	9,750
DIAMOND A INVESTORS L.P	110	325	25,000	$	2/93	1,000
DIAMOND A PARTNERS L.P.	110	325	200,000	$	2/93	1,000
DICKSTEIN & CO. L.P.	=	4	2,000,000	$	4/86	1,000
DNB FUND PARTNERS L.P.	=	294	250,000	$	6/94	1,000
DORAN CAPITAL MGT. L.P.	=	295	250,000	$	6/94	1,000
EAGLE CAPITAL PARTNERS L.P.	=	3	500,000	$	1/91	1,000
EAGLE GLOBAL VALUE FUND LP	111	326	1,000,000	$	7/94	1,000
* EMERGING EUROPE FUND LTD.	64	202	5,000	$	11/93	100
EMERGING GROWTH MANAGEMENT	=	11	500,000	$	1/90	1,000
* ERMITAGE AMERICAS HEDGE FUND LTD.	29	96	10,000	$	11/93	10.00

TABLE A-3 (continued). Performance of Hedge Funds

1/95 NAV/ Unit	2/95 NAV/ Unit	Pct Change 1 Mo	Pct Change 12 Mo	Pct Change YTD	12 Month Rank	Initial Equity (Mil)	Current Equity (Mil)	Type of Fund
2,377	2,321	-2.4	20.6	.5	11	3.30	15.00	US OPPORT.
144	138	-4.7	-16.2	-4.7	207	3.30	35.78	GLOBAL
386	405	4.9	15.3	-1.7	21	1.79	44.23	US OPPORT.
1,055	1,066	1.0		1.6		5.00	31.00	MKT NEUTRAL
7,692	7,696	.1	6.5	9.9	71	.03	69.00	EVENT-DRIV.
135	128	-5.1	8.0	-4.6	64	1.50	40.80	MKT NEUTRAL
122	129	5.9	-.3	.4	123	.65	2.80	US OPPORT.
1,053	1,117	6.1		9.0		10.00	50.00	US OPPORT.
11,625	11,994	3.2	-1.6	3.5	138	2.03	156.20	GL MACRO
1,044	1,098	5.3	-.6	6.9	128	1.40	2.49	MKT NEUTRAL
3,534	3,678	4.1	46.7	5.4	1	2.30	15.05	US OPPORT.
3,193	3,257	2.0	-13.6	-9.5	197	2.30	31.00	US OPPORT.
513	525	2.3	-5.9	-.7	166	10.63	96.50	GL MACRO
891						3.17	2.99	MKT NEUTRAL
110	111	.9	7.2	1.7	68	1.51	9.00	EVENT-DRIV.
94.29	92.29	-2.1		-9.7				GLOBAL
1,917	1,967	2.6	-3.1	.8	149	.80	6.44	US OPPORT.
4,053	4,244	4.7	18.3	-1.8	14	1.00	102.75	GL MACRO
1,786	1,868	4.6	.4	5.4	112	4.30		SHORT
1,047	1,113	6.3	8.4	-1.9	58	6.00	17.25	US OPPORT.
1,035	1,010	-2.4		-4.0		10.26	18.74	GL MACRO
961						2.00	2.51	US OPPORT.
1,274	1,347	5.8	-.1	8.1	120	.75	3.60	US OPPORT.
1.77	1.78	.6	-8.2	1.1	175	2.00	4.10	EVENT-DRIV.
1,314	1,354	3.0	-4.7	-.7	164	.80	3.00	US OPPORT.
16,203	16,898	4.3	8.8	7.3	49	4.00	10.20	GLOBAL
120	123	2.5	2.4	3.6	97	2.87	9.20	EVENT-DRIV.
9.47	9.46	-.1		-3.4		3.00	2.85	MKT NEUTRAL
1,124	1,119	-.4	5.5	-.8	77	6.00	10.00	US OPPORT.
1,234	1,314	6.5	-1.0	3.9	135	1.25	6.38	GLOBAL
2,801	2,983	6.5	-1.0	3.9	133	.10	6.38	GLOBAL
11.01	10.40	-5.5	-14.9	-8.5	205	13.08	19.18	GLOBAL
1,552	1,573	1.3	20.4	.7	12	10.06	16.00	MKT NEUTRAL
1,182	1,188	.5	8.7	1.1	51	11.59	52.00	MKT NEUTRAL
1,026	1,033	.7		1.3		5.54	9.50	MKT NEUTRAL
1,016	1,007	-.9	-.2	-4.0	121	3.42	8.46	MKT NEUTRAL
337	338	.4	9.3	-.9	47	8.43	15.00	GL MACRO
959	984	2.6	-4.0	2.9	156	2.00	5.00	US OPPORT.
1,377	1,404	2.0	7.7	2.7	65	20.00	24.00	EVENT-DRIV.
5,585	5,420	-3.0		-3.8		1.00	9.02	US OPPORT.
6,840	7,318	7.0	23.1	-.9	8	1.91	14.48	US OPPORT.
1,316						3.00		US OPPORT.
1,858	1,803	-3.0	.3	-1.8	114	3.00	5.00	US OPPORT.
1,396	1,422	1.8	1.7	2.5	100	4.64	28.86	MKT NEUTRAL
9.28	9.10	-1.9	-9.9	.7	182	10.00	15.25	MKT NEUTRAL
8,643	8,970	3.8	-11.9	6.0	191	1.50	2.60	GLOBAL
1,267	1,281	1.1	-31.8	6.5	224	.09	.85	US OPPORT.
1,318	1,338	1.5	-30.7	7.6	223	.10	4.80	US OPPORT.
15,375	15,390	.1	2.5	-1.3	96	7.80	181.00	EVENT-DRIV.
1,193	1,167	-2.2		-2.1		1.00	1.50	US OPPORT.
1,193	1,362	14.2		16.3		1.00	4.00	US OPPORT.
2,154	2,209	2.5	8.2	2.9	61	.70	21.00	US OPPORT.
1,097	1,112	1.3		.4		7.00	17.00	US OPPORT.
137	139	1.3	27.8	2.5	5	.17	.23	GLOBAL
3,090	3,214	4.0	17.4	4.6	18	.05	31.37	SHORT-SALES
6.69						10.30		GL MACRO

TABLE A-3 (continued). Performance of Hedge Funds

*ERMITAGE ASIAN HEDGE FUND	29	94	10,000	$	6/93	10.00
*ERMITAGE CROSBY ASIA FUND	=	138	10,000	$	6/91	10.00
*ERMITAGE EMERGING MARKETS FUND LTD.	=	138	10,000	$	12/92	10.00
*ERMITAGE EQUITIES FUND	=	138	10,000	$	7/88	10.00
*ERMITAGE EUROPEAN FUND	=	138	10,000	DM	12/92	10.00
*ERMITAGE INTEREST RATE STRATEGY FUND	37	136	20,000	DM	4/94	10.00
*ERMITAGE INTERNATIONAL BOND FUND	=	302	10,000	$	7/83	10.00
*ERMITAGE MEES & HOPE EMS BOND FUND	=	300	10,000	ECU	7/92	100
*ERMITAGE MEES & HOPE EUROPEAN FUND	=	300	20,000	DM	8/90	100
*ERMITAGE SELZ FUND	29	95	10,000	$	5/84	10.00
*ERMITAGE UK EQUITIES FUND	=	138	10,000	BP	4/91	10.00
EUROPEAN FINANCIAL EQUITIES PLC.	=	280	350,000	$	4/93	99.74
EUROPEAN VALUE FUND L.P. (CLASS A)	76	261	100,000	DM	12/93	2,000
*EUROPEAN VALUE FUND LTD. (CLASS A)	76	261	1,000,000	DM	12/93	2,000
EUROPEAN VALUE FUND L.P. (CLASS B)	76	261	250,000	$	12/93	1,000
*EUROPEAN VALUE FUND LTD (CLASS B)	76	261	1,000,000	$	12/93	1,000
EVEREST CAPITAL FUND L.P.	=	70	2,000,000	$	2/91	100
*EVEREST CAPITAL INTL. LTD.	=	70	2,000,000	$	2/92	104
*THE EXPLORER FUND LTD.	=	260	1,000,000	$	1/94	100
*THE EXPONENTIAL OFFSHORE FUND LTD.	=	20	500,000	$	9/94	100
EXPONENTIAL PTNRS. MAX. CAPITAL	=	20	500,000	$	10/91	1,000
FAMCO CAPITAL PARTNERS L.P.	=	283	1,000,000	$	6/93	1,000
FAMCO INCOME PARTNERS L.P.	=	283	500,000	$	6/93	1,000
FELDMAN-JACINTO L.P.	=	107	100,000	$	7/92	1,000
FENCHURCH BETA FUND	=	30	1,000,000	$	3/87	1,000
*FENCHURCH GAMMA FUND LTD.	=	30	100,000	$	6/87	1,000
*FERRELL GLOBAL TRADING LTD.	65	999	1,000,000	$	8/93	10.00
FINANCIAL PARTNERS I LTD.	=	72	Closed	$	9/93	5,000
FINSBURY PARTNERS L.P.	=	181	1,000,000	$	5/94	1,000
*FIRST EAGLE FUND N.V.	=	60	5,000	$	11/89	37,549
FIXED INCOME OVERLAY STRATEGY	=	21	1,000,000	$	2/93	1,023
*FLA INTERNATIONAL FUND LTD.	=	272	1,000,000	$	10/94	100
*FORTUNA INTERNATIONAL LTD.	23	118	50,000	$	3/94	25.00
FULLY HEDGED PARTNERS	39	143	1,000,000	$	1/93	1.00
GABELLI ASSOCIATES FUND	=	53	1,000,000	$	2/85	1,000
*GABELLI ASSOCIATES LTD.	=	53	1,000,000	$	9/89	100
*GABELLI INTL. GOLD FUND LTD(CLASS B)	=	53	250,000	$	10/94	10.00
*GABELLI INTL. GOLD FUND LTD(CLASS C)	=	53	1,000,000	$	11/94	10.00
*GABELLI INTL. LTD.	=	53	1,000,000	$	2/89	109
GABELLI PERFORMANCE PARTNERSHIP L.P.	=	159	1,000,000	$	1/87	1,000
*GAM ARBITRAGE INC.	62	299	15,000	$	1/84	100
*GAM ASEAN INC.	=	285	15,000	$	6/87	100
*GAM AUSTRALIA INC.	=	285	15,000	$	8/85	100
*GAM BOND FUND INC.(D-MARK)	=	285	15,000	DM	12/85	100
*GAM BOND FUND INC.(POUND STERLING)	=	285	15,000	BP	12/85	100
*GAM BOND FUND INC.(SWISS FRANC)	=	285	15,000	SFR	12/85	100
*GAM CROSS-MARKET INC.	=	285	15,000	$	6/93	100
*GAM EAST ASIA INC.	=	285	15,000	$	8/85	100
*GAMERICA INC.	=	285	15,000	$	6/83	100
*GAM EUROPEAN INC.	=	285	15,000	$	3/89	100
*GAM FRANCE INC.	93	293	100,000	FFR	5/86	1,000
*GAM FRANC-VAL INC.	=	285	25,000	SFR	1/85	100
*GAM GAMCO FUND INC.	93	292	15,000	$	11/87	100
*GAM HIGH YIELD INC.	93	290	15,000	$	8/87	100
*GAM JAPAN INC.	=	285	15,000	$	8/85	100
*GAM MONEY MARKETS FUND (D-MARK)	=	285	15,000	DM	2/87	100
*GAM MONEY MARKETS FUND INC.	=	285	15,000	YEN	2/87	10,000
*GAM MONEY MARKETS FUND (POUND)	=	285	15,000	BP	2/87	100
*GAM MONEY MARKETS FUND(SWISS FRANC)	=	285	15,000	SFR	2/87	100
*GAM OVERSEAS INC.	93	286	15,000	$	10/91	100

TABLE A-3 (continued). Performance of Hedge Funds

8.49	8.25	-2.8	-36.6	-1.8	227		15.88	GL MACRO
14.42	14.80	2.6	-32.8	-13.6	225	4.09	5.52	GLOBAL
15.54	15.06	-3.1	-9.4	-9.4	180	1.35	10.16	GLOBAL
15.27	15.14	-.9	-18.9	-4.7	212	10.14	1.96	GLOBAL
9.00	8.75	-2.8	-38.9	-3.4	228	8.91	33.22	GLOBAL
10.09	10.03	-.6		-1.3		25.50	24.07	MKT NEUTRAL
20.40	20.78	1.9	-17.7	2.2	210	4.00	8.90	GLOBAL
119	118	-.8	-8.7	.0	177		11.08	GLOBAL
91.32	91.34	.0	-23.2	-5.5	217	14.03	5.32	GLOBAL
61.41	62.31	1.5	-7.1	.9	172		182.20	GL MACRO
9.97	10.02	.5	-25.3	-8.3	219	1.32	6.54	GLOBAL
126	129	2.5	-.4	4.3	124		16.40	GLOBAL
2,138	2,071	-3.2	-2.6	-1.0	146	.05	48.15	GLOBAL
2,138	2,071	-3.2	-3.3	-3.1	152			GLOBAL
1,066	1,040	-2.5	-1.8	-.6	139	10.18	91.32	GLOBAL
1,066	1,040	-2.5	-2.3	-2.3	144			GLOBAL
213	215	1.0	-10.9	-2.2	185	10.75	188.40	GLOBAL
120	121	.8	-12.0	-2.8	192	2.00	220.00	GLOBAL
851						115.50	74.70	GLOBAL
103						3.00	4.00	US OPPORT.
1,792						2.20	40.00	US OPPORT.
1,118	1,156	3.5	-14.0	4.4	200	2.32	40.50	US OPPORT.
1,137	1,147	.9	-2.7	2.7	147	3.45	14.50	US OPPORT.
1,425	1,388	-2.6	1.6	3.6	102	.62	3.00	US OPPORT.
3,221	3,147	-2.3	8.5	-.7	57	2.98	134.60	MKT NEUTRAL
3,241	3,169	-2.2	8.0	-.7	63	48.05	537.60	MKT NEUTRAL
7.96	7.75	-2.6	-14.8	-4.0	204	13.50	14.10	GL MACRO
7,421	7,855	5.8	20.9	11.4	10	.65	2.73	US OPPORT.
1,093	1,102	.8		3.4		58.00	78.30	GLOBAL
59,013	59,987	1.6	.1	2.1	119	193.20	246.50	US OPPORT.
1,429	1,435	.4	4.1	.8	86	100.00	100.00	MKT NEUTRAL
98.50						2.00	1.97	US OPPORT.
16.96	13.13	-22.6	-47.5	-17.0	230	15.00	12.00	GL MACRO
1.11	1.12	.9	2.8		93	3.00	5.66	MKT NEUTRAL
2,968							75.00	EVENT-DRIV.
154							3.00	EVENT-DRIV.
8.76						.30	.33	NATURAL
8.71						5.00	4.35	NATURAL
248							21.00	US OPPORT.
1,988						27.00	66.00	US OPPORT.
412	419	1.8	7.0	2.1	69	25.00	50.70	EVENT-DRIV.
367	379	3.4	-25.8	-9.8	220		298.80	GLOBAL
208	194	-6.7	-14.8	-11.4	202		5.50	GLOBAL
119	121	1.1	-1.0	1.9	132		66.60	MKT NEUTRAL
160	162	.8	-3.2	-4.8	151		32.20	MKT NEUTRAL
103	103	.5	-1.0	1.5	134		62.40	MKT NEUTRAL
114	112	-1.3	.8	-.7	107		134.90	GLOBAL
612	632	3.2	-17.8	-9.2	211		33.50	GLOBAL
466	472	1.3	8.7	3.4	52		34.20	US OPPORT.
88.31	89.54	1.4	-4.7	.6	163		68.60	GLOBAL
1,577	1,511	-4.1	-28.4	-7.2	222		10.60	GLOBAL
231	230	-.4	-13.8	-4.9	199		27.80	GLOBAL
218	221	1.1	.6	2.3	110		3.50	US OPPORT.
158	163	3.2	1.2	3.3	104		32.70	US OPPORT.
792	754	-4.8	-11.3	-11.7	186		281.20	GLOBAL
100	101	.3	.1	-1.3	118		30.00	US OPPORT.
10,014	10,026	.1	.2	-.5	116		10.70	US OPPORT.
100	101	.4	.4	-1.4	113		46.20	US OPPORT.
100	100	.2	.1	-1.2	117		110.40	US OPPORT.
168	163	-2.9	-21.6	-.5	214		19.90	GLOBAL

TABLE A-3 (continued).   Performance of Hedge Funds

Fund Name	General Partner	Fund Manager (a)	Minimum Investment Required	Currency	Start Date	Start NAV/ Unit
* GAM PACIFIC INC.	=	285	15,000	$	12/83	100
* GAM RELATIVE VALUE STRAT. FUND INC.	80	285	15,000	$	9/92	100
* GAM SELECTION INC.	93	296	15,000	$	5/84	100
* GAM SINGAPORE/MALAYSIA INC.	=	285	15,000	$	8/85	100
* GAM STERLING SPECIAL BOND FUND INC.	=	285	10,000	BP	12/90	100
* GAM SWISS FRANC SPECIAL BOND FUND	=	285	25,000	SFR	10/88	100
* GAM U.S. INC.	93	284	15,000	$	8/86	100
* GAMUT INVESTMENTS INC.	93	279	15,000	$	7/86	100
* GAM VALUE INC.	93	291	15,000	$	1/89	100
* GAM WHITETHORN FUND INC.	93	288	15,000	$	4/87	100
* GAZELLE GLOBAL FUND LTD.	=	19	1,000,000	$	7/94	1,000
GEM CONVERTIBLE SECURITIES PTNRS.	=	145	250,000	$	7/93	1,000
* GEOPARTNERS L.P.	45	143	1,000,000	$	5/94	1,000
* G.I. MULTI-STRATEGY FUND	=	33	50,000	$	5/91	1,000
* GLENROCK GLOBAL PARTNERS (BVI) INC.	=	281	500,000	$	10/94	95.51
GLENROCK GLOBAL PARTNERS L.P.	=	281	500,000	$	10/94	1,000
GLOBAL FIXED INCOME STRATEGY	=	21	1,000,000	$	4/94	1,000
GLOBAL MAP I L.P.	65	#	500,000	$	12/92	1,000
GRYPHON HIDDEN VALUES LTD	=	327	100,000	$	8/91	1,000
HALCYON ALCHEMY FUND LP	=	327	500,000	$	8/90	1,000
HALCYON ARBITRAGE, L.P.	=	327	500,000	$	1/90	1,000
HALCYON DISTRESSED SECURITIES LP	=	327	500,000	$	1/90	1,000
HALCYON INSTITUTIONAL LP	=	327	500,000	$	1/90	1,000
HALCYON MULTIPLE STRATEGIES LP	=	327	500,000	$	2/90	972
HALCYON PRIVATE PAPER LP	=	327	500,000	$	2/90	1,001
HALCYON SPECIAL SITUATIONS LP	=	327	500,000	$	1/90	1,000
HEARTLAND L.P. I	97	304	250,000	$	3/94	1,000
* HEDGE FUND (STERLING)	13	26	1,500,000	BP	11/92	100
HELLMOLD ASSOC. OPPORTUNITY II L.P.	=	278	500,000	$	12/91	
HIGHBRIDGE CAPITAL CORP.	=	103	1,000,000	$	9/92	10,000
HUDSON VALLEY PARTNERS L.P.	=	22	1,000,000	$	11/87	1,000
HULL LIQUIDITY FUND LP	=	328	500,000	$	1/94	1,000
* III FUND LTD	61	32	250,000	$	7/93	1,000
* III GLOBAL LTD.	61	32	1,000,000	$	6/94	1,000
III L.P.	=	32	1,000,000	$	7/82	1,000
* ILIAD PARTNERS L.P.	55	181	1,000,000	$	1/89	1,000
* INTEGRAL HEDGED ASSETS LTD. EUROPEAN	52	171	25,000	$	6/94	10.00
* INTERMARKET FUND S.A.	=	137	20,000	$	1/88	327
* INTERPORTFOLIO CONVERTIBLE BONDS	=	137	20,000	$	6/93	1,000
* JAGUAR FUND N.V. +	=	37	1,000,000	$	11/92	362
JGM HEDGE FUND L.P.	=	31	50,000	$	5/87	1,000
JLH CAPITAL INVESTMENT LTD.	38	142	100,000	$	1/93	1,000
JRO ASSOCIATES L.P.	=	111	1,000,000	$	8/82	1,000
* THE KIM FUND LTD.	9	23	100,000	$	7/93	1,000
* KLEINWORT BENSON BOND ARB.FUND (ECU)	=	93	250,000	ECU	11/92	10.00
* KLEINWORT BENSON BOND ARBITRAGE (US)	=	93	350,000	$	8/94	10.00
* KLEINWORT BENSON DER. PRODUCTS (DM)	=	93	500,000	DM	2/94	100
* KLEINWORT BENSON DER. PRODUCTS (USD)	=	93	350,000	$	3/94	50.00
* KODIAK INTERNATIONAL LTD.	23	151	Closed	$	11/93	25.00
* KS INTERNATIONAL INC.	=	141	250,000	$	1/93	100
* LA JOLLA INTL. GROWTH FUND LTD.	24	29	250,000	$	12/91	100
LA JOLLA PARTNERS L.P.	=	29	500,000	$	7/90	1,000
* LANE ARBITRAGE LTD. (INTL.)	=	224	1,000,000	$	1/94	1,000
LANE ARBITRAGE LTD.	=	224	1,000,000	$	1/94	1,000
LATINVEST PARTNERS L.P.	=	134	1,000,000	$	2/94	1,090
THE LEXINGTON TRUST	=	62	Closed	$	1/93	100

TABLE A-3 (continued). Performance of Hedge Funds

1/95 NAV/ Unit	2/95 NAV/ Unit	Pct Change 1 Mo	Pct Change 12 Mo	Pct Change YTD	12 Month Rank	Initial Equity (Mil)	Current Equity (Mil)	Type of Fund
842	836	-.8	-6.3	-9.8	167		182.20	GLOBAL
106	106	.3	-11.7	.2	189		40.80	MKT NEUTRAL
602	598	-.7	-13.2	-2.2	195		77.90	GLOBAL
649	696	7.2	-4.4	-7.2	159		17.10	GLOBAL
133	135	1.6	-10.7	-3.6	184		15.40	MKT NEUTRAL
127	129	1.0	-3.7	.0	154		9.10	MKT NEUTRAL
212	222	4.6	6.0	4.0	76		5.00	GLOBAL
860	837	-2.6	3.0	-2.9	92	800.00	734.80	GL MACRO
117	116	-.9	-14.8	-2.9	203		2.00	US OPPORT.
185	181	-2.3	-6.8	-4.5	170		1.10	US OPPORT.
1,410	1,445	2.5		54.9		2.00	2.89	EVENT-DRIV.
1,064	1,073	.9	-5.2	-2.3	165	4.67	14.31	MKT NEUTRAL
1,093	1,104	1.0		2.0		16.27	8.29	MKT NEUTRAL
580	512	-11.7	-53.5	-12.7	231	2.00	.23	GL MACRO
94.89	92.42	-2.6		-.7		1.00	1.70	GLOBAL
1,007	978	-2.9		.0		4.50	5.60	GLOBAL
1,040	1,045	.4		1.2		5.00	25.00	MKT NEUTRAL
934	913	-2.2	-10.7	-2.0	183	8.00	21.20	GL MACRO
1,923	1,996	3.8	9.6	6.3	46	26.00	35.40	EVENT-DRIV.
2,306	2,352	2.0	.8	2.4	108	1.00	7.60	EVENT-DRIV.
2,015	2,049	1.7	15.0	2.7	22	32.20	68.70	EVENT-DRIV.
2,362	2,458	4.0	10.5	5.8	38	25.60	61.40	EVENT-DRIV.
1,797	1,823	1.5	12.2	2.6	30	16.90	16.20	EVENT-DRIV.
1,984	2,031	2.4	10.6	3.5	37	31.10	70.30	EVENT-DRIV.
1,837	1,904	3.6	11.5	4.8	32	12.00	13.60	EVENT-DRIV.
1,797	1,817	1.1	8.5	2.0	56	20.10	21.50	EVENT-DRIV.
1,294	1,369	5.8	36.9	13.3	2	.20	1.87	US OPPORT.
76.97	81.74	6.2	-19.4	4.8	213	40.00	12.32	MKT NEUTRAL
929	966	4.0	-13.2	-1.0	196	40.00	40.00	EVENT-DRIV.
12,253	12,387	1.1	-1.4	3.7	136	32.51	137.12	MKT NEUTRAL
2,199	2,236	1.7	14.6	3.0	23	4.00	35.50	EVENT-DRIV.
1,189	1,212	1.9	18.3	.2	15	6.00	20.43	MKT NEUTRAL
1,208	1,216	.7	9.3	1.5	48	37.81	187.60	MKT NEUTRAL
1,066	1,074	.8		1.2		24.83	167.40	MKT NEUTRAL
8,164	8,225	.8	9.8	1.6	43	10.51	226.00	MKT NEUTRAL
2,372	2,432	2.6	-4.5	3.0	162	53.69	340.50	GL MACRO
10.02	9.87	-1.5		2.0		4.00	12.34	GLOBAL
531	546	2.7	-8.8	2.0	179	3.80	76.70	MKT NEUTRAL
1,144	1,115	-2.6	-17.5	-2.9	209	5.20	19.80	GL MACRO
583	582	-.2	1.3	1.3	103	803.00		GL MACRO
1,458	1,421	-2.5	5.5	-5.9	78	2.70	1.03	GLOBAL
1,599	1,606	.4	19.6	2.8	13	1.40	11.40	MKT NEUTRAL
15,866	15,898	.2	10.4	-.4	39	1.00	124.60	GL MACRO
1,018	1,019	.1	-7.1	1.5	171	3.75	5.72	GL MACRO
12.36	12.41	.4	6.5	1.1	72	5.00	19.97	MKT NEUTRAL
1,000	1,004	.4		9774.1		1.50	14.66	MKT NEUTRAL
102	97.93	-3.7	-1.9	-1.7	142	12.10	11.85	GLOBAL
50.42	48.44	-3.9	-3.1	-1.6	150	1.50	1.64	GLOBAL
31.42	30.45	-3.1	13.8	-3.4	26	3.80	45.50	SHORT-SALES
128	134	4.2	-4.2	5.2	158	3.50	9.50	EVENT-DRIV.
164	177	8.0	-.6	4.2	127	6.90	20.07	GL MACRO
2,237	2,446	9.4	1.6	6.8	101	1.80	27.60	GL MACRO
1,116	1,110	-.6	10.1	.7	41	11.89	27.70	MKT NEUTRAL
1,116	1,110	-.6	10.1	.7	42	11.89	27.70	MKT NEUTRAL
1,202	1,071	-10.9	-.4	-19.7	125	.50	70.00	GLOBAL
115	117	1.7	13.5	3.1	27	40.00	75.00	MKT NEUTRAL

TABLE A-3 (continued).   Performance of Hedge Funds

LINDAHL CAPITAL MGT.	=	66	100,000	$	3/87	1,000
*LS EUROPEAN FUND INC	113	329	100,000	$	11/94	100
LYNX PARTNERS L.P.	1	1	500,000	$	2/91	1,000
*MAGUS INTL. LTD.	=	152	250,000	$	10/94	1,000
CARL MARKS STRATEGIC INVESTMENTS L.P	=	119	1,000,000	$	11/87	
*MAVERICK FUND	=	173	1,000,000	$	4/90	1,000
MAVERICK FUND USA	=	173	1,000,000	$	4/90	1,000
MAYBERRY FUND L.P.	=	135	20,000	$	6/93	1,000
*MCD FINANCIAL ARBITRAGE FUND LTD.	16	30	10,000	$	2/84	10.00
*MCD MERGER ARBITRAGE FUND LTD.	=	197	10,000	$	12/83	10.00
*MCD U.S. EQUITY FUND LTD.	=	197	10,000	$	1/90	10.00
*McGINNIS GLOBAL FUND LTD.	=	218	500,000	$	11/93	1,000
McGINNIS PARTNERS FOCUS FUND L.P.	94	218	2,000,000	$	2/90	1,000
*M.D. SASS RE/ENTERPRISE INTL. LTD.	=	73	500,000	$	7/93	1,000
M.D. SASS RE/ENTERPRISE PARTNERS L.P	=	73	725,000	$	10/89	1,000
MERGER ARBITRAGE PROGRAM	114	#	5,000,000	$	1/87	1,000
METEORIC L.P.	=	17	500,000	$	12/90	1,000
MIDWEST HARVEST FUND L.P.	43	999	250,000	$	3/94	1,000
MILLENNIUM PARTNERS L.P.	=	305	1,000,000	$	1/90	1,000
*MINNISINK INTERNATIONAL LTD.	=	129	250,000	$	5/93	1,000
MINNISINK PARTNERS L.P.	=	129	1,000,000	$	2/93	1,018
*MOMENTUM GUILD LTD.	11	25	100,000	$	1/92	100
*MOMENTUM NAVELIER PERFORMANCE FUND	11	25	25,000	$	1/94	100
*MOMENTUM STOCKMASTER FUND	11	25	50,000	$	3/94	162
MONTGOMERY CAPITAL PARTNERS L.P.	=	2	500,000	$	7/93	1,000
MONTGOMERY EMERGING WORLD PTNRS.	=	2	500,000	$	10/93	1,000
MONTGOMERY GROWTH PARTNERS L.P.	=	2	500,000	$	7/91	1,000
MONTGOMERY GROWTH PARTNERS II L.P.	2	2	500,000	$	1/92	1,000
MOORE GLOBAL INVESTMENT +	=	67	Closed	$	7/90	1,867
NAPOLI INVESTMENT PARTNERS L.P.	=	191	250,000	$	1/94	1,000
NEEDHAM MGT GROWTH PARTNERS	115	334	250,000	$	1/93	1,000
NEW WORLD PARTNERS (SPH) L.P.	75	258	500,000	$	1/89	1,000
NIPPON PERFORMANCE FUND LTD.	=	190	100,000	$	11/93	100
*NORDIC HEDGE FUND LTD.	47	155	50,000	SEK	4/93	1.00
OAK HALL INVESTORS L.P.	=	266	500,000	$	4/93	1,000
OAK TREE PARTNERS L.P.	=	145	3,000,000	$	11/91	1,000
*ODEY EUROPEAN (DM) INC.	=	114	50,000	DM	6/92	100
*ODEY EUROPEAN (US$) INC.	=	114	50,000	$	3/94	173
*OMEGA OVERSEAS PARTNERS LTD. +	=	64	1,000,000	$	11/92	106
OPPORTUNITIES II FUND L.P.	=	106	25,000	$	1/94	1,000
*THE OPTIMA EMERALD FUND LTD.	15	335	250,000	$	2/94	10.10
OTTER CREEK PARTNERS I L.P.	=	71	500,000	$	8/91	1,000
OVERTURE FUND LP	=	336	500,000	$	1/95	1,000
THE PANTHER FUND LTD.	=	314	500,000	$	5/94	10.00
PARAMETRIC FUND L.P.	42	146	250,000	$	1/93	1,000
PARK PLACE INTERNATIONAL LTD	=	327	250,000	$	11/94	1,000
PEREGRINE CAPITAL PARTNERS	=	35	250,000	$	12/91	1,000
*PEREGRINE OPTIONS & DERIVATIVES FUND	10	24	5,000	$	3/93	1,000
PERKINS PARTNERS I LTD.	26	72	100,000	$	10/92	1,000
*PERMAL EUROMIR (ECU) LTD.	=	42	25,000	$	9/89	1,000
*PERMAL MEDIA & COMMUNICATIONS LTD.	=	41	25,000	$	9/89	1,000
*PERMAL NOSCAL LTD.	67	51	25,000	$	1/88	1,000
PHILBECK INVESTMENT FUND I L.P.	▪	132	200,000	$	4/94	10,000
J. PHILIP FUND PARTNERS L.P.	≠	168	250,000	$	6/94	1,000
*THE PLATINUM FUND LTD	15	170	500,000	$	6/94	1,000
PONTE VEDRA FUND L.P.	=	13	200,000	$	10/92	1,000
PORPOISE INVESTORS I L.P.	=	110	500,000	$	4/93	1,000
QUANTITATIVE LONG/SHORT	=	6	1,000,000	$	9/92	1,000
*QUANTUM EMERGING GROWTH FUND N.V.	=	38	Closed	$	2/92	108
*QUANTUM FUND N.V.	=	38	Closed	$	3/85	3,252

TABLE A-3 (continued).   Performance of Hedge Funds

2,175	2,221	2.2	8.2	3.4	62	25.00	160.00	MKT NEUTRAL
126	151	20.0		19.9		.38	.80	GLOBAL
1,098	1,106	.8	23.6	5.0	7	2.10	2.50	SHORT-SALES
1,021	1,020	-.1		1.0		1.00	1.00	GLOBAL
1,908	1,963	2.9	3.4	2.6	89	1.00	87.90	US OPPORT.
3,743	3,870	3.4	-6.7	2.1	168	6.00	51.00	GLOBAL
3,914	4,039	3.2	-1.4	1.8	137	6.00	43.00	GLOBAL
1,048						.03	.47	MKT NEUTRAL
58.20	56.87	-2.3	6.9	-.9	70	.78	5.90	MKT NEUTRAL
35.09	35.72	1.8	9.6	3.3	45	1.99	2.30	US OPPORT.
12.98	13.52	4.2	4.5	6.6	84	3.89	2.60	US OPPORT.
1,273	1,231	-3.2	-2.5	-7.5	145	3.20	17.00	GLOBAL
6,363	6,116	-3.9	-13.0	-8.4	194	1.00	44.80	GLOBAL
1,333	1,427	7.1	6.3	10.5	74	3.57	56.71	EVENT-DRIV.
2,799	3,019	7.9	10.3	10.7	40	9.20	130.92	EVENT-DRIV.
2,378	2,404	1.1	8.7	1.6	53	2.00	22.00	MKT NEUTRAL
1,242	1,202	-3.2	-22.8	-8.7	216	1.80	10.38	GL MACRO
1,155	1,226	6.1	22.6	2.3	9	.50	5.00	US OPPORT.
2,060	2,101	2.0	9.6	4.5	44	3.00	81.71	MKT NEUTRAL
1,124	1,056	-6.1	-3.6	-6.9	153	1.00	18.10	GLOBAL
1,251	1,172	-6.3	-4.4	-7.5	160	3.30	21.30	GLOBAL
80.91						20.00	6.00	GL MACRO
92.16	94.43	2.5	-6.8	-6.7	169	10.00	11.00	US OPPORT.
160	160	.2	-.8	1.5	130	8.00	14.00	GL MACRO
1,454	1,479	1.7	16.6	.8	20	2.95	41.73	GL MACRO
1,078	1,088	.9	-8.1	-8.4	174	1.90	7.66	GLOBAL
1,983	2,140	7.9	3.6	15.6	88	2.92	13.83	US OPPORT.
1,440	1,529	6.1	-.4	12.3	126	10.47	25.98	US OPPORT.
4,422	4,300	-2.8	-12.3	-3.7	193	210.00	2500.00	GL MACRO
1,299						1.00	1.79	MKT NEUTRAL
1,586	1,679	5.9	29.3	7.5	4	6.16	41.44	US OPPORT.
2,085	2,091	.3	-1.9	.8	141	1.00	12.00	MKT NEUTRAL
76.32	76.10	-.3	-24.7	25.8	218	3.43	3.42	GLOBAL
2.01	1.88	-6.5	.5	-2.1	111	.05	5.17	GLOBAL
1,422	1,416	-.4	-26.0	-9.5	221	1.25	5.01	US OPPORT.
2,061	2,368	14.9	8.5	2.8	55	14.32	103.00	US OPPORT.
105	103	-1.8	-40.3	-.8	229	2.00	65.00	GLOBAL
111	112	.6	-35.3	5.3	226	10.00	5.00	GLOBAL
149	150	.5	-9.7	2.3	181	41.00	1800.00	GL MACRO
1,055	1,075	1.9	4.1	2.2	85	1.50	6.73	GL MACRO
10.78	10.93	1.4	8.8	1.8	50	7.50	15.00	US OPPORT.
1,717	1,738	1.3	8.3	1.2	60	.80	10.00	EVENT-DRIV.
995	1,030	3.5		3.0		7.00	13.40	MKT NEUTRAL
10.42	10.86	4.2		3.4		.50	1.10	GL MACRO
825	770	-6.6	-11.7	-10.6	188	.80	1.00	US OPPORT.
1,052	1,052	.0		3.5		10.57	11.04	GLOBAL
2,121	2,134	.6	10.6	2.5	36	.15	8.19	US OPPORT.
1,324						11.15	6.09	GL MACRO
1,027	1,038	1.0	5.1	3.8	80	3.71	8.60	US OPPORT.
1,446	1,528	5.7	-15.4	3.7	206	5.00	113.80	GL MACRO
971	1,012	4.3	-8.8	-1.2	178	3.00	46.00	SHORT-SALES
1,837	1,848	.6	3.7	1.3	87	5.18	84.00	SHORT-SALES
9,723	9,714	-.1		.9		4.00	1.98	GL MACRO
1,282	1,273	-.8		-.4		.30	.37	US OPPORT.
1,047	1,062	1.5		-.7		38.00	114.00	GLOBAL
1,611	1,571	-2.5	-7.9	-9.2	173	1.03	2.50	US OPPORT.
1,271	1,233	-3.0	-11.5	2.0	187	3.50	15.00	EVENT-DRIV.
1,127	1,135	.7	.7	.1	109	49.73	417.71	MKT NEUTRAL
172	168	-1.8	-13.7	-9.8	198	437.00	1900.00	GLOBAL
16,422	16,504	.5	.8	-5.7	106		4900.00	GL MACRO

TABLE A-3 (continued).   Performance of Hedge Funds

Fund Name	General Partner	Fund Manager (a)	Minimum Investment Required	Currency	Start Date	Start NAV/ Unit
* QUANTUM INDUSTRIAL FUND	=	38	Closed	$	5/94	102
QUEST CAPITAL PARTNERS L.P.	30	104	250,000	$	2/94	100
RAINIER EMERGING GROWTH FUND L.P.	43	999	250,000	$	1/95	1,000
RAINIER MPT GROWTH FUND L.P.	43	150	250,000	$	11/91	1,000
RAINIER MPT TRADING FUND L.P.	43	150	250,000	$	6/94	1,000
RAINIER SHORT SELLING FUND	43	999	150,000	$	7/87	1,000
* REALTY TRUST	=	38	Closed	$	4/93	104
REGAL TRADING PARTNERS LTD.	=	12	500,000	$	1/86	1,000
REGENT PACIFIC HEDGE FUND	=	113	100,000	$	11/93	100
* RESOLUTE HEDGE FUND	=	196	150,000	$	4/94	1,000
ROANOKE PARTNERS L.P.	=	28	250,000	$	2/91	1,197
ROSEBURY L.P.	=	17	500,000	$	7/91	1,000
RUSSIA VALUE FUND L.P.	91	218	100,000	$	9/94	1,000
* SAGE INTERNATIONAL FUND LTD.	57	185	250,000	$	10/92	100
* SALUS INTERNATIONAL FUND LTD.	57	183	250,000	$	7/93	100
* THE S.A.M. GLOBAL FUND LTD.	=	63	500,000	$	9/93	1,000
SANT CASSIA INVESTMENT MGT. LTD.	70	999	1,500,000	$	1/94	1,000
SAUSALITO CAPITAL ASSETS L.P.	33	112	250,000	$	10/91	1,000
* SBC CURRENCY PORTFOLIO LTD.	=	160	10,000,000	$	9/93	1,000
IBJ SCHRODER HEDGED EQUITY PRODUCT	116	338	2,000,000	$	4/92	1,000
SELECT STRATEGIC PARTNERS L.P.	31	105	250,000	$	3/91	1,000
* SENTRY SELECT LTD.	106	316	100,000	$	7/94	500
SHAREVEST PARTNERS L.P.	6	14	250,000	$	2/87	1,040
SINTRA FUND LTD.	=	306	500,000	$	4/89	1.79
* SIRIUS INTL. LTD.	105	312	100,000	$	2/95	25.00
SKYE SHORT-SELLING FUND L.P.	=	311	100,000	$	7/90	1,000
SMC PARTNERS L.P.	117	339,340	250,000	$	9/93	1,000
* SOUTHBRIDGE FUND INC.	=	10	5,000,000	$	10/92	1,000
* SOUTHPORT PARTNERS INTL. LTD.	=	5	1,000,000	$	8/94	1,000
SOUTHPORT PARTNERS L.P.	=	5	250,000	$	10/92	1,000
THE SPX TRADER	73	223	10,000	$	1/94	1,000
STEEL PARTNERS II L.P.	=	210	500,000	$	10/93	1,000
* STROME OFFSHORE LTD. +	=	65	100,000	$	4/92	103
* TAI CHI EQUITY LTD.	99	307	25,000	$	2/94	100
TARGAT ASSOCIATES L.P.	=	16	500,000	$	10/81	1,000
TECHNOLOGY YIELD FUND	88	157	250,000	$	7/89	100
TEXAS HEDGE FUND LTD.	=	139	50,000	$	1/94	1,000
TGT CAPITAL PARTERNS L.P	118	341,342	250,000	$	10/91	1,000
* TITAN EURO-EQUITY FUND LTD.	=	308	25,000	$	10/94	100
TRT GOLD STOCK	=	348	1,000,000	$	2/88	1,000
* TSG GENERAL FUND (GBP UNITS)	=	343	10,000	$	11/93	1,102
* TSG GENERAL FUND (USD UNITS)	=	343	10,000	$	11/93	1,639
TSG LEVERAGED FUND (GBP UNITS)	=	343	10,000	$	8/93	753
TSG LEVERAGED FUND (USD UNITS)	=	343	10,000	$	8/93	1,099
TURKEY VULTURE FUND XIII LTD	=	344	100,000	$	2/95	100
* ULTRA CERBERUS FUND	119	345	250,000	$	1/93	1,000
* ULTRA SECTOR FUND	119	346	500,000	$	1/93	1,000
* U.S. FINANCIAL EQUITIES PLC.	=	280	350,000	$	11/94	100
THE VIPER FUND L.P.	44	153	250,000	$	2/94	1,000
WATERFALL FUND L.P.	43	147	250,000	$	1/94	1,000
WCM PARTNERS L.P.	=	22	250,000	$	9/88	1,000
WESTBRIDGE PARTNERS FUND L.P.	68	10	3,000,000	$	3/94	1,000
WEST BROADWAY PARTNERS L.P.	=	69	100,000	$	1/93	1,000
WESTCLIFF LONG/SHORT L.P.	=	275	250,000	$	7/93	1,000
WESTCLIFF PARTNERS L.P.	=	275	250,000	$	7/93	1,000
YERBA BUENA INVESTORS L.P.	=	216	250,000	$	8/94	1,000

TABLE A-3 (continued). Performance of Hedge Funds

1/95 NAV/ Unit	2/95 NAV/ Unit	Pct Change 1 Mo	Pct Change 12 Mo	Pct Change YTD	12 Month Rank	Initial Equity (Mil)	Current Equity (Mil)	Type of Fund
102	102	-.1		-3:6				GLOBAL
95.09	101	6.2	-.8	.7	131	.70	1.04	US OPPORT.
988	1,052	6.5		5.2		1.00	1.00	US OPPORT.
1,211	1,195	-1.3	-11.9	-12.2	190	2.10	4.00	US OPPORT.
1,096	1,074	-2.0		-14.3		.40	2.00	US OPPORT.
1,225	1,195	-2.4	17.2	1.2	19	.50	3.00	SHORT-SALES
136	137	.9	1.7	-1.7	99		655.00	EVENT-DRIV.
4,904	4,856	-1.0	.9	-.9	105	3.70	137.00	GL MACRO
119	112	-6.2	-2.0	-13.1	143	41.10	225.00	GL MACRO
967	965	-.2		-1.1		.33	1.05	GL MACRO
3,459	3,489	.9	-1.8	1.2	140	2.03	11.00	US OPPORT.
1,151	1,114	-3.2	-14.7	-8.1	201	7.70	18.00	GL MACRO
671	584	-13.1		-23.5		54.00	40.60	GLOBAL
112	111	-.8	-4.1	-2.0	157	3.90	67.43	MKT NEUTRAL
115	113	-1.5	3.2	.3	90	3.60	20.00	MKT NEUTRAL
1,295	1,287	-.6	14.5	.9	24	65.27	176.00	GL MACRO
1,116	1,107	-.7	6.2	1.0	75	1.50	75.00	GL MACRO
1,463	1,426	-2.5	-.7	-5.2	129	.55	11.00	US OPPORT.
1,170	1,186	1.4	11.3	5.0	33	46.00	304.00	GL MACRO
1,214	1,245	2.5	2.0	2.4	98	4.83	44.24	MKT NEUTRAL
1,481	1,497	1.1	2.6	-.6	94	.75	3.66	GL MACRO
518	521	.6		1.3		3.13	6.93	US OPPORT.
2,399	2,427	1.2	-3.8	4.2	155	5.43	32.44	US OPPORT.
13.06	11.80	-9.6	-22.5	-15.1	215	5.00	34.30	GLOBAL
25.00	25.23	.9				1.00	1.00	US OPPORT.
1,197	1,203	.5	27.0	5.4	6	.08	2.59	SHORT-SALES
1,040	1,025	-1.5	-8.4	-3.6	176	1.56	10.20	US OPPORT.
1,706	1,527	-10.5	5.3	8.0	79	12.57	85.00	GL MACRO
1,025	1,039	1.4		2.5		4.70	4.80	MKT NEUTRAL
1,305	1,339	2.7	2.6	7.3	95	.44	6.75	MKT NEUTRAL
1,161	1,125	-3.2	7.7	-3.5	66	.03	300.00	US OPPORT.
1,349	1,372	1.7	31.7	8.4	3	3.39	20.40	US OPPORT.
170						67.00	460.00	GL MACRO
97.64	99.16	1.6	-.2	-1.7	122	2.00	2.01	GLOBAL
6,626	6,819	2.9	.3	3.7	115	5.31	57.70	US OPPORT.
242	252	4.0	-4.5	4.6	161	4.30	20.42	US OPPORT.
1,136	1,136	.0	11.1	4.0	35			US OPPORT.
2,372	2,508	5.7	4.7	6.9	82	1.00	13.00	EVENT-DRIV.
103	102	-.6		2.1		.10	.10	GLOBAL
3,068	3,040	-.9	3.0	-9.1	91	1.50	12.00	NATURAL
1,160	1,213	4.5	11.2	6.3	34			US OPPORT.
1,834	1,920	4.7	18.2	7.5	16			US OPPORT.
721	784	8.7	5.0	12.9	81			GLOBAL
1,139	1,233	8.3	13.0	13.6	29			GLOBAL
100	92.99	-7.0				6.41	9.81	US OPPORT.
1,213	1,259	3.7	7.4	2.3	67	.90	11.45	EVENT-DRIV.
1,113	1,135	2.0	-3.0	2.8	148	.49	5.84	GLOBAL
101	103	2.0		3.3		32.50	33.75	US OPPORT.
875	831	-5.1	-17.3	-2.9	208	15.00	2.00	GL MACRO
1,051	1,041	-1.0	8.4	5.0	59	1.00	4.00	SHORT-SALES
1,841	1,866	1.4	8.6	2.2	54	2.00	5.60	EVENT-DRIV.
1,186	1,063	-10.4	6.3	5.4	73	20.00	29.00	GL MACRO
1,414	1,451	2.6	13.2	5.4	28	1.82	12.00	EVENT-DRIV.
1,156	1,156	.0	17.8	-4.9	17	.36	8.23	US OPPORT.
1,078	1,093	1.4	4.6	-8.0	83	.59	3.42	US OPPORT.
1,074	1,125	4.8		7.4		.80	1.50	MKT NEUTRAL

TABLE A-3 (continued).   Performance of Hedge Funds

YORK CAPITAL MGT.	=	262	500,000	$	10/91	1,000
* YORK INVESTMENT LTD.	=	263	500,000	$	10/91	1,000

TABLE A-3 (continued).   Performance of Hedge Funds

2,151	2,160	.4	11.5	3.7	31	5.00	47.00	EVENT-DRIV.
2,196	2,212	.7	14.2	3.3	25	5.00	22.50	EVENT-DRIV.

(a) Names of General Partner and Fund Manager can be found in the key.

\# Multiple Fund Managers.

* Funds open to non-US investors only.

= General Partner is the same as designated Fund Manager.

+ Estimated Asset Size.

TABLE A-4. Performance of Funds of Funds

Fund Name	General Partner	Fund Manager (a)	Minimum Investment Required	Currency	Start Date	Start NAV/ Unit
* ADVANCED STRATEGIES LTD.	106	998,317	100,000	$	5/91	100
ALL SEASONS FUND LTD.	69	301,998	250,000	$	1/94	1,000
* ALPHA GLOBAL FUND LTD.	=	998	250,000	$	10/88	500
* ANABASIS FUND INC.	7	999	100,000	$	1/90	1,000
ARDEN ADVISERS L.P.	104	999	500,000	$	10/93	1,000
BANC FUND L.P.	56	998	100,000	$	7/93	1,000
BIRCHWOOD ASSOCIATES	=	998,276	500,000	$	12/84	1,000
* BLACKSTONE GLOBAL PARK AVENUE FUND	60	998	1,000,000	$	1/95	1,000
* BLACKSTONE PTNRS GLOBAL INVEST. FUND	60	998	100,000	$	4/93	1,000
BLACKSTONE PARTNERS INVEST. FUND L.P	60	998	10,000,000	$	9/90	1,000
CENTENNIAL PARTNERS I L.P.	18	998,999	500,000	$	4/94	1,000
CENTENNIAL PARTNERS II L.P.	18	998,999	500,000	$	7/94	1,000
THE COMMON FUND	103	998,999	100,000	$	4/94	1,000
COMPLETE MANAGER FUND	22	999	1,000,000	$	7/92	26,379
* COMPLETE MANAGER GLOBAL FUND LTD.	22	999	100,000	$	10/93	10,000
* CONCERTO LTD.	=	998,179	100,000	$	4/94	100
DIVERSIFIED INVESTMENTS ASSOCIATES	3	998,#	100,000	$	10/89	1,000
* EAGLE CAPITAL INTERNATIONAL FUND LTD	92	998,277	100,000	$	1/94	100
* ENIGMA DIVERSIFIED FUND LTD	23	152	50,000	$	11/91	25.00
EQUITY FUND L.P.	56	998,999	100,000	$	1/92	1,000
EVEREST EMERGING MARKETS FUND L.P.	=	267	100,000	$	6/94	1,000
FIDUCIARY PARTNERS L.P.	41	999	500,000	$	1/94	1,000
* GAM ALLOCATED MULTI-FUND INC.	80	285,998	15,000	$	1/90	100
* GAM COMBINED FUND INC.	80	998,285	25,000	DM	1/93	100
* GAM EMERGING MARKETS MULTI-FUND INC.	80	285,998	15,000	$	4/92	100
* GAM MULTI-EUROPE (DM) FUND INC.	80	285,998	25,000	DM	6/92	100
* GAM MULTI-EUROPE (US$) FUND INC.	80	285,998	15,000	$	10/91	100
* GAM MULTI-GLOBAL (US$) FUND INC.	80	285,998	15,000	$	1/90	100
* GAM TRADING DM FUND INC.	80	285,998	25,000	DM	10/92	100
* GAM TRADING US$ FUND INC.	80	285,998	15,000	$	5/90	100
* GAM UNIVERSAL US$ INC.	=	998,285	15,000	$	9/90	100
* GEMINI CAYS LTD.	102	998,999	250,000	$	6/92	5,000
* GEMS PROGRESSIVE FUND LTD. "D"	8	999	100,000	$	5/92	1,000
* GEMS PROGRESSIVE FUND LTD. "J"	8	999	100,000	$	5/92	1,000
* GEMS PROGRESSIVE FUND LTD. "T"	8	999	100,000	$	5/92	1,000
* GENESEE FUND LTD. (PORTFOLIO A)	19	998,#	250,000	$	12/91	1,000
GLENWOOD PARTNERS L.P.	74	998,225	500,000	$	1/87	1,000
GLOBAL HIGH PERFORMANCE FUND L.P.	56	998,999	100,000	$	10/93	1,000
GOLDEN EAGLE PARTNERS, L.P.	=	347	250,000	$	7/94	1,000
* GOVETT DOLLAR GL. BAL. HEDGE FUND	=	998,195	20,000	$	4/93	9.54
* GOVETT STERLING GL. BAL. HEDGE FUND	=	998,195	10,000	BP	12/93	10.00
* GOVETT SWISS FRANC GL.BAL.HEDGE FUND	=	998,195	20,000	SFR	12/93	10.00
* GSAM COMPOSITE INC.	93	998,287	15,000	$	2/86	100
HALCYON/SLIFKA BAL. MULTI-MGR FUND	=	327	500,000	$	1/90	1,000
* HAUSSMANN HOLDINGS N.V.	21	998,#	25,000	$	12/82	75.00
HEDGE VENTURES L.P.	27	998,#	500,000	$	3/91	1,000
HORIZON ONE LTD.	96	998,999	100,000	$	7/94	1,000
INTERNATIONAL FUND L.P.	56	998,999	100,000	$	7/93	1,000
IVY ASSET MGT. CORP.	=	998,276	500,000	$	12/84	1,000
JCI FRONTIER FUND L.P.	101	999	100,000	$	2/93	1,000
* KEY ASIA HOLDINGS INC.	32	#	500,000	$	6/94	100
* KEY GLOBAL HEDGE INC.	32	#	500,000	$	6/92	180
* KEY HEDGE FUND INC.	32	74,111,188	500,000	$	4/90	100
* MAGNUM AGGRESSIVE GROWTH FUND LTD.	=	998,303	200,000	$	4/94	100
* MAGNUM FUND LTD.	=	998,303	100,000	$	4/94	100
* MAGNUM MULTI-FUND LTD.	=	998,303	100,000	$	4/94	100

TABLE A-4 (continued). Performance of Funds of Funds

1/95 NAV/ Unit	2/95 NAV/ Unit	Pct Change 1 Mo	Pct Change 12 Mo	Pct Change YTD	12 Month Rank	Initial Equity (Mil)	Current Equity (Mil)	Type of Fund
162	162	.1	2.1	.9	8	4.20	81.87	
932	880	-5.6	-10.7	-7.7	36	3.29	9.50	
873	856	-1.9	-15.3	-4.8	55		45.57	
1,599	1,605	.4	-8.5	-.5	32	4.93	37.00	
1,175	1,185	.8	12.1	2.2	1	2.00	15.00	
1,147	1,166	1.7	1.3	2.4	9	.51	1.11	
2,632	2,666	1.3	-.8	2.2	13	.90	29.00	
993	1,002	.9		.2		12.00	44.00	
1,137	1,147	.9	-2.8	.7	18	10.62	45.00	
1,645	1,660	.9	-5.4	.4	27	10.39	275.00	
1,086	1,068	-1.6		.7		36.88	61.72	
1,000	1,014	1.4		1.9		10.00	10.34	
1,038	1,048	1.0		2.5		51.00	126.40	
31,815	31,818	.0	-13.5	-2.0	46	4.20	55.00	
9,071	9,072	.0	-12.5	-1.7	41	15.85	25.00	
91.46	92.10	.7		.5		28.25	27.72	
1,110	1,113	.3	-13.8	.3	48	1.39	.87	
88.42						6.70	8.11	
28.19	27.13	-3.8	-17.0	-2.3	58	1.10	3.00	
1,357	1,375	1.4	6.4	2.1	5	4.05	3.77	
1,017	920	-9.6		-18.8		.95	2.44	
942	971	3.0	-8.4	-1.5	31	4.80	11.40	
155	154	-.9	-13.4	-1.2	45	5.00	5.30	
116	113	-2.8	-23.6	-5.2	63		27.20	
161	153	-5.1	-18.5	-10.7	60	5.00	70.50	
121	120	-.1	-16.6	-.3	57	97.00	32.10	
120	120	.1	-17.0	.0	59	5.00	53.10	
164	163	-.6	-14.5	-1.3	52	100.00	478.80	
121	118	-2.8	-12.6	-3.3	42	100.00	172.50	
171	170	-.5	-2.0	1.5	15	110.00	245.50	
146	148	1.0	-10.0	3.3	35		7.10	
5,389	5,215	-3.2	-9.2	-1.0	34	4.58	21.38	
1,172	1,174	.2	-14.6	-2.2	53	11.97	30.00	
1,518	1,521	.2	-2.1	1.6	16	1.00	4.42	
1,043	1,030	-1.2	-3.6	1.1	21	2.00	7.50	
1,522						2.08	25.00	
2,469	2,465	-.2	-4.5	-.1	23	4.53	112.00	
1,063	966	-9.2	-16.2	-21.4	56	.89	2.40	
948	947	-.1		1.5				
10.91	11.10	1.7	-4.1	.1	22	2.86	3.90	
8.80	8.95	1.7	-13.7	-2.9	47	.77	.70	
8.83	8.83	.0	-13.0	-4.8	43	2.20	2.30	
320	314	-1.9	-14.1	-3.5	49		145.60	
1,571						32.90	24.10	
604	608	.6	-6.9	-.3	29	65.69	1900.00	
1,834	1,839	.3	-12.3	-.8	40	1.55	29.74	
1,012	1,034	2.2		1.3		.50	3.00	
1,248	1,161	-6.9	-8.9	-12.8	33	2.49	4.55	
2,973	3,011	1.3	-.2	2.3	12	.90	397.00	
1,367	1,384	1.2	-3.6	3.3	20	.14	4.00	
97.50	96.41	-1.1		-2.8		4.30	7.00	
237	235	-.7	-14.5	-2.7	51	4.00	33.00	
149	150	.4	1.2	.2	10	4.50	32.00	
87.23						5.56	9.94	
84.31						14.34	15.63	
89.43						4.49	4.82	

TABLE A-4 (continued). Performance of Funds of Funds

MESIROW ALTERNATIVE STRATEGIES FUND	100	309,998	5,000,000	$	4/94	1,000
MILLBURN MULTI-STRATEGY PORTFOLIO	=	313	250,000	$	1/95	1,000
* MOMENTUM RAINBOW FUND	11	25	25,000	$	10/93	124
OAKWOOD ASSOCIATES	=	998,276	500,000	$	4/87	1,000
* OLYMPIA STARS EMERGING MARKETS	40	998,92	250,000	$	1/94	1,000
* OLYMPIA STARS GLOBAL HEDGE SERIES	40	998,#	250,000	$	1/93	1,000
OPTIMA FUND L.P.	15	999	1,000,000	$	1/89	1,000
* THE OPTIMA FUND LTD.	15	999	500,000	$	1/89	10.00
OPTIMA GLOBAL FUND L.P.	15	999	500,000	$	9/92	1,000
* THE OPTMA GLOBAL FUND LTD.	15	999	250,000	$	2/93	10.04
THE OPTIMA SHORT FUND L.P.	15	999	1,000,000	$	8/90	1,000
* THE OPTIMA SHORT FUND LTD.	15	999	500,000	$	7/90	10.11
PAN DOMESTIC L.P.	86	998,999	250,000	$	1/91	1,000
PANPIPES INTERNATIONAL L.P.	86	998,999	250,000	$	1/94	1,000
* PERMAL INVESTMENT HOLDINGS N.V.	20	998,#	25,000	$	4/92	1,000
* PRIME ADVISORS FUND LTD.	=	271	100,000	$	9/94	100
* QUASAR INTL. FUND N.V.	=	998,38	Closed	$	5/91	100
* QUOTA FUND N.V.	=	998,38	Closed	$	2/92	99.88
RAINIER PARTNERS	43	999	150,000	$	1/88	1,000
ROSEWOOD ASSOCIATES	=	998,276	3,000,000	$	12/88	1,000
RSM SECTOR PARTNERSHIP	12	998,#	Closed	$	9/93	1,000
THE SEEDLING FUND L.P.	=	276	500,000	$	1/95	100
SOUTHWIND PARTNERS L.P.	18	998,999	1,000,000	$	10/92	1,000
STONEWALL PARTNERS L.P.	54	998,#	250,000	$	1/94	1,000
SUMMIT PRIVATE INVESTMENTS L.P.	=	269	500,000	$	1/91	1,000
* TITAN HEDGE FUND LTD.	=	308,998	25,000	$	12/94	100
YANKEE GROWTH PARTNERS	49	998,#	1,000,000	$	1/93	1,000

TABLE A-4 (continued). Performance of Funds of Funds

1,048	1,056	.8		1.3		7.50	158.00
987	1,014	2.8		1.4		.50	.50
109	109	-.2	-14.9	-.9	54	9.50	17.00
1,664	1,679	.9	-2.3	1.5	17	.80	35.00
842	803	-4.6	-19.6	-11.1	61	25.06	21.43
967	953	-1.4	-20.4	-2.2	62	34.17	38.08
1,728	1,745	1.0	-6.0	.9	28	22.00	91.00
17.40	17.59	1.1	-4.8	1.3	24		59.50
1,320	1,304	-1.2	-14.2	-5.5	50	5.00	15.80
12.90	12.69	-1.6	-13.0	-5.9	44		16.70
640	618	-3.4	10.6	-4.2	3		5.50
7.20	6.99	-2.9	11.3	-3.5	2		11.50
1,769	1,742	-1.5	-.8	-1.9	14	1.50	12.00
932	904	-3.0	-11.2	-8.1	39		2.00
1,274	1,286	.9	-7.5	-.8	30	1040.00	1200.00
108						.54	1.00
155	157	1.3	4.1	-.3	6	771.00	1500.00
128	129	.8	-10.8	-9.5	37	250.00	1050.00
1,653	1,631	-1.3	.5	-.5	11	1.70	6.00
1,605	1,621	1.0	-5.3	1.8	26	3.60	107.00
1,062	1,082	1.9	-5.1	-.7	25	.50	1.91
101	103	1.8		3.0		11.00	16.00
1,209	1,198	-.9	7.9	.2	4	32.97	56.31
1,041	1,047	.6	2.9	1.2	7	2.50	9.80
1,883	1,892	.5	-3.1	-.1	19	.75	30.00
96.21	96.50	.3		-3.3		5.00	.30
904	932	3.1	-11.0	1.7	38	.19	1.40

Index

Lookout Mountain

Hedge Fund
R   E   V   I   E   W

Prudent hedge fund evaluation is far more difficult than evaluating publicly traded securities or mutual funds. The *Lookout Mountain Hedge Fund Review* is an edification tool. We began publishing in March of 1994, under the presumption that the investing public has a genuine need for greater *insight* regarding hedge funds . . . insight clearly lacking in the financial press.

We believe that hedge fund statistics, although useful in very general terms, are seldom accurate and often misleading. We also believe hedge fund performance rankings grossly oversimplify historical performance, and offer no utility for future performance estimations. You will find neither in our publication. Nor will you find hedge fund listings or phone numbers there.

We are not indiscriminate defenders of hedge funds, but rather prudent advocates for an investment form that has provided some of the best returns over the past half century. We probe the primary determinants for superior performance, and the problems that may impede performance or investor satisfaction. Our periodic "media check" commentary sheds light on unbalanced or misleading reports in the financial press.

Our goal is simple. When readers finish our newsletter, we want them to feel they have gained something useful, just a little better perspective of hedge funds.

The *Lookout Mountain Hedge Fund Review* is published quarterly by Lookout Mountain Capital, Inc., a registered investment advisor. Although the majority of our subscribers are individual and institutional investors, a large number of hedge fund managers, U.S. and foreign banks, brokerage firms, and investment advisors also subscribe. We would welcome your subscription at (615) 629-4226.

Ted Caldwell, President
Lookout Mountain Capital, Inc.